Chasing *the* Ghost Birds

Saving swans and cranes from extinction

by David Sakrison

Contents

International Crane Foundation
E11376 Shady Lane Road
P.O. Box 447
Baraboo, Wisconsin 53913-0447 USA
www.savingcranes.org

Terry and Mary Kohler
Photo, © International Crane Foundation, Baraboo, WI.

Foreword

By Mary and Terry Kohler

WHEN WE WERE IN GRADE SCHOOL IN 1941, the only remaining wild flock of Whooping Cranes was wintering in the Aransas National Wildlife Refuge (ANWR) in Texas, and its numbers had dwindled to fewer than 20 individuals, maybe as few as 14. No one (except a few natives in Canada's far north) knew where they summered and nested, although they were known to migrate north and south through the Platte River in Nebraska. Historically, Whooping Cranes migrated and nested through much of North America but they had been hunted nearly to extinction by the year 1900. There were once non-migratory flocks in Florida, Louisiana, and probably in other parts of the southern United States. They, too, had disappeared a century ago, hunted to extinction or driven out by loss of their wetland habitats.

Today, you can see and hear wild Whooping Cranes in Wisconsin, in Florida, and along the 1,000-mile migration route in between. There aren't many of them, yet—a hundred or so, compared to the thousands that used to inhabit this flyway. But their numbers are growing.

The Whoopers are back because of the determined efforts of the

i

International Crane Foundation (ICF), the US Fish & Wildlife Service, and an army of avian biologists, conservationists, volunteers, and donors.

Trumpeter Swans had not been seen or heard in our native Wisconsin and surrounding states for more than a century. Once common here, they had disappeared east of the Rocky Mountains. Today, the Trumpeters are back, thanks to a partnership of local, state, and federal agencies, public and private organizations and determined individuals. Trumpeter Swan reintroduction in the Midwest Flyway has been a huge success, far outstripping its original goals.

We have been privileged to play a small part in these projects. We've had some wonderful adventures and gained many friends, human and avian, along the way.

In the beginning, it was a request from our friend, Wisconsin Governor Tommy Thompson that brought us into the Trumpeter Swan project, flying swan eggs from Alaska to Wisconsin in our company's jet.

Neither of us can remember when we first became aware of the critical status of the Whooping Crane. We have long supported the ICF with financial contributions, and our active involvement began almost by accident. It has grown into a passion—one that has brought us a huge amount of satisfaction and a whole lot of fun. Through our work with ICF and its amazing and tireless director, George Archibald, we have flown our company jet to the farthest reaches of Siberia, in aid of Russian efforts to preserve the beautiful Siberian Crane, one of the most endangered crane species.

Working with Trumpeter Swans, Whooping Cranes, and Siberian Cranes is an experience that has provided almost weekly excitement in our lives for nearly 20 years. Over the years, we've tried thousands of times to come up with a coherent answer to the question, "What do you two do with those Whooping Cranes?" This book is our latest attempt at an answer. And we hope it is more than that.

We want to tell the wider story—of the Trumpeters, Sibes, and Whoopers, and of the many people and organizations that are working so hard to protect these majestic threatened birds. What do we two do with those Whooping Cranes and other birds? We play a tiny part in species recovery projects that have spanned more than 60 years. These are projects that must and will continue long after our small parts are acted out.

We also hope this book will inspire you to get involved, to discover the passion and the rewards that we have discovered in the course of this adventure over the past two decades. The wild things and wild places in this world need your help if they are to endure for your grandchildren and their grandchildren.

Finally, we offer this book as a "thank you" for the enjoyment we've had in the Trumpeters, Whoopers, and Sibes, and in the people they have introduced us to.

HUMAN BEINGS POSSESS MOST OF THE INTELLIGENCE on this planet, or at least we like to think so. It is our job to be stewards of the environment. Migratory birds like the Whooping Crane are very fragile. They are the first to suffer when we pollute or damage their habitats. They offer visible signs that we may be doing something wrong to our environment. It is critically important for us to study them, learn from them, and use the knowledge we gain from them to correct our environmental mistakes. It's up to each of us to help make things right again.

Sadly, the Siberian Cranes are hanging on by the thinnest thread. Their numbers, about 3,000, are expected to decline rapidly as human pressures disrupt their habitats in Russia, China, and Central Asia.

So far, the Trumpeter Swan and the Whooping Crane are environmental success stories. Twenty years ago, wild Trumpeter Swans hadn't been seen east of the Rocky Mountains since the 1880s. Today, there are close to 5,000 of them in the Midwest Flyway. Wild Whooping Cranes hadn't been seen in the eastern United States for 100 years. Today, the Whooper is on its way to being taken off the Endangered Species List—an objective once widely thought impossible.

Continued success depends on continued stewardship. Please lend your hand to help preserve and protect God's wondrous creatures and the wild places where they live.

Long live the Trumpeters, the Sibes, and the Whoopers!

Mary and Terry Kohler
Puerto Montt, Chile
January 2007

Introduction

by George W. Archibald
Co-founder and Senior Conservationist
The International Crane Foundation,
Baraboo, Wisconsin
www.savingcranes.org

"SIBES!" I COULD HEAR TERRY KOHLER'S EXCITED ROAR, even over the roar of the gigantic and ancient Russian helicopter. Peering from a small circular window in the helicopter's cabin, Terry had spotted two rare Siberian cranes on the tundra a few hundred feet below us. Locating those white birds against the white snow was no small accomplishment, given our speed and our limited field of vision from the helicopter's cabin. It seemed like a miracle sighting. And though we were in the heart of the Sibes' nesting grounds in Yakutia, in far northeastern Siberia, those two were the only Siberian cranes we saw that June day in 1997.

Our Russian pilots set us down near a low hill, where a house trailer on skis served as a field research station for Kytalic Nature Reserve, a protected area for nesting Siberian cranes, far above the Arctic Circle in eastern Russia. After the helicopter departed, the silence was broken only by the scolding calls of a rough-legged hawk and the more distant trumpeting of Sandhill cranes. Like us, the Sandhill cranes were visitors from North America. Their primeval calls color our Wisconsin landscapes. In this remote place, half a world away from home, we felt as if we had met old friends.

We searched with spotting scopes for the Sandhills but saw none. Mary Kohler and I ventured out onto the tundra along a ridge top, searching for more ornithological treasures. Mary is an avid, lifelong birder, and her tenacity was impressive. Our search was rewarded by the sight of a screaming peregrine and several Sandhills.

The Sandhill cranes we encountered in Siberia had migrated thousands of miles, from wintering grounds in Texas, through Canada and Alaska, and across the Bering Sea, to nest here in the Siberian Arctic. We—my wife Kyoko and I, and Mary and Terry Kohler of Sheboygan, Wisconsin—had flown across the North Atlantic and Europe, to Moscow, then on to Siberia, in the Kohlers' private jet. We brought with us precious Siberian crane eggs from captive Sibes at Baraboo, Wisconsin.

We visited the crane conservation/restoration program at Russia's Oka Nature Reserve, near Moscow. Then, in the pleasant company of Russian colleagues, including crane specialists Vladimir Flint and Sasha Sorokin, we flew on to visit the three nesting grounds of the only remaining flocks of Siberian cranes—one of the three most endangered species of cranes. In one of those nesting areas, we placed our Sibe eggs in the nests of Eurasian cranes, in the hopes that these "foster-parents" would raise new Siberian cranes to sustain the rapidly dwindling western and central flocks of Sibes.

The days of our journey were filled with flights across the vastness of half a world—15 time zones, in all—social gatherings with old and new Russian friends, and caring for our captive-produced Sibe eggs. It was a historic flight across a country that just a few years before was closed to foreigners. We landed in places that had not been visited by an American aircraft since World War Two, more than fifty years earlier. During the Cold War, which ended less than a decade before our journey, our American-registered airplane would have been a military target. Now we were welcomed as goodwill ambassadors and as friends.

Leaving Yakutia, northeastern Siberia, we followed the Sandhills' migration route across Alaska, then veered east and home to Baraboo. There, the Kohlers dropped Kyoko and me at the tiny airport from which, 11 days before, with precious Sibe eggs in a portable incubator, we had departed to the east on our round-the-world journey. The trip was a gift to the International Crane Foundation from Terry and Mary Kohler. It was a wonderful journey that gave me new insights into the world of Siberian cranes and into the character of a most remarkable couple.

The Kohlers are world travelers involved in a diversity of issues related to politics, sports, business, and conservation. They have supported and participated in conservation programs of the Wisconsin and Michigan Departments of Natural Resources, the US Fish & Wildlife Service, the ICF, the Milwaukee County Zoo, and other public and private organizations. Mary was instrumental in the creation of the Riveredge Nature Center, a conservation education center for public schools in east central Wisconsin.

Bob Hallam, a former Director of Development at the International Crane Foundation (ICF), arranged my first meeting with the Kohlers in the early 1990s. A federal election was in the wind, and Mary was wearing the colors of the Republican Party.

The Kohlers' enthusiasm for the work of the ICF was obvious. Our meeting hatched a friendship and helped to bring about Terry and Mary's in-depth involvement in the conservation of whooping cranes and Siberian cranes.

In 1989, Terry introduced me to the award-winning film "C'mon Geese" by Canadian artist, pilot, and conservationist, Bill Lishman. This captivating 28-minute video tells the story of a flock of hand-reared Canada Geese trained by Lishman to follow an ultra-light aircraft. Terry is an active pilot and aviation enthusiast, and he posed a question to me: Could Lishman's methods be used to teach captive-raised whooping cranes how to migrate? Less than a year later, I showed the video to my fellow members of the International Whooping Crane Recovery Team.? At that meeting, I was pretty sure what the rest of the team was thinking: "Here we go again with one of George's out-of-the box ideas."

But the crazy idea struck a chord. With financial backing from Terry and Mary, "out-of-the-box" got off the ground. By 2001, Bill Lishman and his colleague, Joe Duff, the co-founders of Operation Migration, were leading whooping cranes behind ultra-lights, successfully teaching the birds to migrate from Wisconsin to Florida. By 2005, we had successfully established a new, wild population of whooping cranes, migrating between Florida and Wisconsin.

The Kohlers have used their own Windway Capital Corp. aircraft and corporate pilots to bring eggs to breeding centers, to move chicks to release sites, and to track and monitor released cranes throughout their wide ranges. On occasion, they have sent a plane to rescue a migrating crane that wandered far off course. Terry and Mary have provided major financial support to ICF and our partner Operation Migration, allowing us to meet our budgets and continue our crane recovery and conservation programs. A long and complicated chain of people and events has brought about a significant conservation success story—the return of wild whooping cranes to eastern North America. Through their enthusiasm and their considerable financial and material support, the Kohlers have been—and remain—a critical link in that chain.

Chasing the Ghost Birds chronicles just three of the conservation projects to which the Kohlers have lent substantial support; there are many more. Knowing Mary and Terry, I was not surprised that they did not want to be the main characters of this book. That role, they insisted, was for the cranes, the swans, and the many other people who took part in these efforts. The author has honored that wish, and it is the Kohlers' sincere hope that the story of these three conservation projects will inspire others to learn about, and become involved in, programs to preserve wildlife and wild habitats.

Intellectually and motivationally gifted, warm and unpretentious, and blessed with resources to realize their dreams, the Kohlers are also committed Christians who begin meals with prayer and who are faithful members of the Anglican church. As fellow believers, Kyoko and I have found much enjoyment in the Christian fellowship and friendship we have shared with this most remarkable couple, on an amazing journey.

George W. Archibald
Baraboo, Wisconsin

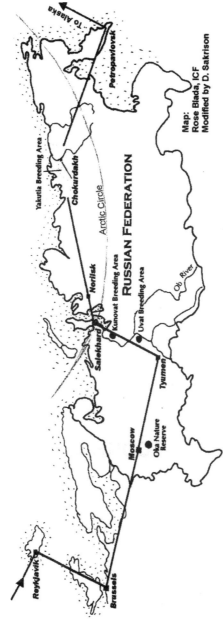

Map:
Rose Blada, ICF
Modified by D. Sakrison

Starting and ending at Baraboo, Wisconsin, the Kohler's 1997 Siberian Odyssey round-the-world flight took 13 days, and covered more than 13,000 miles. Total flight time: 39.2 hours.

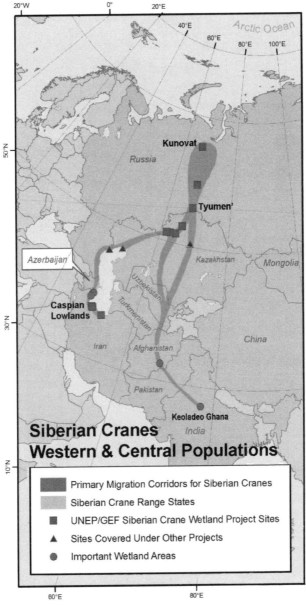

Siberian Cranes
Western & Central Populations

Primary Migration Corridors for Siberian Cranes
Siberian Crane Range States
■ UNEP/GEF Siberian Crane Wetland Project Sites
▲ Sites Covered Under Other Projects
● Important Wetland Areas

Map by the International Crane Foundation 2005
Cartographer: Zoë Rickenbach

XI

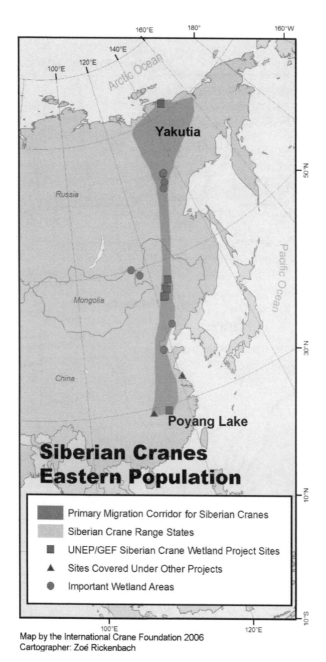

Map by the International Crane Foundation 2006
Cartographer: Zoé Rickenbach

Fort Smith, NWT

Wood Buffalo
National Park

ALBERTA

SASK.

MT

SD

WY

NE

Whooping Crane
Range

CO

Aransas-Wood Buffalo
Flock

KS

OK

TEXAS

D. Sakrison

Corpus Christi

Aransas
NWR

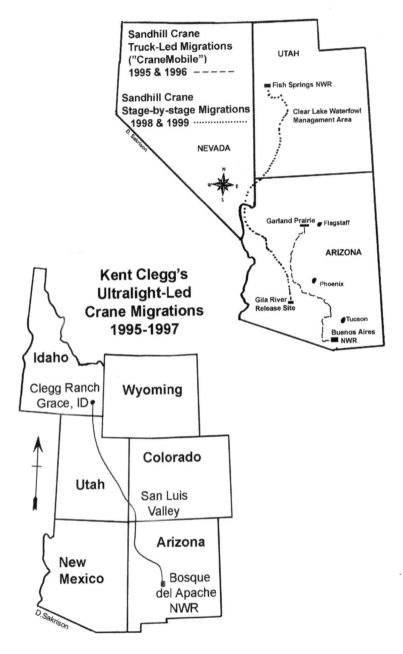

Sandhill Crane
Truck-Led Migrations
("CraneMobile")
1995 & 1996 – – – – –

Sandhill Crane
Stage-by-stage Migrations
1998 & 1999 ·············

D. Sakrison

UTAH

NEVADA

Fish Springs NWR

Clear Lake Waterfowl
Management Area

N
W   E
S

Garland Prairie   Flagstaff

ARIZONA

Phoenix

Gila River
Release Site

Tucson

Buenos Aires
NWR

Kent Clegg's
Ultralight-Led
Crane Migrations
1995-1997

Idaho

Clegg Ranch
Grace, ID

Wyoming

Utah

Colorado

San Luis
Valley

Arizona

New
Mexico

Bosque
del Apache
NWR

D. Sakrison

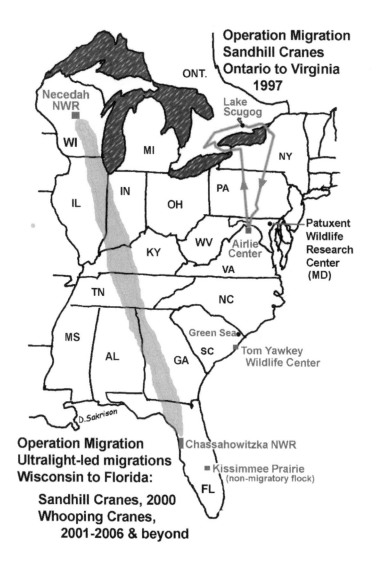

Operation Migration
Sandhill Cranes
Ontario to Virginia
1997

ONT.

Necedah
NWR

Lake
Scugog

WI

MI

NY

IL

IN

OH

PA

Patuxent
Wildlife
Research
Center
(MD)

KY

WV

Airlie
Center

VA

TN

NC

MS

Green Sea

SC

Tom Yawkey
Wildlife Center

AL

GA

D.Sakrison

Operation Migration
Ultralight-led migrations
Wisconsin to Florida:

Chassahowitzka NWR

Kissimmee Prairie
(non-migratory flock)

FL

Sandhill Cranes, 2000
Whooping Cranes,
2001-2006 & beyond

Ghost Birds

Photo © www.operationmigration.org

A SIBERIAN LEGEND SAYS THAT CRANES are not birds, at all. They are brave warriors who were slain in battle. Instead of going to their graves, these heroes returned to life as majestic white birds—ghost birds.

Cultures all over the world, from ancient Greeks to American Indians, have revered the crane as a symbol of longevity and purity. In China, cranes are called "the patriarch of the feathered tribe," and are symbols of wisdom. In Europe, where they often appeared in heraldry, cranes were symbols of vigilance and loyalty, and were seen as protectors. An ancient legend common to many cultures says that the first alphabet was inspired by the sight of a **V** of cranes flying overhead. A Japanese creation story tells of an ancient warrior who expanded the kingdom of Japan. When he died in battle, his soul became a white crane and flew away. The crane dance is common to every culture where cranes are known, often as a celebration of vitality and joy of life. Naturalist and author Aldo Leopold spoke with an ancient and timeless voice when he called the crane, "no mere bird."

SWANS, TOO, HAVE A CENTRAL PLACE IN THE MYTHS and stories of many cultures around the world. They often symbolize light. To the Greeks, swans were associated with the sun god, Apollo. In other cultures, the moon goddess was a swan. As a female symbol, the swan represented grace, inspiration, and intuition. As a male, it symbolized fire. To alchemists, swans represented the merging of

1

male and female, dark and light.

Swans even have their own constellation—one of the 88 catalogued by the astronomer Ptolemy (90-168 A.D.). Visible in the Northern Hemisphere's summer sky, "Cygnus" spreads its wings gracefully over the Milky Way.*

The myth of the swan maiden is common to many cultures. Like the Scottish "Selkie," or "seal woman," the swan maiden can transform herself into a graceful, alluring young woman by removing her feathered skin. If a man steals her swan skin and hides it from her, she is bound to him and will forget her life as a swan, though she may spend much time walking and daydreaming at the water's edge. And woe to the man who doesn't hide her feathered skin well enough. For if she finds it, she cannot help but try it on for all its beauty. And then she returns to her home on the water.

Something in swans and cranes—their size, their beauty, their haunting calls; their fidelity to their mates; their exuberance in dance or in flight—touches the soul and imagination of mankind in some inexpressible way, and leaves us better for it. But for all that humans revere and celebrate the swans and cranes, we have not always treated them with reverence. The trumpeter swan, North America's largest waterfowl, was hunted nearly to extinction a hundred years ago. The whooping crane, the rarest and most endangered crane species, was reduced to a mere handful of survivors by 1940. The Siberian crane, deprived of habitat, faces the very real prospect of extinction in the near future.

Through carelessness and neglect, we nearly made ghosts of them. But humans have the capacity to change, however reluctantly. And sometimes, with enough brains, resources, determination, and hard work, we can undo our mistakes. In less than a score of years, the trumpeter swans have come back to the Midwest Flyway and are thriving there. Whooping cranes have grown to number more than 500 and are living wild in the Eastern United States for the first time in more than a century. The "Sibes" are still dwindling under enormous pressures from human encroachment in Russia, China, India, and Central Asia. But dogged efforts and lessons learned among the whoopers may yet save Siberia's ghost bird from the void.

---

* Because of its shape, the constellation is also called "the Northern Cross." "Cygnus" is a much older appellation.

THIS BOOK DESCRIBES THREE major conservation projects: the reintroduction of trumpeter swans to the Midwestern United States, efforts to preserve the seriously-threatened Siberian crane in Russia, and reintroduction of the whooping crane to the Eastern United States. Researching and writing about these projects, one is struck by a common thread that runs through them: With all our technology and all our supposedly superior intelligence, humans could not simply drag these species back from the brink of extinction with our own methods and tools. We first had to learn from the birds, tease out their secrets, learn their habits, and let them show us the way. We marveled at their beauty, their instincts, their capabilities, and their social complexity. In that process, we have learned something about ourselves, if only that, as American inventor Samuel Morse once said, "Human beings don't know one millionth of one tenth of a percent about anything."

The story of these three conservation projects offers up heroes aplenty—many of them ordinary folks, who together are accomplishing extraordinary things. The next time you hear the clear, bell-like call of a trumpeter swan or the haunting whoop of a whooping crane, remember that these birds were almost gone. Like the ghost birds of the legend, they are returning. And like the dancing cranes, their wild, ancient voices call to each of us to treasure and celebrate life in all its varieties.

Part One: Swan Song

© Greg Erlandson

"Birds are indicators of the environment. If they are in trouble, we know we'll soon be in trouble."
—Roger Tory Peterson

"Tug on anything at all and you'll find it connected to everything else in the universe."
—John Muir

Chapter 1
Trumpet Call

IT IS EARLY MORNING ON THE SOUTHERN EDGE of a marsh in North Central Wisconsin. The marsh hasn't iced over yet, but there is ice around its edges and frost on the long grass. The steam in our breath and the numbness in our toes tell us that winter can't be far off, despite the bright late-October sunshine.

It is a noisy place. Canada geese, herons, egrets, cormorants, ducks, a few snow geese, the occasional rattle of Sandhill cranes, and the cries of a hawk—they all add up to something like a noisy cocktail party, with the most raucous hilarity coming from a large flock of mallard ducks nearby. If we're lucky this morning—very, very lucky—we might spot one of the rare whooping cranes that now nest in Wisconsin, thanks to the efforts of the International Crane Foundation (ICF) and the Eastern Whooping Crane Partnership, among others. (As it turns out, on this day we're not that lucky.) We're here this morning to try to spot another majestic bird, the largest waterfowl in North America.

After what seems like a long, chilly wait, we hear the call; deep and loud, resonant and trumpet-like, it stands out above the cocktail chatter. The birds come into view flying low over the marsh—five trumpeter swans in flight. They might be a breeding pair and three cygnets (young swans), or maybe a sibling group, independent from their parents but not yet paired with mates. Snowy white, with adult wing spans of nearly eight feet, (2.4 meters) the birds are breathtakingly beautiful—all the more so because, by some accounts, they shouldn't be here at all. Until a few years ago, wild, free trumpeter swans had not been seen in midwestern skies for nearly 120 years.

The French explorers and trappers who first ventured into the

Great Lakes region (the old Northwest Territory) some 300 years ago found swans in large numbers throughout Michigan, Wisconsin, and Minnesota. Found only in North America, trumpeter swans were common throughout the central United States and Canada, and they may have numbered as many as 130,000 birds, in nesting ranges from the eastern foothills of the Rocky Mountains to Lake Michigan and James Bay (on the southern end of Hudson Bay). Their wintering ranges extended from Texas to the Atlantic coasts of Virginia and North Carolina.[1]

The French soldier and explorer Antoine de la Mothe Cadillac founded Fort Pontchartrain in 1701 on the future site of the city of Detroit, Michigan. In a letter of October 1701, he described the area to his employers. He wrote, in part:

> "Swans are in such profusion that they might be taken for the lily rushes in which they gather. The chattering goose, the duck, the teal, and the bustard are so numerous that I must use the expression of an Indian whom I asked, before coming here, if there was much feathered game. There is so much, he said, that they have to open a way in order for the canoes to pass."

Today, it is unknown whether the swans that Cadillac saw in such profusion were trumpeters, tundra swans, or both. Nonetheless, trumpeters may have been common in the Great Lakes region when the first Europeans arrived here.

Trumpeter swans are large birds; adults stand up to five feet (150 cm) tall and weigh up to 35 pounds (15 kg). They are slow in flight, making them easy targets for settlers and hunters. Through the 1700s, they were hunted for their meat and for the writing quills

---

[1] Evidence that trumpeters may have nested throughout Eastern U.S. and Canada is controversial. Some point to historic evidence of trumpeter sightings all along the Eastern Seaboard, from Nova Scotia to Florida.

Others say that evidence is far from conclusive, that pre-extirpation sightings in the 17th and 18th centuries failed to differentiate between nesting and migrating swans, or between trumpeters and tundra swans. Tundra swans are known to be native to the east coast. More conclusive evidence, some experts argue, puts the eastern limit of the trumpeter's historic nesting range along a line from James Bay to northwestern Indiana. Recent efforts to establish new nesting populations of trumpeters around Chesapeake Bay and elsewhere in eastern North America have only added heat to the debate.

John James Audubon (1785-1851), the revered American wildlife artist, was indirectly responsible for the killing of thousands of trumpeter swans, when he declared their quills as superior to all others for his finely detailed sketches of American birds. Photo: Wisconsin Dept. of Natural Resources

Stacked trophies from a swan hunt, around 1900. Legal hunting ended when the trumpeter became an internationally protected species in 1919. Photo: Wisconsin DNR.

made from their feathers. Even naturalist John James Audubon helped fuel the traffic in trumpeter swans; he declared their quills as superior to all others for his finely detailed sketches of American birds. To meet a growing demand for swans down, the Hudson's Bay Company, the huge Canadian fur trader founded in 1670, began harvesting trumpeter swans in the late 1700s. In the 1800s, commercial hunters pursued the trumpeter to meet a continued demand for swans down, and to supply a new American and European fashion for feathered hats and swan skin powder puffs.

Meanwhile, settlers hunted trumpeter swans for food, and as they cleared the land, they drained and filled the trumpeters' wetland habitats. Today, some Midwestern states have lost up to 90 percent of the wetlands that existed 200 years ago.

By the late 1880s, it was widely assumed that the trumpeter swan was extinct in the wild.

Then, in 1919, two trumpeter swan nests were found in Yellowstone National Park. Sixty-nine trumpeters were discovered nesting nearby at Montana's Red Rock Lakes in 1932. These birds ranged over parts of Idaho, Montana, and Wyoming. Three years later, in 1935, Congress created the Red Rock Lakes National Wildlife Refuge in Montana's Centennial Valley, to protect what were then believed to be the only wild trumpeter swans left in North America. The refuge managers provided winter food for the swans, restricted cattle grazing and hay cutting in the marshes, controlled predators, and took other steps to improve the swans' habitat. By the late 1950s, there were more than 600 trumpeters at Red Rock Lakes and nearby Yellowstone Park.

In the 1950s, several thousand trumpeter swans were discovered nesting in east central Alaska, and about 1,000 more trumpeters were counted in northwestern Canada. These birds had been protected from hunters and hidden from wildlife biologists by the isolation and inaccessibility of their range.

The 1919 International Migratory Bird Treaty, signed by Canada, Mexico, and the United States, made the trumpeter swan (Cygnus buccinator) a protected species in all three countries. The success of the Montana/Wyoming birds and the discovery of large flocks in Alaska and Canada kept the trumpeter off the U.S. lists of threatened or endangered species, even though everywhere east of the Rocky Mountains, they were long gone.

IN 1984, THE CANADIAN WILDLIFE SERVICE and the U.S. Fish and Wildlife Service released a cooperative North American Management Plan for Trumpeter Swans, part of the joint North American Waterfowl Management Plan. To aid in management, the trumpeter plan recognized three separate populations. The trumpeters that summer in Alaska and winter in British Columbia were designated as the Pacific Coast Population. Migratory trumpeters that breed in north central Canada and winter in the tri-state region (Idaho-Montana-Wyoming), and non-migratory trumpeters living in the tri-state region were grouped into the Rocky Mountain Population. Minnesota's Hennepin County Parks had begun a trumpeter restoration project eight years earlier; those birds became the Interior Population, which would also include future restored flocks in Iowa, Wisconsin, Michigan, and other midwestern states. After the federal Management Plan was published, several states followed suit by creating their own trumpeter restoration plans. Today, Indiana, Iowa, Michigan, Minnesota, Nebraska, Ohio, South Dakota, and Wisconsin all have active trumpeter swan restoration programs, as do the Canadian provinces of Ontario and Alberta.

Some biologists were concerned that habitat loss would be the biggest obstacle to restoring wild trumpeter swans. Many of the wetlands that once supported wild flocks of trumpeters were gone. In Michigan and Wisconsin, half the wetlands—potential historic nesting areas—had been drained or filled since the mid-19th century.

Farther south, in the swans' historic wintering grounds, the situation was even worse. Ohio, Iowa, and other central states had lost up to 90 percent of their wetlands, mainly to farmland. Could trumpeters survive in a landscape that had changed so radically?

And yet, the region supported and continues to support healthy populations of tundra swans and mute swans. Some people argued that hunting, not habitat loss was the main reason that trumpeter swans had disappeared from the region more than 100 years earlier. The trumpeter swan was now protected, they said. Imposing penalties for killing the swans, and educating hunters, should curtail both accidental and vandalistic shooting of the swans.[2]

MINNESOTA'S THREE RIVERS PARK DISTRICT (formerly the Hennepin County Parks District) launched the first trumpeter swan recovery project in the Midwest, in 1966. At that time, the trumpeter swans in Yellowstone and Montana were the only surviving wild trumpeters in the lower 48 United States. The park district, located in Minneapolis-St.Paul, obtained 40 swans from the Montana's Red Rock Lakes to establish a captive breeding flock in the Twin Cities' parks and wetlands. Over the next 20 years, Three Rivers built up a population of nearly 100 trumpeters, including 13 breeding pairs. Cygnets and eggs came to the park district from Montana, Minnesota zoos, and Chicago's Brookfield Zoo.

Encouraged by the park district's success, the Minnesota Department of Natural Resources (DNR) began reintroducing trumpeters to wetland areas in northern and southern Minnesota. Reintroduction programs also were getting underway in Iowa, Wisconsin, and Michigan.

At first, the Minnesota DNR relied on Montana wildlife refuges, public zoos, and private swan propagators for its trumpeter swan eggs. But those sources could only provide a limited number of eggs and cygnets. The 10,000 wild trumpeters that nested in Alaska every summer could produce enough trumpeter eggs for all of the trum-

---

[2] Hunters often mistake trumpeter swans for tundra swans or snow geese, or so they claim. Tundra swans closely resemble the larger trumpeters. Snow geese (Chen caerulescens) are white with conspicuously black wing tips, have a typically goose-like call, and are less than half the size of an adult trumpeter, with a wingspan of about three feet. Snow geese can be hunted legally in most states; tundra swans, in a handful of states. Trumpeters are protected throughout their range.

peter restoration programs in Canada and lower 48 United States. The Alaskan trumpeters were also much more genetically diverse than Montana's wild swans. Their genetic diversity would help to ensure that the Interior flocks that were being created in Iowa, Minnesota, Wisconsin, and Michigan would be healthy and robust.

In the wild, each pair of Alaskan trumpeters rears an average of 2.2 cygnets per year, out of an average clutch of five eggs. Avian biologists believed that removing "surplus" eggs while leaving at least two viable eggs in each nest, would not affect the productivity of the wild trumpeters. This belief was confirmed by later surveys of the Alaskan flock.

Ornithologists from the Minnesota DNR began collecting trumpeter eggs in Alaska in 1986, under license from the Alaska DNR. Fifty Alaskan trumpeter eggs were collected each year from 1986 through 1988. Incubated and hatched at the Carlos Avery Wildlife Management Center in St. Paul, cygnets from the Alaskan eggs were released at state and national refuges around Minnesota. The first release was in the spring of 1987 when 21 two-year-old trumpeters were released near the Tamarac National Wildlife Refuge in Minnesota's Becker County. The birds migrated south in the fall and wintered in widely scattered areas around the Midwest. Several pairs returned to Minnesota and nested the following summer.

HATCHING AND RAISING YOUNG SWANS IN CAPTIVITY for release into the wild is a complex and expensive undertaking. When the Michigan DNR began its trumpeter swan restoration program in 1986, avian biologists there proposed a different approach, one that would take advantage of the state's existing population of mute swans.

Besides the trumpeter, only one other swan species is native to North America: the tundra swan

Trumpeter

Tundra (Whistling)

Mute

Source: Wisconsin DNR

(Cygnus columbianus), also known as the "whistling swan." Tundra swans and trumpeters are almost identical in appearance. The tundra swan is smaller, weighing 13 to 20 pounds (6-9 kg), and standing about four feet (120 cm) tall, with a wingspan over five feet (150 cm). Both tundra and trumpeter cygnets are grayish tan, though trumpeter cygnets tend to be a little sootier. The most reliable way to tell trumpeters and tundra swans apart is by their calls. The trumpeter has a distinct trumpet-like call that is sometimes compared to the note of a French horn. Tundra swans sound more like Canada geese.

The mute swan (Cygnus olor) is perhaps the most familiar of the swan species; it is the one that usually appears in greeting cards, paintings, and storybooks. It is an invasive European species, imported into this country in the late 1800s as a domestic bird.[3] Nearly as large as the trumpeter, the mute swan has a distinct orange bill with a black fleshy knob that extends from the back of its bill to the top of its forehead. On the ground or in the water, the mute swan holds its neck in an S-shape, with its bill pointing downward. The trumpeter swan usually holds its neck and head upright. The mute swan isn't really mute, but its calls are subdued, consisting mostly of snorts and grunts.

In Michigan and Wisconsin, DNR biologists placed trumpeter swan eggs into the nests of wild mute swans. The Michigan DNR's main partner in the program was Michigan State University's Kellogg Bird Sanctuary at Kalamazoo.[4] The program was led by Joe Johnson, chief wildlife biologist at the sanctuary, and a member of the Midwest Flyway Trumpeter Swan Technical Committee.

In both states, trumpeter eggs came from zoos, from private game farms, and from wild swan nests in Alaska.

Johnson traveled around the central and eastern U.S. to find wild mute swan nests in which to place the trumpeter swan eggs. He recalled: "I placed 48 eggs under mute swans and they hatched 30, which wasn't bad. But only six survived to fly."

The Wisconsin DNR placed 35 trumpeter swan eggs in the nests

---

[3] Most of the wild populations of mute swans in North America began with birds that escaped captivity or were accidentally released. It is an aggressive species that harasses other waterfowl and tears up the wetland vegetation that other birds rely on for food. Enshrined though it may be in folklore and art, the mute swan is widely considered by ornithologists and conservationists to be an undesirable pest.

[4] The Bird Sanctuary is part of the university's Kellogg Biological Station (KBS), located on 4,065 acres (16.5 km2) between Kalamazoo and Battle Creek, Michigan. W.K. Kellogg, founder of the breakfast cereal empire, was a philanthropist and environmentalist. He created the bird sanctuary in 1926, along with several other facilities and tracts that now make up the KBS, including the Kellogg Farm, the Kellogg Biological Laboratories, the KBS Conference Center, Extension and Outreach offices, the Lux Arbor Reserve, and the nearby Kellogg Experimental Forest. Today, the entire complex is owned and operated by Michigan State University.

of wild mute swans on Phantom Lake in Waukesha County, in Southeastern Wisconsin. The eggs came from private game farms and from zoos in Milwaukee and Chicago. From 35 eggs, the foster-parent swans at Phantom Lake produced only one surviving cygnet.

Under the best of conditions, cygnets (swans less than a year old) face a host of threats to their survival in the wild. They hatch in June, each weighing about half a pound (220 grams). After a day or two of drying off and resting, the cygnets begin swimming and eating duck-weed and aquatic insects. They gradually learn feeding habits from their parents, and by four to six weeks of age, they are feeding almost entirely on water plants. On this protein-rich diet, their weight increases about 20 percent each day. Swans are attentive parents, protecting their cygnets and teaching them what foods to eat. Young swans stay partly dependent on their parents for most of the first year of life, gradually learning to fend for themselves.

Threats to the cygnets' survival come from predators, disease, illegal or accidental shooting by hunters, power lines, entanglement with discarded fishing lines, vehicular collisions, and on rare occasions collisions with power boats. Predators include snapping turtles during the cygnets' first few weeks, as well as mink, raccoon, red fox, coyote, and occasionally a bald eagle.

Lead poisoning is a serious environmental risk for all North American waterfowl, including the trumpeter swan. Though hunting with lead shot has been banned nation-wide since 1991, lead pellets and lead fishing sinkers can be found in abundance in every wetland where gun hunting or fishing has occurred in the past.[5] Swans and other birds can ingest lead pellets and sinkers as they forage for underwater plants and search for grit—such as pondweed seeds—to aid their digestion.

Trumpeter swans are especially susceptible to lead poisoning; ingesting one or two pellets of lead shot can cause an adult trumpeter to sicken and die. Lead shot may be the single most serious threat to the trumpeter's survival in the Midwest. In wetlands that are heavily contaminated with lead shot, the mortality rate for swan cygnets, from lead poisoning, can be as high as 90 percent.

In the Michigan and Wisconsin cross-fostering experiments, predation and lead poisoning took a heavy toll. Phantom Lake, where

---

[5] Several states are currently considering a ban on lead fishing sinkers; a few have banned them already.

Photo: *Wisconsin DNR*

Wisconsin's mute swan foster parents nested, turned out to be "a snapping turtle Mecca," according to officials there. Two other factors contributed significantly to the lack of success in both cross-fostering programs:

First, captive trumpeters lay their eggs about three weeks later than wild mute swans, so the trumpeter cygnets mature and fledge later. That makes them more vulnerable to snapping turtles and other predators. Mute swan cygnets sometimes climb onto their parents' backs to escape snapping turtles; trumpeters rarely do so.

Second, mute swans frequently feed on plant leaves and stems. While trumpeters will also eat leaves, they prefer seeds and tubers. This makes trumpeters more susceptible to lead poisoning, since they are more likely than mute swans to swallow lead pellets from the marshy bottoms. At Phantom Lake, where several trumpeter cygnets succumbed to lead poisoning, few of the mute swans had high levels of lead in their blood.

The International Crane Foundation has successfully cross-fostered captive cranes in captivity at Baraboo, Johnson notes. But in the wild, he said, "you have no control over the parents or the cygnets," and cross fostering has not been successful. "For 17 years, they tried cross-fostering whooping cranes under Sandhill cranes out west, and that did not work."

"I tried [cross fostering] for three years," Johnson said, Wisconsin's DNR "tried it for two, and we decided this is just not going to work. It was a romantic thing to do; it was inexpensive. We thought, 'Man, this is the Dutchman's way out of this, it's cheap.' But we had parental rejection at Day One and parental abandonment at about five to six weeks of age when the cygnets are just stupid."

By 1989 both Michigan and Wisconsin had abandoned cross fostering of trumpeters. In Canada, Ontario tried cross fostering for one more year. In 1990, none of Ontario's cross-fostered trumpeters survived.

Cross fostering was "a great idea," Johnson concludes. " It didn't work worth a damn."

AFTER GIVING UP ON CROSS FOSTERING, Michigan began incubating trumpeter eggs and raising the cygnets in captivity at the Kellogg Bird Sanctuary. Those cygnets were raised in isolation from humans "as much as possible," Johnson said. "Staff were threatened with death if they spoke to the birds." Every attempt was made to minimize human contact, especially after the birds reached five weeks of age. By that time, they had grown large enough that they didn't need to be warmed and could be put in predator-proof pens at the water's edge. After that, the only human contact was someone coming out to the pen and putting food in a bin.

To keep the young birds from flying away, the flight feathers of all the brooder-raised cygnets were clipped at 15 weeks of age, then again at 11 months of age. "And every time you captured those buggers and clipped their feathers, they started to not like you," Johnson said. That seems to have counteracted some of the cygnets' socialization to humans. "I think our techniques were right on," he added.

Raised in broods of seven or eight, the cygnets were released into the wild at two years of age. Michigan's original goal was to establish three wild flocks on its wetlands, totaling 200 trumpeter swans, with 30 nesting pairs, by the year 2000. Those flocks were to be established by releasing trumpeter cygnets at three wetland areas in the state: in southwest Michigan, west of Kalamazoo; in northeast Lower Michigan in and near the Au Sable State Forest; and at Seney National Wildlife Refuge (NWR) in Schoolcraft County in the central Upper Peninsula.

The 2000 bird census in Michigan counted 401 trumpeter swans in the state—twice the goal for that year—including 39 nesting pairs. The largest and most successful of the three flocks is at Seney NWR. Johnson counts off the reasons for that success: "It's a national wildlife refuge; there is little or no lead poisoning, little or no vandalistic shooting, and no high tension wires to run into." Those are all major causes of death among swans and other large birds in southern Michigan. Johnson added:

"The growing season is shorter in the Upper Peninsula, the wetlands aren't as productive, the clutch sizes and brood sizes are smaller, but the rate of survival is far greater among the Schoolcraft County flock than among birds in southern Michigan. Swans from Seney [NWR] are nesting all over the eastern Upper Peninsula now."

IN IOWA, THE DNR WORKED WITH PRIVATE landowners to establish more than 50 "trumpeter swan breeder pair partnership sites." These were privately owned ponds and wetlands where flightless pairs of trumpeters could nest and raise free-flying cygnets. The first of these sites was established in 1989. The breeding pairs came from a variety of sources including zoos, private propagators, and other states' swan restoration programs. Iowa also obtained 30 trumpeter eggs from Alaska over two years, brought back by the Wisconsin DNR.

Cygnets produced in the partnership site program were kept flightless and were left with their parents until they were a year old, then moved to other wetland sites around the state and released.

Most of Iowa's trumpeters winter in northwestern Missouri and northeastern Kansas, though they have been seen as far south as Oklahoma and Arkansas. When they can find open water, many of the Iowa trumpeters winter in Iowa. Like other migratory birds, most trumpeters have an instinctive urge to migrate, but learn migration routes from their parents. When Midwestern biologists and conservationists first began releasing captive-raised two-year-old trumpeters into the wild, there was widespread concern that the birds might be unable to migrate south, without wild parents to show them the way. For the most part, those fears proved unfounded. Released in areas shared by Canada geese, ducks, herons, and other migrating waterfowl, many of the trumpeter swans followed other species as they migrated south in the fall.

Some of the released trumpeters venture only as far as they need to, to find open water. More than a century ago, before wild trumpeters disappeared from the Midwest, finding open water in the winter months meant migrating several hundred miles south. Today nuclear power plants, coal-fired power plants, water and sewage treatment plants, and other man-made facilities discharge warm water, creating suitable year-round open-water habitats far north of the swans' historic wintering grounds.

THE WISCONSIN TRUMPETER SWAN RECOVERY PLAN, published in 1986, set a goal of at least 20 wild trumpeter breeding pairs nesting in the state by the year 2000. To implement the plan, the Wisconsin Department of Natural Resources (WDNR) Bureau of Endangered Resources partnered with the Milwaukee County Zoo and the Zoological Society of Milwaukee County to set up a captive breeding and rearing program. Cygnets from that program were to be released at protected sites around the state.

Eggs for the program—at least 50 a year—would come initially from two breeding pairs at the Milwaukee County Zoo, from captive birds at Chicago's Lincoln Park Zoo, and from wild trumpeter swans in Alaska. Collecting eggs from Alaskan swans offered some real advantages. The large Alaskan flocks could provide plenty of eggs without threatening their own survival; the genetic diversity of the Alaskan swans would help to ensure healthy birds in the Midwest; and the Alaskan swans possessed strong migratory instincts that the Midwestern birds would need to chart new migration routes without parents to guide them.

The Wisconsin DNR forged an agreement with Alaska's DNR: WDNR could collect wild trumpeter swan eggs in Alaska, leaving at least two viable eggs in each affected nest. In exchange, Wisconsin would pay for two aerial surveys each year in which it gathered eggs—an early survey of nesting pairs in the proposed collection area, and a later "productivity survey" to count the number of cygnets produced by nesting pairs in the collection area. Biologists would also survey a "control area" where no eggs had been collected. With that data, Alaska's DNR could reliably measure the impact of egg collection on the affected flocks. The Minnesota and Michigan DNRs penned similar agreements with Alaska, to gather eggs for their trumpeter swan recovery programs.

Chapter 2
Eggs-Pedition to Alaska

IN 1985, AS A YOUNG AVIAN ECOLOGIST with the Wisconsin Department of Natural Resources (WDNR) Sumner Matteson was assigned to write a recovery plan for an endangered species. His administrators mulled over the choice between the trumpeter swan and the whooping crane, and chose the former. That decision propelled Matteson into an adventure that has lasted more than 20 years. The WDNR published his Wisconsin Trumpeter Swan Recovery Plan in 1986.

The Recovery Plan called for Wisconsin to obtain trumpeter eggs from Alaska and from captive breeding pairs. Some of the eggs would be cross-fostered by placing them in wild mute swan nests. The rest would be incubated and reared in controlled conditions, for later release into the wild.

In 1987, Matteson helped to lead an International Crane Foundation trip to China's Pyong Lake Nature Preserve, where ICF volunteers and others counted Siberian and other cranes on their wintering grounds. Mary Kohler, of Sheboygan Wisconsin, was one of the volunteers on that trip and she and Matteson became friends during the weeklong project.

"Mary is a very independent person and very persuasive," Matteson said. "She's a strong individual with a vibrant personality, and she was willing to do anything asked of her on that trip. She is also a very good birder."

Two years later, in early 1989, as Matteson and his colleagues prepared to collect trumpeter eggs from Alaska, they began looking for transportation. Wisconsin Governor Tommy Thompson learned of their search. Mary and her husband Terry Kohler were both actively involved in Thompson's 1986 election to the governorship, and in April 1989 Thompson made a call to Terry. According to Terry's notes, their conversation went something like this:

Thompson: "Terry, our Wisconsin DNR has put together a plan to re-establish trumpeter swans into Wisconsin. We are going to be collecting the swan eggs in Alaska with the help of the U.S. Fish & Wildlife Service, and then we have to transport them back to Wisconsin to the Milwaukee Zoo to incubate and hatch them before releasing them into the wild here.

"The major problem we have is that a commercial flight down from Alaska involves many hours and multiple transfers, all the time carrying a box of 50 to 60 swan eggs in one's lap on the airplane. I know your company has a Citation V that you fly all the time. Is there any chance you might be willing to fly up there with our guys, and help them out by bringing the eggs back?"

Terry: "When do we leave?"

Mary Kohler called Matteson the next day and told him that she and Terry would commit to flying the WDNR to Alaska for the next nine years, in their company's Cessna Citation business jet. Matteson was astounded, he recalls. "It was the answer to our prayers, and proved to be a hell of a lot of fun, to boot."

Mary is an avid, lifelong birder. She was one of the first teacher-naturalists trained by Wisconsin's Riveredge Nature Center. She has taught summer ecology classes and set up outdoor education programs for grade school students, mothers, and teachers, and served on the Riveredge board for 14 years. She has taken part in more than a dozen dinosaur digs with the Milwaukee Public Museum and the Museum of the Rockies. And she has served on the boards of, among others, the Nature Conservancy (Wisconsin Chapter), the Coastal Management Council, Nashota House (an Episcopal Seminary), and the Wisconsin Women's Council.

Terry Kohler is an active outdoorsman, and a life member of

Ducks Unlimited and the National Rifle Association. He has served on the board of the Trout and Salmon Foundation for two decades. He has also been a sailor most of his life. In 1978, he skippered his boat, "A'gape," to defend the Canada's Cup for the United States, and his company, North Sails Group, is the world's leading manufacturer of America's Cup sails.

Terry's activities in support of conservation have been many and varied. And when he talks about the projects he has been involved in, he reveals a deep reverence for the natural world and simple delight in participating and in seeing first-hand how conservation projects work.

He has flown his Bell 407 helicopter in surveys and videotaping of Montana trout streams for the Trout and Salmon Foundation, and of Wisconsin trout streams for the Wisconsin Coastal Survey. To help promote Wisconsin's Ice Age Trail, he flew video missions along much of the trail's length, at times carrying a film crew from the National Geographic Society. For the Museum of the Rockies, he flew aerial surveys of ancient coal beds in Montana, helping paleontologists searching for clues to the extinction of the dinosaurs. In Chile, where the Kohlers owned a fishing lodge at Puerto Montt, Terry flew helicopter surveys of black-necked swans for a local conservation project. He also flew "all kinds of medevac flights down there."

For the Riveredge Nature Center, he once flew an extensive survey of the Cedarburg Marsh in Southeastern Wisconsin, looking for purple loosestrife, an invasive plant that crowds out cattails and other wetland plants. The director of the Riveredge Center, "used to call me periodically," Terry recalls. "He'd say, 'I've got another project; are you interested in doing it?'" Terry adds, "My usual reaction was, 'When do we leave?'"

His love of flying certainly played a part; many of his conservation activities have involved aircraft in some way, often with Terry in the pilot's seat. He learned to fly during a tour in the U.S. Air Force from 1955 to 1959. Trained as a jet fighter pilot, he served as a B-47 bomber combat pilot in the Strategic Air Command. He has been an active aviator ever since.

Talking about their conservation activities, both Mary and Terry are apt to defer the credit to others, and to downplay their own contributions. But virtually every biologist, aviculturist, and conservationist interviewed for this book gave the Kohlers a great deal of credit. They also spoke of Mary and Terry with affection, describing them as warm, generous, unpretentious, and very likable people.

THE AIRCRAFT THAT WOULD TAKE SUMNER Matteson to Alaska and return with trumpeter swan eggs was Windway Capital Corporation's Cessna Citation 560. It was a twin-engine business jet with room for two pilots and eight passengers. It cruised at 375 to 400 knots, or 430 to 460 miles per hour (690 to 740 kilometers per hour), at up to 45,000 feet (13,700 m) of altitude. It had a maximum range of more than 2,200 miles (3,540 km) between fuel stops. The Citation's passenger cabin was comfortable, if not exactly roomy. Over the years, Terry took the airplane south all the way to Chile and north to Prudhoe Bay, Alaska.

Cessna Citation V

The Citation's first trip to Alaska to gather trumpeter swan eggs was scheduled for early June 1989, when the eggs would be 20 to 25 days old. On June 7, the Kohlers flew the Citation to Kalamazoo, Michigan to pick up Joe Johnson, who would bring back 20 eggs for Michigan's trumpeter swan reintroduction program. Terry was in the pilot's seat; Mary flew as his co-pilot. From Kalamazoo, they flew the Citation to Madison, Wisconsin to pick up Matteson and Randy Jurewicz, a staff biologist from the WDNR's Bureau of Endangered Resources. With two fuel stops, in Lewiston, Montana and Ketchikan, Alaska, the flight to Fairbanks, Alaska took about nine hours. Landing in Fairbanks in evening twilight at a quarter to midnight local time, Terry taxied the Citation to a parking area, slipped the jet into an empty spot, and shut down the engines. Johnson continued the story:

"We were just starting to climb out of the airplane when three police vehicles came up, sirens going and lights flashing. I think they thought we were drug smugglers." This was years before 9/11 and the heightened security that followed that event.

The police informed Terry that the airplane was in the Commuter

Lot, where it didn't belong, and that it was pointed in the wrong direction for the prevailing winds. The airplane was moved to a proper parking place and pointed in the right direction.

At eight o'clock the next morning, the team was met by US Fish & Wildlife Service pilot and biologist Rod King, whom they promptly dubbed, "Sky King." Matteson, Jurewicz, and Johnson flew in King's Cessna 185 float plane to an isolated DNR cabin in the Minto Flats State Game Refuge, which lies about 50 miles (80 km) west of Fairbanks. A Cessna 185 has four seats. In Johnson's plane, the rear seat had been replaced with a jump seat made of wooden rods and canvas. Terry remembers it as "terrible to sit on." The plane was modified with a STOL (short takeoff & landing) wing that allowed it to fly in and out of small lakes and rivers.

Covering half a million acres (2,000 km2), the Minto Flats is the nesting area for the largest group of wild trumpeter swans in North America. Other bird species commonly seen there include ducks (150,000 new ducklings a year), geese, Sandhill cranes, loons, bald eagles, peregrine falcons, grouse, ptarmigan, passerines, and small owls. This mosaic of streams, ponds, oxbows, and wetland and upland meadows also supports large numbers of moose, black bear, beaver, muskrat, river otter, lynx, wolverine, red fox, mink, and marten. Northern pike, turbot, grayling, whitefish, and blackfish thrive in the Flats' rivers and shallow lakes, while Chinook, chum, and Coho salmon migrate through here. Deer flies, black flies, mosquitoes (the unofficial "state bird" of Alaska), and biting "no-see-ums" provide entertainment during the warm months.

Minto Flats was and remains a traditional hunting and fishing grounds for the Athabaskan Indians who now live in and around the nearby towns of Minto and Nenana. Under state management, the refuge is also an important resource for hunters, trappers, and fishermen from the Fairbanks area and beyond. There are no campgrounds or other public-use developments in the refuge, and only a single road enters the refuge, from Fairbanks. Most access is by boat or float-plane in the summer and by snowmobile, dogsled, or ski plane in the winter. Weather on the Flats is typical for the Alaskan interior. Summers are short and warm, winters are long and numbingly cold, and precipitation is low year-round. Minto Flats is also known for its steady high winds.

A week before Matteson, Jurewicz, and Johnson arrived, King had found, by aerial survey, more than two dozen trumpeter swan nests in the area, that appeared to be accessible from the water, and he had marked their locations on a topographical map.

The team brought with them three black egg-collecting boxes on loan from the Minnesota DNR, which had used the same boxes in their egg collection efforts. Padded with foam and warmed by hot water bottles, these containers would keep the eggs warm and snug during the long trip from Minto Flats to the Milwaukee County Zoo. Matteson carried a fourth container, a small padded gray suitcase for collecting the eggs. To minimize the time between nest and incubator, the egg collection would be a single all-day marathon, followed by a race back to Fairbanks and a quick departure in the Citation for an overnight flight to Milwaukee.

The timing of the trip was important. Matteson wanted to collect the eggs when they were 20 to 25 days old. Lots of research has shown that the best results come from eggs that have been at least partially incubated by parents—wild or captive. Trumpeter eggs hatch after 30 to 35 days of gestation; by 20 to 25 days, Matteson and his colleagues reasoned, the embryos should be robust enough to survive the long flight to Milwaukee and Michigan and to do well in the artificial incubators.

MATTESON HAS AN INNER EAR CONDITION that makes him especially prone to motion sickness. The 1989 trip from Fairbanks to Minto Flats in Rod King's Cessna 185 floatplane was only his second trip in a bush plane. During his first bush flight 20 years earlier, Matteson had unceremoniously "lost my lunch." Anticipating similar trouble in Alaska, he sought advice prior to the trip. The results were contradictory and not much help. In Fairbanks, on the morning of the egg collection, he ate a light breakfast—and lost it less than an hour into the flight. Sick and dehydrated, he struggled through 13 straight hours of egg collection, nearly passing out at one point. Sometime during the afternoon, King asked him, "You're not going to die on me are you?" He survived, collecting a total of 60 eggs that day—40 for Wisconsin and 20 for Michigan. In succeeding years, a patch, worn behind Matteson's ear, controlled his motion sickness and made his flights in the bush planes much less of an ordeal.

King first flew the team out to a remote DNR cabin in Minto Flats. Johnson and Jurewicz spent the day there, tending the eggs that King and Matteson collected from nests located all around the flats. Terry and Mary Kohler spent the day in Fairbanks, sleeping and rest

This wilderness cabin at Minto Flats was the base of operations for egg-collecting missions.
Photo: Wisconsin DNR

Sumner Matteson, pilot Rod King, and Randy Jurewicz with King's floatplane.
Photo: Wisconsin Dept. of Natural Resources

ing for an overnight return flight to Wisconsin.

To collect the eggs, King landed on the water near a selected nest, then taxied the floatplane as close to the nest as possible. Matteson climbed out of the airplane and onto a floating bog mat, checking his footing at each step. Much of the "terrain" at Minto Flats is made up of floating mats of vegetation, from a few inches to several feet thick. Walking there can be like walking on a waterbed. Before Matteson left the plane, he donned a flotation vest. "If you break through the mat," King told him, "just pull the lanyard. The vest will inflate and you'll pop right back up."

Trumpeters like to build their nests atop muskrat or beaver lodges. If there are no accommodating muskrats or beavers in the neighborhood, the swans will pile up mounds of sedges and cattails, usually in open water where predators would have a hard time sneaking up on the nest. The male (called a "cob") pulls up vegetation and brings it to the female (called a "pen"), who arranges it around herself to create a mounded nest with a shallow bowl in the middle. The finished nest may be six feet (180 cm) across. A trumpeter pair's nesting territory may be as small as six acres or as large as 150 acres (0.024 to 0.6 km2), depending on the quantity and quality of food plants available. A mating pair may use the same nest year after year, especially if they have successfully raised a brood there. Trumpeter swans can be very aggressive in defending their nesting territories. They will drive off or even kill other swans and Canada geese, though they are usually tolerant of smaller waterfowl.

Eggs begin to appear in late April or early May, one every other day. A pen typically lays between five and nine eggs each spring, each weighing about 12 ounces (340 g). Her first year of nesting, she will lay fewer eggs and they will probably be infertile. Once the eggs are laid, the pen incubates them for about 33 days, while the cob stands guard, challenging any and all intruders. From time to time, the pen will leave the nest to feed or to bathe and preen her feathers. Before she leaves, she covers the eggs with nest material, and while she is away, the cob stands guard on or near the nest.

At each stop on the day-long egg hunt, Matteson climbed out of King's airplane and made his way cautiously to the nest. He carried a canoe paddle in one hand—to feel his way across the boggy ground and to ward off attacks from the guarding cob. In his other hand, he carried his small gray suitcase for the eggs and an egg candler.

Crossing a floating mat of vegetation to reach the nest was a balancing act. To his surprise, Matteson recalls, given how woozy he felt from the flying, he lost his balance only once, near the first nest. "At that point I jumped for the nest edge and almost landed in the nest cup. Luckily, I didn't crush any eggs—that would not have been a good way to begin our first egg collection trip."

At each nest he candled[6] each egg to see if it was good. That way, the eggs he collected were likely to be healthy and at least two healthy eggs would be left in the nest. "I never knew for sure," he said, "because I had never done this in the wild before, only at a game farm. I was a basket case that first year."

He measured each egg with a caliper and took the larger eggs, since it was assumed they would travel better. Each collected egg was marked with an alphanumeric code that identified the nest it came from.

A wild trumpeter swan nest, with eggs and the black egg candler.   Photo: Wisconsin DNR

---

[6] The candler Matteson used on loan from the Minnesota DNR and was had been used in previous egg collecting missions Alaska. It was a black hollow cylinder about the size of a coffee can, with black rubber stretched over both ends. One end had an opening a little smaller than a swan egg, the other, a viewing hole. Matteson held each egg against the wide opening, pointed the candler at the sunlight, and peered through the viewing hole. Against the light, a healthy, developed egg looks partially dark. If an egg is close to hatching, one might see the chick's egg tooth moving at the edge of the air

Then Matteson placed the collected eggs in the small gray suit-case and cautiously made his way back to the floatplane. There Rod King placed each egg into one of the large black suitcase-like boxes. Each black suitcase had red hot-water bottles inside. A Radio Shack® electronic digital thermometer strapped to the outside of each suitcase kept accurate temperature readings via heat sensors attached to a cord inside. When the suitcases were filled, King and Matteson flew them back to the cabin base camp and turned the eggs over to the care of Jurewicz and Johnson. Then King and Matteson flew off for more eggs, while Jurewicz and Johnson stayed at the cabin, monitoring temperatures in the boxes and feeding the wood stove to keep the hot water bottles hot. They also turned the eggs every two to three hours, to keep the embryos from adhering to one side of the shell.

Trumpeter swans can be very aggressive when protecting their nests from predators or from egg-marauding ecologists. During the nesting season, they become increasingly territorial and increasingly aggressive, though aggressive behavior varies widely among individual swans. At the approach of an intruder, some birds stand on the nest and make noisy threat displays, hissing, fluffing their feathers, and shaking their wings. Others will charge and attack, beating the intruder with their wings. It is no empty threat; a blow from a trumpeter's wing can break human bones. One USFWS biologist who was knocked down and pinned to the ground by an angry cob recalled that the beating he took felt like being pounded with a baseball bat.

At one of the nests King and Matteson visited, the guarding swans didn't wait for Matteson to approach the nest. Matteson recalls:

> "At around 10:00 p.m. Rod landed the plane, and was coasting about 100 meters from the nest. The

---

cell. An egg that appears transparent might be infertile or might be very early in embryonic development. ("I've been fooled over the years," Matteson said.)

A bird's "egg tooth" is not a true tooth. It's more of a "horn"—a sharp bump on the top of the chick's beak. The chick uses the egg tooth to break through its eggshell, in a process called "pipping." The egg tooth falls off two or three days after the chick emerges from the shell. Some crane chicks pip by breaking a small hole and then enlarging it until it is big enough to crawl through. Other chicks start with a small hole, and then follow a crack around the circumference of the shell until a section of the shell falls away. Either method is exhausting, and not all chicks survive the ordeal.

> cob was some distance away, flying parallel to the plane's course, when it suddenly veered toward the airplane, heading right toward the propeller. Rod turned the plane sharply to the right to avoid a collision, and we heard a tremendous thud from the rear of the plane. Rod turned to me and said, 'My God, we've just been attacked by a trumpeter!'"

On reaching the nest, Matteson and King jumped out and looked back. The two adult swans were swimming away side by side and there was no sign that either bird was injured. But in its attack, the cob had snapped the communications antennas off the back of the plane. Before King flew the egg collecting crew back to Fairbanks that evening, he had to call his wife on the base camp cabin's short wave radio, and ask her to call the airport, to let the airport staff and the Kohlers know what time the eggs would arrive there. At the end of the day, the score stood at: Swans, one, Airplanes, zero.

On that first "eggs-pedition" in 1989, Matteson visited 27 trumpeter nests and candled 134 eggs, collecting 60 of them. Three out of four of the eggs he candled were viable; half the nests he visited contained at least one non-viable egg.

After a long, grueling, and—for Matteson—groggy 13 hours of collecting, the team headed back to Fairbanks to rendezvous with the Kohlers for the overnight flight to Milwaukee.

The Citation's normal cruising level is around 35,000 feet above sea level. At that altitude, the plane's interior is pressurized to the equivalent of about 8,000 feet above sea level. Terry was concerned that the low cabin pressure might damage the eggs. On the trip home, he maintained a higher pressure in the cabin by flying at 27,000 feet, hoping that would put less stress on the eggs.

From Fairbanks, Terry had planned a fuel stop in Ketchikan, but headed for Juneau, Alaska instead, because of "really bad weather" at Ketchikan. Joe Johnson remembers the approach to Juneau as "kind of exciting:"

> "We had a beautiful flight over the mountains, looked at the glaciers, got down around Juneau, and it was totally fogged and clouded in. We could see mountain peaks sticking up through the clouds and a huge band of clouds below us. Terry dove right

down through those clouds and was practically skipping the waves over the water. We could see mountainsides to the right and to the left and we could see a mountain straight ahead of us with a great big flashing arrow—'TURN RIGHT'—it was huge! It was there to help airplanes find the airport."

The next stop was Great Falls, Montana, for fuel, then on to Milwaukee. Matteson, Jurewicz, and Johnson spent the trip monitoring and regulating the temperatures in the egg boxes. When the temperatures dropped, the crew used an electric coffee warmer to heat water for the hot water bottles. When a fresh hot water bottle caused the temperature in an egg box to rise too high, the box was opened a crack to let some of the heat escape.

Early on the morning of June 9, the Citation, with its tired crew and passengers and its precious cargo of eggs, touched down in Milwaukee. The eggs collected for Wisconsin were checked, loaded into a zoo van, driven to the zoo's aviary, and placed in large incubators there. Joe Johnson and his 20 eggs were transferred to a Michigan DNR aircraft and flown to Kalamazoo, where one more twist was thrown into the adventure. Johnson recalled:

> "Just as we were approaching the Kalamazoo airport, the DNR pilot got a call on the radio: 'Land that thing or get out of the way!' We landed, and five Blue Angels [U.S. Navy Flight Demonstration Squadron] flew over us. We had arrived the day before the Kalamazoo Air Show, and five jet fighter pilots practicing for the air show had ended up right on our tail. Why the tower didn't tell us about that, I don't know, but it was close."

OF THE 60 EGGS COLLECTED IN ALASKA that year, one was found to be bad before the group left Fairbanks. Jurewicz would later kid Matteson: "If your sense of smell had been working that day, you would have known it was bad!" Of Wisconsin's 39 eggs, 38 hatched. Of Michigan's 20 eggs, 19 hatched—overall, a success rate of 94.8 percent. In the wild, about 60 to 80 percent of trumpeter eggs hatch successfully. "Not bad for a rookie," Matteson said, adding that the transportation provided by the Kohlers and the expert care provided by the staff at Milwaukee County Zoo were largely responsible for that 94.8 percent success rate.

Joe Johnson did not accompany the Wisconsin group after the first "eggs-pedition" in 1989. Instead, Johnson and the Michigan DNR went looking for a Michigan-based aircraft to make the annual trip to Alaska. "The Kohlers' Citation was pretty cramped with three 'gorillas' and all our gear," Johnson explained. "I was looking for another way to get there, and in February 1990, a member of the Michigan Audubon Society suggested I contact Edgar Prince," founder and CEO of the Holland, Michigan-based Prince Corporation, a manufacturer of automobile parts.

Bruce Wickmann, who was then the chief pilot for Prince Corp., remembers a call from the State of Michigan, asking about using one of Prince's aircraft for the Alaska egg collection. "I went to Mr. Prince and asked him if he'd be interested in the project," Wickmann recalled. "He said it sounded like it would be fun to do. He was a wonderful man and he loved to see things like that happen."[7]

The passenger list eventually included Edgar Prince and his wife, another Prince Corp. executive and his wife, plus Johnson and two other DNR biologists. Wickmann captained the flight, with another company pilot in the right seat. With seats for 13 passengers, the company's Gulfstream II was roomier than the Kohlers' Citation, and had a longer range. "We flew from Holland [Michigan] to Minot, North Dakota—a fuel stop—then direct to Fairbanks," Wickmann said. "We left the biologists there and flew down to Anchorage for a couple of days, and then back to Fairbanks to pick up Joe [Johnson] and his crew." Johnson had brought along a portable electric incubator that he plugged into the Gulfstream's AC outlet. That kept the eggs at a constant temperature all the way home. "We had favorable winds," Wickmann said, "and we flew non-stop from Fairbanks to Battle Creek [Michigan] in five and a half hours. We took off out of Fairbanks in late afternoon, and the sun really never set, it just kind of clocked around the horizon. We landed in Battle Creek just about the time the sun was coming up."

The Prince Gulfstream made only one trip to Alaska. By 1991, the auto industry was entering a downturn and, Johnson explained, "Prince couldn't justify flying a $20,000 charter to Alaska while they

---

[7] Edgar Prince died in 1995, still leading the company he had founded. Prince Corporation was sold two years later to Johnson Controls, Inc.

were laying off workers." So in 1991, Johnson and his Alaskan eggs traveled on Northwest Airlines. "I went passenger class on the way up and first class on the way back." That flight took 18 hours from Fairbanks, to Seattle, to Minneapolis, to Kalamazoo. "The eggs did-n't mind," he said. "We hatched every damn egg we brought back."

Minnesota, Wisconsin, Michigan, Iowa, Ohio, and Ontario all obtained eggs from Alaska, Johnson said, adding:

> "I think the bottom line is: if you look at these states, we all hatched almost 90 percent of the eggs. [That rate of success] was just an awesome boost to all of our efforts. Some 70 percent of the birds released in Wisconsin were of Alaskan origin and 40 percent in Michigan. [Alaskan eggs were] very, very important to our programs."

In 1990, the Kohlers flew Matteson and Jurewicz to Glenallen, Alaska to gather eggs in the Nelchina Basin—the upper watershed of Alaska's Copper River. Covering more than 22,000 square miles (57,000 sq km), the upper Copper River Basin is a crazy quilt of shrub tundra, cottonwoods, open spruce forests, bogs, alpine tundra, alpine barrens, and glaciers. Permafrost and poor drainage form hundreds of small lakes and bogs, and the basin is crisscrossed with an untold number of rivers, streams, and creeks. Hemmed in by the Talkeetna Mountains, the Alaska Range, and the Wrangell-St Elias Range, the basin drains through a single deep canyon in the Chugach Range, to the south.[8]

Downriver, the lower Copper River watershed reaches from the Chugach Range to the Gulf of Alaska. Together, the upper and lower Copper River encompasses what may be the most diverse ecosystem of interrelated environments anywhere on the Pacific Rim.

During the Pleistocene Era, the Nelchina basin was a huge glacial lake, now called Lake Ahtna. Its outlet through the Chugach Range

---

[8] The mountains ringing the basin include four of the fifteen highest peaks in North America. Four glacier-covered volcanoes loom over the basin: Mt. Drum, 12,010' (3,660 m), Mt. Wrangell, 14,163' (4,317 m), Mt. Sanford, 16,237' (4,949 m), and Mt. Blackburn, 16,390' (4,996 m). Mt. Wrangell occasionally spits out hot gases and light ash falls. Earthquakes are common here, in one of the most tectonically active places in the world. In the past 40 years more than 35 earthquakes measuring at least 5.0 on the Richter scale have occurred in the region.

was dammed by ice. Geologists believe the lake filled and catastroph-ically emptied several times. Those glacial floods shaped the land south of the Chugach Range and formed the Copper River Delta, the largest contiguous wetlands on North America's Pacific Coast. At its deepest, Lake Ahtna may have been 500 to 1,000 feet (150-300 m) deep, its shoreline reaching up the mountain slopes to an elevation of 2,400 feet (730 m). About 10,000 years ago, the ice dam melted once more, draining Lake Ahtna for the last time.

Today the Nelchina Basin is a flat and gently rolling plain, com-pletely encircled by mountains, volcanoes, and some of the world's largest glaciers and ice fields.[9]

Most of the rivers and lakes in the basin are frozen from November to April. Summers can be warm, with high temperatures above 90° F. (around 35° C.). In general, the waters are clearer here than at Minto Flats, and less nutrient-rich. Still, the Nelchina Basin supports 45 species of mammals, from mice to moose, and 200 species of birds.[10] The Nelchina caribou herd—some 40,000 cari-bou—migrates through the basin's western edge. King and sockeye salmon spawn in the Copper River and its tributaries. The trumpeter swans' nesting grounds are mainly in the north central part of the basin.

In 1990, the first year of collecting eggs in the Nelchina Basin, Terry suggested to Matteson that, since they were going all the way to Alaska, they should fly up a day early and combine the egg-collect-ing mission with some serious goofing off. "I couldn't complain," Matteson said, "especially when Terry arranged and paid for a day of fishing for king salmon." Goofing off on the team's future trips to Alaska included more salmon fishing, as well as visits to Denali Park, the Pribiloff Islands, and Prudhoe Bay on the North Slope, via the ice highway from Fairbanks northward.

On the day of the 1990 egg collection, Alaska DNR pilot Lee Hodgekiss picked up Matteson, Jurewicz, and the egg containers at Glenallen, and flew them into the basin in his Cessna 206 amphibi-ous floatplane. The Cessna 206 was larger and heavier than "Sky" King's Cessna 185. It could land only on the largest lakes in the basin.

---

[9] The Bering Glacier-Beagley Icefield is the largest ice field in the world, outside of Greenland and the polar ice caps. It covers 2,300 square miles (5,950 sq km).

[10] Mammals found in the region include moose, caribou, Dall sheep, mountain goat, bison, deer, brown and black bear, grey wolf, coyote, fox, wolverine, lynx, martin, otter, mink, muskrat, beaver, shrews, voles, bats, hares, marmot, and lemming.

That left many of the nests out of reach, and by the morning's end the team had collected only 19 eggs—far short of their goal. At mid-day, they decided to return to Glenallen. Hodgekiss advanced the throttle and began his takeoff run across the glassy lake. But the plane was too heavy; with its three occupants and all of their cargo, the amphibious C-206 could not lift off the glassy-smooth lake.

Lee Hodgekiss' Cessna 206 on amphibious floats. L-R: Terry Kohler, unidentified, Lee Hodgekiss, Mary Kohler.

Photo: *Wisconsin Dept. of Natural Resources*

To take off, a floatplane must gain enough speed to break the surface tension of the water and begin hydroplaning on the bottom surface of the floats. Only then can it accelerate to takeoff speed. Waves and swells can help lift the floats and break the surface tension. On smooth water, getting the floats "up on the step" requires more speed and more power. The fully loaded Cessna 206 amphibian was too heavy to break free of the lake's glassy smooth surface.

Hodgekiss taxied up and down the lake at full power, yanking the plane's nose up, or rocking its wings to try to break the floats free one at a time. He taxied in circles and tried to take off over his own wake, hoping that those ripples would help the floats break free. None of it worked.

Finally he turned to his passengers and told them, "I'm never supposed to do this, but I'm going to have to leave one of you behind and come back for you—or we're never going to get off this lake." As the larger of the two passengers, Randy Jurewicz earned the dubious honor of waiting an hour or so in the middle of the marsh for "the next plane out." Hodgekiss left him on an island, with a flotation vest and bits and pieces of survival gear. "He didn't leave me a rifle, Jurewicz recalled. "I was really wishing that he had left me a rifle." In an environment where some of the inhabitants might consider him edible, being on an isolated island offered at least some protection—or so he hoped.

From where he stood on the shore, Jurewicz could see trails crisscrossing the island. With an hour's time to kill, he decided to do some exploring.

A few minutes down the path that led into the island's interior, he noticed bits of what looked like horsehair hanging from branches overhead. "I thought, the birds must have put it there," he said, "but I couldn't figure out why, and there was so much of it." Then the cerebral light bulb came on. "It was moose hair. The branches over my head had scraped it off the back of a moose." That was enough exploring for one day. He turned around and headed back to the shore. Hodgekiss returned in about an hour and flew Jurewicz back to Glenallen, none the worse for wear.

Worried that they might not achieve their objective of 40 eggs, Matteson and Jurewicz discussed the situation with Terry, who called and contracted for two local bush pilots with smaller planes. While awaiting the arrival of the two new planes, Hodgekiss told Matteson he knew of a nest on a small bog lake in the middle of an island. He said he could fly Matteson to the island; did Matteson want to collect eggs there? Matteson agreed that it was worth a try.

Hodgekiss flew Matteson to the island, mooring the plane at the water's edge. He would stay with the airplane, while Matteson collected the eggs. As Matteson climbed out onto the plane's float and prepared to set off into the island's interior, Hodgekiss' final word of advice was, "Watch out for critters."

Matteson recalled:

> "I walked for some time over fallen trees and
> through dense brush until I heard a trumpeter
> swan's call echoing through the woods. Coming out
> of the woods through an opening, I saw a small lake
> rimmed by sphagnum moss, with a mound—a trum-

peter nest—in the middle of the lake. I really wanted to get to that nest. But the only way to get there was to swim."

Reluctantly, Matteson took off his clothes. Carrying only the candler, a pencil, and a zip-lock bag, he slipped into the frigid water. He swam out to the nest and scrambled out of the water onto the mound. The nest held just three eggs, and he would have to leave at least two healthy eggs behind. If only one egg proved infertile, his cold swim would be for naught.

"As soon as I got out of the water, deerflies and horseflies started biting the soles of my feet. I was shivering from the cold, trying to keep the flies off me, and trying to candle the eggs. I candled the first egg—good. I candled the second egg—good. I candled the third egg, and it was good. So I could take one egg from the nest."

He carefully placed the largest egg in the zip-lock bag and turned back toward the shore, with the bag in his teeth. "I did not want to go back in that water; it was freezing. But there was no other way to get back."

He swam awkwardly back toward land, holding the egg up with one hand to keep it out of the frigid water. Approaching the shore, he heard something move in the brush ahead but could see nothing. Reaching the pond's edge, he tried to climb out of the water, but the floating mat of vegetation that formed the shoreline gave him no foothold, and with one hand occupied, he could not get up onto that mat. After several tries, he finally managed to crawl and drag himself partway up the mat. It sank under his weight and he continued to struggle up the slippery mat, through the icy water, until he reached the upland and relatively solid ground. Soaking wet and covered with frigid slime from the floating mat, he was catching his breath when the sound he had heard earlier seemed to come closer. Looking up, he found himself staring into the face of a bull moose.

Visitors to Alaska seem to worry most about bears. But Alaskans know that the most dangerous animal in the woods—the animal that inflicts the highest number of serious injuries and fatalities on humans—is the moose. Normally rather shy, moose can be very aggressive when they are tired, hungry, nervous, or startled.[11]

"I froze," Matteson recalled. "After staring at me awhile, the moose ambled away." Matteson quickly pulled on his clothes and wasted no time tramping back across the island to the waiting airplane. He found Hodgekiss "sunning himself" on one of the airplane's floats. Matteson related to the pilot what he had just been through. "All Hodgekiss said was, 'Darn! I wish I'd had the video camera!'"

"I'm happy to report," Matteson said, "that that egg made it back to Wisconsin and hatched. And the cygnet fledged and was released into the wild."

Back in Glenallen that afternoon Al and Jerry Lee, a father/son bush pilot team, arrived to complete the egg collection. They brought a 150-horsepower Piper PA-18 Super Cub and special hybrid airplane called a "Producer," a four-seat aircraft with excellent STOL performance. Both aircraft were on floats and were able to get in and out of smaller lakes in the basin. With Matteson and Jurewicz gathering eggs simultaneously from the two planes, they collected another 19 eggs in just three hours.

"Hiring those aircraft was really above and beyond the call of duty," Matteson said. "Over and over again, the Kohlers went way out of their way to help make the project work."

"The bush planes were great," Jurewicz recalled. Matteson was especially enthusiastic about flying in them; he describes them as, "like dragonflies."

With Matteson and Jurewicz both out on the egg hunt, the task of tending the eggs that had already been collected fell to Terry and Mary. They were kept busy monitoring temperatures and refilling hot water bottles. By the time the bush planes returned, Terry was determined to find a better, easier way.

One of the companies owned by Kohler's Windway Capital Corporation is the Vollrath Company, a manufacturer of commercial food service equipment, including portable insulated food carriers. After returning from Alaska, Terry called Bob Moran, a product engineer at Vollrath. He asked Moran to design and build a portable container to carry trumpeter swan eggs. Matteson met with Moran

---

[11] A bull moose can weigh more than 1,200 pounds (550 kg) and stand more than seven feet tall (over 2 meters) at the shoulder. Though their eyesight is poor, their hearing and sense of smell are excellent. They are good swimmers and can run up to 35 mph (55 km/h).

and model maker Bill Kuitert to help work out the design.

Moran and Kuitert started with an off-the-shelf item from the Vollrath catalog—a Side Load Food Carrier. It was similar to a large plastic insulated ice chest with a drop-down door on its long side, and walls made of rigid insulating foam sandwiched between inner and outer plastic shells. The inside walls were ribbed to hold stainless steel serving pans. Working with Matteson, the Vollrath engineers designed special trays to hold the eggs in contoured foam inserts. They carved out the container's insulation to create ducts for warm air, and attached a Coleman electric heater to the back of the carrier. Nine electronic temperature probes inside the carrier were linked to nine digital displays in a console on top of the carrier, so temperatures inside could be precisely monitored. The entire system—heater and probes—could be powered by a motorcycle battery or plugged into the cigarette lighter/power outlet in a car or an airplane. It took about six months to design, build, and test three egg carriers, each holding up to thirty eggs. Terry Kohler and the Vollrath Company donated all of the time and materials used in manufacturing and testing the egg carriers.

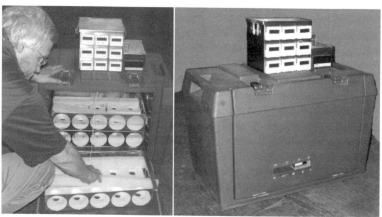

The author inspects a Vollrath Egg Carrier — Temperature readouts and motorcycle battery box are on top; stainless steel trays with plastic foam inserts hold up to 30 eggs per carrier. Nine electronic probes allowed for precise monitoring of the temperatures in the trays. The carriers transported trumpeter swan, Siberian crane, and whooping crane eggs in the Kohlers' Citation.

Photos: Jerry Baumann.

In 1991, as the date of the annual egg collection trip approached, the Kohlers' Citation was in Texas getting a new paint job and new engines. Terry expected the work to be finished in time for the Alaska trip, but as the date drew nearer, it was clear that the aircraft would not be ready. Matteson began looking for commercial flights and mentioned this to Terry. According to Matteson:

> "Terry said, 'No. I promised to get you to Alaska every year and I'll do it. When you're ready to go, there will be a plane waiting for you at Madison.' At his own expense, Terry chartered a jet and two pilots out of Chicago to fly us to Glenallen and back to Milwaukee that year. He insisted on it."

The following year, 1992, the Citation was back in operation and Terry and Mary were back in the pilot's and copilot's seats.

In early June of 1991, Matteson and Jurewicz again collected eggs from the Nelchina Basin. It was snowing in the Basin the night they arrived in Glenallen. The following morning, Rod King told the biologists he wouldn't fly that day, until and unless the temperature reached 50° F. (10° C.) At colder temperatures, and with the sky overcast, King was afraid that the swan eggs would become too chilled when the parents were driven from the nests.

All morning, the mercury crept slowly up through the 30s and 40s. At two o'clock that afternoon, it stood at 48° F. (8.9° C.) "That's close enough," King told them. "Let's go." From 2:30 until 10:30, they collected eggs—40 in all—working through the long daylight of the sub arctic.

At 4:30 the next morning, they left Glenellen for Milwaukee. "The Vollrath Egg Carriers worked beautifully," Matteson recalled. "They were really portable incubators." In tests, the temperatures inside the containers never varied by more than a degree and a half. Operating off the Citation's power system, the egg carriers kept the precious cargo safe and warm. The eggs still had to be turned every couple of hours but the constant temperature made the trip far less stressful for the precious embryos and their fellow travelers.

From 1992 on, the annual flights to Alaska became "almost routine," according to Matteson and Jurewicz. Everyone knew what to expect (more or less) and everyone enjoyed the experiences and the camaraderie that the trips provided. The Vollrath egg carriers allowed the team to collect eggs one day, get a good night's sleep, and fly home the next day. Not having to replenish hot water bottles cut the workload and made the trip back to Wisconsin much easier.

Milwaukee County Zoo's Curator of Birds Ed Diebold went along in 1993. Diebold was in charge of the trumpeter swan activities at the zoo. At the time, he was also working with another research group studying South America's Humboldt penguins.

"This was the most endangered of all the penguin species," Diebold said, "But in 1992, no one knew much about them; there was little information about their biology and behaviors." The staff at the Milwaukee County Zoo formed a five-member research group to study the penguins. Diebold recalled:

> "In 1992 the research group made two trips to Peru and Chile, to study birds and gather blood samples. In 1993, on the way to Alaska in the Kohlers' Citation, I was telling Sumner [Matteson] about the project and how we wanted to expand it. Sumner told me that Mary and Terry owned a fishing lodge in Chile, and he said I should tell them about the penguin project. Over lunch the next day, I described the project to the Kohlers, and Mary said to me, 'Write it up.'"

Diebold had explained to the Kohlers that the research group had other grants to fund the study itself, but getting to and from South America twice a year was a sticking point. It was politically difficult for a publicly funded zoo to justify international travel on public funds. "So we asked the Kohlers to help us get there and back. I was thinking maybe we could ride along on their trips to their lodge in Chile." Instead, the Kohlers made a five-year commitment to pay for airline travel for three researchers to make two trips a year. "As a result," Diebold said, "there is a lot more information about Humboldt penguins in the scientific literature today than there was five years ago."

When Diebold made his request to the Kohlers in 1993, there was no formal process for requesting a contribution from them. Diebold asked Terry what his research group needed to do to request funds. "Terry simply told me, 'You ask for the money and you say, thank you, when you get it,'" Diebold recalled. "But for all their generosity, the Kohlers consistently refused to be acknowledged publicly for their contributions."

MATTESON, JUREWICZ, AND THE KOHLERS RETURNED to Minto Flats in 1994. Accompanying them that year were Jurewicz' son, Jericho, Andy Larson, director of the River Edge Nature Center,[12] and Bill Roach, a professional video photographer. Roach's footage includes views of the DNR cabin that served as a base camp, brief interviews with Matteson and with Terry and Mary Kohler, views from the Citation en route, local wildlife, and step-by-step egg collection. Some of that footage appeared in a story later broadcast by a television station in Madison, Wisconsin.

Denali, also known as Mt. McKinley, is at 20,320 feet (6,194 m) the highest mountain peak in North America. Most of the time, it is shrouded in clouds. As the egg collecting team prepared to depart Fairbanks for Milwaukee in June 1994, Terry learned that the weather around Denali was clear. He requested and received clearance to circle the mountain in the Citation. The images Roach captured on videotape are stunning. From an altitude of about 25,000 feet (7,620 m), the passengers could see climbers and climbing camps scattered around the mountain. Matteson and Jurewicz were both struck by the beauty, immensity, and isolation of that landscape.

They also experienced a strong feeling of spatial disorientation. As the aircraft circled the peak in a gently banking turn, centrifugal force and the seats of their pants told them the plane was level, but the view out the window was down, not sideways. Up the in the cockpit, the Kohlers had the horizon ahead to keep them visually oriented, but the passengers' only view was out the side windows, and that view disagreed with what their inner ears and backsides were telling them. It was an unsettling feeling, Jurewicz said. "Our brains couldn't quite process it." Matteson agreed, "It was pretty disorienting. We just hoped Terry was still oriented up in the cockpit."

After a long, slow circuit of Denali—Athabaskan for "the high one"—the Citation leveled off and headed southeast for Montana.

Thanks to the Kohlers and their business jet, the eggs were nestled into the incubators at Milwaukee County Zoo less than 12 hours

---

[12] Mary Kohler played a key role in the creation of River Edge Nature Center and taught there for several years.

Located in Newburg, WI, the Center is a 350-acre (1.4 km2) wildlife sanctuary and "living classroom." Its primary goal is to provide environmental education to schools, teachers, and the public. It offers school programs to some 10,000 students each school year, as well summer camps, weekend family programs, teacher education, and curriculum development.

after the last egg was collected—somewhat more than half the time it would have taken if the swan eggs had traveled to Wisconsin on commercial flights.

On all of the Alaska trips, the Kohlers donated their time and expenses for the flights, plus a lot of extras.

"We wouldn't do this if there weren't some good—some serious good—coming out of it," Mary Kohler told Bill Roach, the video photographer who accompanied the group in 1994. "But it's fun to have fun while you're doing good."

Terry told Roach: "It's incredible biological science, it's helping to replenish a bird species that's been gone from Wisconsin, and it's really a lot of fun just learning how these projects actually work."

In nine annual trips to Alaska, Matteson and Jurewicz collected a total of 385 eggs for Wisconsin, delivering them to incubators at the Milwaukee County Zoo. The zoo received another 120 from other sources during those years. (Joe Johnson made just one more trip to Alaska to collect trumpeter eggs for Michigan's recovery program, traveling on commercial flights.)

In the wild, 60 to 80 percent of trumpeter swan eggs hatch from year to year. Out of the total of 505 trumpeter eggs collected for Wisconsin's recovery program between 1989 and 1997, 450 were artificially incubated in the Aviary at Milwaukee County Zoo, and 94 percent of those hatched successfully. Only 10 of the 505 eggs were found to be infertile or addled on arrival at Milwaukee.

Meanwhile, in Alaska, the annual productivity surveys were confirming what many people involved in the project had predicted: that nine years of egg collection had absolutely no negative effect on the population or productivity of Alaska's trumpeter swans.

Chapter 3
Learning to Be Wild

ED DIEBOLD IS THE DIRECTOR OF ANIMAL COLLECTIONS at the Riverbanks Zoo & Gardens in Columbia, South Carolina. He was the Curator of Birds at the Milwaukee County Zoo from 1986 until August 1995, and he was involved in Wisconsin's Trumpeter Swan Restoration Project from the beginning.

When Sumner Matteson was writing the Wisconsin Trumpeter Swan Recovery Plan, in 1986, he called Diebold at the zoo. "Sumner and the DNR were looking for a facility where swan eggs could be incubated," Diebold recalled. "He was also looking for information and expertise relating to egg candling, transporting eggs and cygnets, and managing captive and wild cygnets." The zoo staff was able to provide most of what Matteson needed. The Milwaukee County Zoological Society, the non-profit foundation that helps support the zoo, stepped forward and funded several student interns for the project.

The timing of Matteson's call was "interesting," according to Diebold.

> "The zoo's bird house needed work and it was closed to the public for the first few years of the trumpeter swan project. That gave us access to large, ready-made indoor enclosures with ponds and brooding areas where we could raise the cygnets in isolation from human beings."

By the time the bird house reopened to the public, the trumpeter swan project was winding down, and the project was moved to the basement of the zoo's primate house.

As part of its contract with DNR, the zoo agreed to keep a captive pair of trumpeters, to produce eggs for the project. Wisconsin's first trumpeter swan eggs came from that breeding pair and from a pair of trumpeters at Chicago's Lincoln Park Zoo. Later, eggs also came from wild trumpeter nests in Alaska.

Eggs arrived at the zoo 21 to 26 days after they were laid. Some began hatching within a day or two of arrival; most hatched within a week or so.

During incubation at the zoo, the eggs were candled each day and turned every few hours. When candling revealed that the eggs were just a few days from hatching, the embryos were exposed to taped trumpeter swan calls for about an hour, three times a day, until they hatched.

Trumpeter swan eggs hatch about 30 to 34 days after they are laid. On average, it takes the hatchling about 48 hours to break out and emerge from the egg. A few of the stronger hatchlings break out in about 24 hours. Some chicks take up to 72 hours to break free. "It can be agonizing to watch," Diebold said.

Within 24 hours after hatching at the zoo, each "class" of chicks was divided roughly in half. Half the class went to brooder boxes and the other half went to be decoy-raised.

FOR BROODER-RAISING (ALSO CALLED "HOLD-AND-RELEASE"), the chicks were moved to brooder boxes at the zoo and raised there for about three weeks. There were four to six brooder boxes, each containing four to five chicks.

"We matched the chicks, size-wise," said Diebold, "with the largest chicks in one brooder box, the smallest chicks in one box, and so on." That helped to ensure that the chicks in each brooder box would grow and progress at the same pace. Each brooder box was roughly six by eight feet (175 x 225 cm) with walls 18 inches (45 cm) high. About half the box was a "loafing area," with a ramp leading to a shallow swimming pool.

The brooder boxes were isolated from all human activity. Keepers who entered the box for routine cleaning, feeding, or weighing of the chicks wore "swan suits"—neutral colored gowns and beekeeper helmets with one-way viewing glass. No talking was allowed. On the rare occasions when chicks had to be exposed to humans, alarm calls were played to teach the cygnets to avoid contact with humans.

At three weeks of age (one week of age, later in the life of the program) the chicks were moved from the brooder boxes to an over-wintering site owned by General Electric Medical Systems, near Pewaukee, Wisconsin, just west of Milwaukee. "That site was chosen," Diebold explained, "because it had man-made ponds that were recently-built and had never been hunted—we knew there wouldn't be any lead shot in the pond bottoms."

The isolation of the Pewaukee site, and careful attention to isolation protocol by the human keepers, kept many of the birds from becoming tame, but some did habituate to human presence. "They stayed at the site for two years before they were released," he said. "There were concerns about the swans becoming accustomed to humans, so we were very careful to keep them as isolated as possible."

At the Pewaukee site, the cygnets stayed in large pens, monitored and managed by zoo and WDNR staff until they were about 23 months old—the age at which most wild trumpeters choose mates. They were allowed to pair off, choosing their own mates. Then they were given a complete physical examination, including blood, fecal and cloacal samples, and released into the wild at selected marsh sites around the state, mostly in northern and northwestern Wisconsin. Each released swan carried a USFWS leg band that gave the bird a unique identification code. The WDNR attached bright-colored plastic neck collars that made it easy to identify each bird from a distance.

Just before the birds were released into the wild, their flight feathers were clipped. That prevented the swans from leaving the release site immediately, and gave them time to imprint on the site. Matteson and his colleagues hoped that at least some of the newly released swans would return to their release sites—not to Pewaukee—the next spring, after migrating south for the winter. In the two to three weeks it took for their feathers to grow back, the birds were flightless but still large enough and strong enough to protect themselves from predators.

"There were real questions about what these birds would do after they were released," Diebold recalled. "There were proposals to lead them by ultralight to wintering sites, but we were worried about trying to teach a 30-pound bird to follow an ultralight aircraft. If they collided, it could be a disaster for both of them."

Someone even proposed a fixed-wing, radio-controlled swan decoy to lead the decoy-raised cygnets on their first migration southward. That idea never got off the paper.

In the end, the birds solved the problem on their own. When the time came, their migratory instincts took over and they headed south, following the geese, ducks, and tundra swans down the Mississippi Flyway to wintering grounds from southern Wisconsin to northern

Texas. (One large group that nested in northwestern Wisconsin migrated only a short distance to open water near Hudson, Wisconsin.) In the spring, many of the trumpeters returned to Wisconsin, often to the same lakes and marshes where they had been released.

WHILE HALF THE CYGNETS FROM EACH "CLASS" of hatchlings was brooder-raised, the other half was decoy-raised, using techniques developed for the swan project by University of Wisconsin (UW) graduate student, Becky Abel, with assistance from WDNR research biologist Michael Mossman. As an undergraduate, Abel worked for the WDNR, overseeing the cross-fostering project that put trumpeter swan eggs in the nests of wild mute swans. When cross fostering proved unsuccessful, Abel went to see Stan Temple, a UW professor of Wildlife Ecology. She proposed a study for her graduate degree, documenting and analyzing the failure of the cross-fostering experiment. Instead, Temple suggested to her that she "go one better" and develop a decoy-raising program for the swans.

Temple's specialty is working with wildlife recovery and reintroduction programs, especially with birds. When Abel approached him about the swan project, he had just recently been working on using puppets to rear Andean condors, a study that would eventually lead to the reintroduction of California condors. Temple and ICF's George Archibald had been office-mates at Cornell University and had often discussed ideas about puppet rearing and decoy-rearing of birds for reintroduction into the wild.

Abel took Temple's idea and turned it into a very successful decoy-rearing program for trumpeter swans. Temple describes Abel as, "very skillful as a manager of projects and a manager of birds." Much of the success of the decoy-rearing project, he said, "owes a lot to Becky's ability to take a good idea and actually implement it in the field."

The trumpeter swan chicks were decoy-raised in two or three groups of eight to 10 birds each—fewer groups than the brooder-raised chicks because decoy raising was so much more labor-intensive. The cygnets' rearing area was a 50 x 4-foot (15 x 1.2 m) indoor, carpeted runway surrounded by visual barriers and containing a life-size trumpeter swan decoy. Ropes and pulleys allowed a hidden operator (usually a student intern) to move the decoy back and forth along the length of the runway. A speaker in the decoy's neck produced "follow-me" swan calls. Hardly realistic to human eyes, the decoy was good enough for the cygnets, who quickly imprinted on it and learned to follow it. Food was placed at various spots along the runway, the decoy led the chicks to those spots, and the chicks quickly learned to associate following the decoy with finding food. Most of the time the decoy was stationary. "Follow-me" exercises occurred four to eight times a day and lasted about 15 minutes each. Contact between humans and the chicks was rare and was always accompanied by alarm calls from the decoy.

A hidden operator uses ropes and pulleys to move the he swan decoy up and down the "runway."   Photo: Wisconsin DNR

After three to five days in the runway, each group of cygnets and their decoy were flown to one of several carefully selected release sites in northern Wisconsin.

Decoy training continued over the summer at those sites. Each decoy was manipulated by an intern in a "floating blind"—waders and an inner tube camouflaged to look like a mound of vegetation. The intern led the cygnets around the marsh with follow-me calls from the decoy, which was trailed along behind the floating blind. Leading the cygnets to food plants, the intern would bob the decoy's moveable head and neck to imitate feeding. When a potential predator came near, the decoy gave out alarm calls and the intern in the blind led the cygnets to safety.

Swan decoy and the DNR intern's floating blind (above and below), in and out of the water.
Photo: Wisconsin Dept. of Natural Resources

At night, wild adult swans protect their young cygnets from predators and use their own body heat to keep the cygnets warm. The decoy-raised cygnets spent their nights in heated cages until they grew large enough to maintain their own body heat and cope with the local riff-raff.

By autumn, the decoy-raised cygnets had become completely self-sufficient. They were left on their own, monitored and protected, until freeze-up cut off their food supply of aquatic plants and forced them to fly south. Swans need open, ice-free water at their wintering grounds, so they can feed on aquatic plants through the winter. Nesting pairs will return to the same wintering grounds each year, which makes preservation of their winter wetlands critical for the trumpeter's reintroduction and survival.

The first year of the program, some avian biologists were concerned about the decoy-raised cygnets' ability to migrate all on their own. Here, the migratory instincts inherited from their Alaskan parents took hold. In the first year of the program, most of the cygnets migrated south, as far as Texas—about 15 miles (24 km) north of Dallas. Many of the birds released that first year and in following years returned to their release sites in the spring—as wild migratory trumpeter swans.

IN ADDITION TO THE CYGNETS HATCHED AND RAISED at the Milwaukee County Zoo, a few of Wisconsin's new trumpeter swans came from five captive breeding pairs at private game farms and private wetlands. The landowners and game farm owners agreed to maintain each pair in isolation from human activity. Cygnets produced by these five breeding pairs were captured at about ten months of age by DNR staff. They were given health examinations and then released into the wild at various sites.

EVERY SUMMER, TEAMS OF DNR AVIAN SPECIALISTS, managers, technicians, volunteers, and student interns fan out around northern Wisconsin to round up unbanded wild trumpeter cygnets, to screen them for lead poisoning and avian diseases and to mark them for identification. The roundup takes place before the cygnets begin flying, when they are much easier to catch.

Spotters in light airplanes locate the birds and use radios to direct several canoes or kayaks to the catch. The birds are carefully trapped with large nets, of the kind you might use to land a big fish. Once they are netted and lifted gently into a canoe, the swans become surprisingly docile and cooperative. Drawing blood samples, completing the health check, and attaching USFWS leg bands and WDNR collars, takes about 30 minutes, after which the swans are released back into the water with no ill effects. In the twenty years of Wisconsin's Trumpeter Swan Restoration Program, only one swan has been lost during capture.

In spite of all the precautions taken against imprinting or socializing the birds to humans, every state experienced some problems with brooder-raised or decoy-raised swans becoming accustomed to human contact. The Trumpeter Swan Society's Madeline Link recalled, "We used to pick up a few of [Wisconsin's] birds that were walking around in supermarket parking lots. They just didn't know they were swans. But then the second and third generation, raised in the wild, did much better."

Wisconsin also had to remove a few swans that had attacked people.

According to Iowa DNR biologist Ron Andrews, Iowa's captive-raised trumpeter swans were not strictly raised in isolation from human contact. Many of the breeding pairs were in locations where the public could easily view them. "The public wanted so strongly to help out, to jump on the swan bandwagon, that we didn't want to deny them the opportunity and the excitement of seeing these birds," Andrews said. "Obviously that [human contact] could create some problems, but we found that the problems have been minimal in terms of any human imprinting."

In Michigan, Joe Johnson maintains, there were "few problems" caused by released swans associating with humans. "I have often said [Michigan's captive-raised trumpeters] were socialized, but they were not imprinted," he added. "We probably removed three birds [from the wild] out of a total of 123 that were released—birds that would come up to somebody and sit on a beach towel in a public park." Many of Michigan's birds were released at the Seney National Wildlife Refuge, near Manistique in the Michigan's central Upper Peninsula. That probably helped minimize the problems with social-ized birds, Johnson said, "because there's nobody up there for them to mess with." In more populous Lower Michigan, some of the swans wandered into state parks and campgrounds or "ended up on the ice begging mealworms from fishermen." Nearly all of the problem birds turned out to be swans that, as captive cygnets, had become sick and were removed from their brooder groups to be treated in the veteri-nary center for eight to ten days. "We didn't know it at the time, but that kind of messed them up," said Johnson. They became much more socialized than typical brooder-raised cygnets.

Chapter 4
SWAN SONG: REPRISE

A DEBATE PERSISTS AMONG CONSERVATIONISTS, over whether or not birds as large, as territorial, and as aggressive as trumpeter swans should be reintroduced to the nation's much-diminished wetlands—areas where other wetland species may be struggling to hold on.

Trumpeters are very territorial during nesting season, driving away other swans and geese. In the fall, they become much more gregarious and more tolerant of other large birds.

In Wisconsin, Matteson said, the trumpeters compete for nesting territory with mute swans and Canada geese, but "we haven't seen any problems whatsoever with competition with other species." The swans ignore the ducks, loons, terns, and other marsh birds, he added, and Wisconsin's wetland habitats are large enough and diverse enough to support them all.

In Michigan, Joe Johnson said, the trumpeter swans are not driving out other desirable waterfowl species. "They kill or displace mute swans, and that's a plus; and they kill or drive off Canada geese" which have become a pest throughout much of the region. Trumpeters also eat ducklings, as a high-protein "tidbit," but only until the ducklings are about four days old, and agile enough to evade the swans. The swans "get along fine" with the loons and other native waterfowl—"no impact at all," Johnson said, and they are a food source for the bald eagles that are repopulating the Upper Peninsula. "There are so many bald eagles now that they think those cygnets are just like eating escargot." The DNR reported predation on trumpeters by bald eagles at several sites in the Seney refuge in 2005.

In Iowa, where 90 percent of the pre-settlement wetlands had disappeared, finding enough habitat was a critical issue. There, strong public support for the trumpeters has also supported the creation of new wetlands. The restored wetlands tend to be small, but trumpeters can nest on small ponds. And wetland restorations on a relatively small scale can create suitable nesting habitat for a variety of marshland species. What's more, many of those new wetlands lack a history of hunting or fishing, so they are free of lead shot and sinkers.

In the beginning, Johnson said, DNR biologists worried a lot about letting swans nest in many of the state's wetlands because of the waterfowl hunting that had gone on for a hundred years—hunting that left high levels of lead in the clay soils. They tried to avoid releasing swans in areas where they knew there were high concentrations of lead. Still, he added, "We knew some of the birds would get [lead poisoning], but it wasn't going to stop us from trying to restore a bird that had been missing for a hundred years."

Wildlife managers in several states are also worried about the possibility of avian flu attacking the birds. Each state will be monitoring its respective swan population in the coming years, hoping that maintaining geographically separate sub-flocks within each state and region might prevent influenza or some other epidemic from decimating the flocks.

For the Three Rivers Park District in Minnesota, one of the biggest management challenges has been getting its growing flock of trumpeter swans to disperse to new and safe wintering and nesting areas. That's because Three Rivers' original breeding pairs came from the non-migrating flock in Montana. The park district never incubated eggs imported from Alaska or anywhere else. (Like other migratory birds, swans' urge to migrate is instinctive, but they learn where to migrate from their parents.)

"We're managing whatever we can to reduce mortality," said the district's Madeline Link. "Power line collisions are huge," but power companies have been "pretty cooperative," marking lines in key areas with flappers or streamers. Recently, new economic development has brought more power lines to the state. And November and December 2006 were unseasonably warm in Minnesota; which left a lot of rivers and lakes open. That meant the swans were dispersed more widely than usual around the state, and were moving around. Together, more power lines and more movement have added up to a steady increase in power line collisions for the swans.

Lead poisoning is still a problem in Minnesota, but hunting has decreased as a cause of swan mortality there. (Hunting of tundra swans is illegal in Minnesota.)

Sumner Matteson cites three key factors to be considered in reintroducing trumpeters to any area: First, were trumpeters there historically? That question is at the heart of an ongoing controversy about introducing trumpeters along the east coasts of the U.S. and Canada.

Second, is there sufficient habitat to support the swans? Before Wisconsin began reintroducing trumpeters, DNR researchers looked carefully at potential release sites, and concluded that there was an abundance of suitable breeding habitat in the state—large wetland complexes with a variety of wetland habitats.

The third factor to consider, said Matteson, is hunting:

> "If there is a tundra swan [hunting] season, as there is in some eastern states, trumpeters can easily be mistaken for tundra swans, and shot by hunters. If there had been a tundra swan [hunting] season in Wisconsin, I don't think we would ever have gone forward with trumpeter swan reintroductions here. But the driving factor is habitat, and that's something we evaluated very carefully before we went to Alaska."

Vandalistic hunting continues to a serious problem for swan restoration programs. Johnson explained:

> "Every state went through that. Wisconsin thought they were terribly persecuted in 1998-99, so I compared Wisconsin's data to the rest of the flyway. And it was right around 20 to 22 percent of annual deaths that were caused by vandalistic shooting. The further east you went, into Ohio, Michigan, and Ontario, the higher the proportion that died from lead poisoning," [rather than shooting.]

Shooting of trumpeters tends to decline in each state as hunter education catches up with restoration efforts, Johnson added, but "we all agonized for the first seven or eight years," and the hunting problem "seemed to bust loose" in Wisconsin and Michigan in the late 1990s. "Iowa and Ohio are just now going through that agony [in 2005]."

Iowa's Ron Andrews said shooting of trumpeter swans by "poachers" was a significant problem in the early years of his state's program, but public education has improved the situation. "I prefer to call it 'poaching' rather than 'hunting,'" he said, "because I don't think we should lambaste the legitimate sportsmen." Poaching is a problem that every state's trumpeter swan program has faced in its early stages, he agrees. "It's an education issue more than anything else." In Iowa, anyone caught shooting, killing, or injuring a trumpeter swan can be assessed up to $1,500 in damages and a $180 fine, plus court costs.[13] Other states impose similar penalties.

On the many threats to the swans, Johnson reflected,

> "You worry a lot the first three or four years [of a swan restoration program] because the swans don't mature until they are three or four years old, or they aren't very good parents the first couple of years, and it's just agonizing."

IN THE SUMMER OF 2005 THE MICHIGAN DNR counted 345 trumpeter swans in the Upper Peninsula, including 19 successful nesting pairs, producing 54 cygnets. That was the most recent "official" count, said Johnson, and the population of that flock "is just mushrooming."

The southwest Michigan flock is also growing, though not as quickly. That flock, too, is considered self-sustaining. There in 2005, the DNR counted 222 trumpeter swans, and 28 successful nesting pairs with 91 cygnets. A "successful pair" is a nesting pair that has raised at least one cygnet to fledging.

In northeastern Lower Michigan, where environmental lead poisoning and vandalistic shooting are still major problems, there were 161 trumpeters, including 14 successful nesting pairs, with 43 cygnets. "Until that flock can sustain more than 15 successful pairs," Johnson added, "we're not really comfortable."

The 2005 totals for the entire state of Michigan were 728 trumpeters, 61 successful pairs, and 188 cygnets.

The Michigan DNR plans no more releases of trumpeter swans.

---

[13] The Iowa DNR maintains a toll-free Turn-in-Poachers (TIP) hotline, at 1-800-532-2020. Callers can anonymously report poaching or other wildlife violations.

"We'll just monitor the swans' progress from here on," Johnson said. "With nearly 5,000 swans in the flyway, against a goal of 2,000, we're way ahead." Future trumpeter swan surveys will focus mainly on successful nesting pairs, since they are the easiest to count and offer the clearest indication of the flocks' productivity. The counts will come from a combination of aerial surveys and a huge "phone tree" of federal and state officials and private landowners who have reported the birds to the DNR in the past.

Johnson said no one knows where most of the Michigan swans winter. "We had some of them marked the first few years. A few of them tried to winter on the Beaver Islands [in Lake Michigan], which is not a smart thing to do. Some of them came down to Cheboygan," on the northern edge of Lower Michigan. "We think quite a few of them winter right on up in the eastern Upper Peninsula on open rivers." Winters there are getting warmer, he said, "There is open water everywhere." A few marked birds from the Upper Peninsula have wintered in Missouri and Arkansas. But overall, Johnson said, the swans are "reluctant migrants."

He noted in particular that swans hatched from the eggs that Mary and Terry Kohler brought back from Alaska—he calls them the "Kohler birds"—were critical to the success of Michigan's trumpeter swan project. Sixteen Kohler birds were released at Seney NWR in 1991, as two-year-olds. Another 27 Kohler birds were released at Seney in 1992, for a total of 43 swans released. The first nesting of wild trumpeters at Seney occurred in 1992, by Kohler birds that produced two cygnets. That was the first wild trumpeter nest anywhere in Michigan in more than a century. In 2005, there were 294 trumpeter swans at Seney and in surrounding Schoolcraft County, including 16 successful pairs with 47 cygnets. Many more pairs were nesting, but they either didn't produce cygnets or their cygnets were lost to predation. All of these swans are descended from the 43 Kohler birds released at Seney NWR in 1991-92. Clearly, said Johnson, the Seney National Wildlife Refuge flock and the Schoolcraft county flock are "the shining star" of Michigan's trumpeter swan restoration efforts. And the Kohler birds are the core of those flocks.

WISCONSIN'S WILD TRUMPETER SWANS HAVE PRODUCED more than 1,000 wild cygnets, as of the fall of 2006. The state's trumpeter swan population is now self-sustaining and growing, Matteson said, with more than 500 swans and nearly 100 nesting pairs.

Wisconsin's trumpeter swans migrate mainly to western Wisconsin, southeastern Minnesota, southern and east-central Illinois, Missouri, to southwestern Indiana, and as far south as Tennessee and Arkansas. On rare occasions, the state's trumpeters have been seen as far west as Nebraska and northeastern New Mexico and as far east as the Chesapeake Bay.

In late 2006, Matteson and Randy Jurewicz said they expect the trumpeter swan to be removed from Wisconsin's list of endangered species within the next two or three years. WDNR will continue to monitor the swans for five years after they are "de-listed," to help ensure the flock's long-term survival.

In the summer, one of the best places to see trumpeter swans in Wisconsin is the Crex Meadows Wildlife Area, in Burnett County in northwestern Wisconsin. The Sandhill Wildlife Area and nearby Cranmoor Township in central Wisconsin, and the northeastern counties along the Wisconsin/Upper Michigan border are also good places to see trumpeters in the summer.

In the winter, large numbers of trumpeter swans congregate on Lake Mallalieu in Hudson, Wisconsin, just east of Minneapolis/St.Paul.

IN MINNESOTA, THE THREE RIVERS PARK DISTRICT'S flock is now considered self-sustaining, and the park district is no longer rearing and releasing cygnets. Program cuts and budget constraints have made it harder for the Minnesota DNR to accurately survey and count the state's trumpeter swans, and the park district no longer bands its young birds, so they cannot be tracked. "We found that banding was too disruptive to the young birds and to their parents, and it's also very labor-intensive," the park district's Madeline Link explained. "So we stopped banding them a few years ago. And the state only marks the birds that are released along the Iowa border."

At Monticello, on the Mississippi River about 30 miles northwest of St Paul, the river stays open all winter, warmed by outflow from the Xcel Energy nuclear generating plant. In the mid-1980s, a few homeowners along the river began setting out grain for ducks and geese that wintered there. Two trumpeters from the Three Rivers flock showed up at Monticello in the spring of 1986. By 1988, there were 15 trumpeters wintering at Monticello. In the winter of 2004-2005, there were 1,220 trumpeters counted there and local officials expect as many as 1,600 trumpeters to congregate there in early

2007. [14]

The other large congregation of trumpeters in Minnesota is on the Otter Tail River, near Fergus Falls, where about 400 trumpeters spend the winter.

Swans, geese, & ducks mix at Monticello, MN. Nearly 1,600 trumpeter swans congregated there in early 2007. Photo, © Emily L. Spoo

Except in the park district and surrounding areas, the summer population statistics for trumpeters are "fuzzy," but the winter counts are fairly decent, according to Link. The Minnesota DNR estimates the total winter population of trumpeters in the state at about 2,000 individuals.

The park district still has a few captive nesting pairs, and cygnets from those pairs have been given to Iowa, for release along the Missouri border. As adults, some of those cygnets have nested in

[14] A Monticello resident known as "the Swan Lady" puts out 1,200 lbs of cracked corn per day during the peak season, November to February. She used to carry the corn in buckets from her driveway down to the riverbank. A few years ago, she installed a custom-built conveyer system to automatically move the grain from a bulk wagon to the river. For information on viewing the swans in Monticello, contact the Chamber of Commerce at (763) 295-2700, or visit www.monticellochamber.com.

Iowa, and some have returned to nest in Minnesota. The hope is that swans released in southern Iowa will find wintering areas farther south, where the weather is less harsh than Minnesota winters. And there is now a major wintering site near Heber Springs, Arkansas, about 75 miles (125 km) north of Little Rock. First occupied by two Minnesota trumpeters, this privately owned marsh is now the winter home for about 110 trumpeter swans.

The best places to see trumpeter swans in Minnesota at various times of the year are listed on the Three Rivers Park District Web site.[15] During the summer, swans can be seen from the hiking trails in the parks. During the winter, they can be seen on a few of the parks' ponds that don't freeze over. Also in the winter, the Otter Tail River is a good spot to see the swans, and the huge congregation of birds at Monticello is truly an impressive sight.

IN IOWA, THE MORTALITY RATE AMONG THE WILD or released swans was higher than expected in recent years. Lead poisoning, power line collisions, hunters, disease, malnutrition, and unknown causes have all taken their toll. But Iowa's population of trumpeters is growing, and more and more areas of the state are seeing the return of wild trumpeter swans. Although drought conditions during the summer of 2006 limited the available nesting habitats, there were 28 nesting attempts in the wild that year. Twenty wild nests produced at least once cygnet that survived to fly in the fall. The Iowa DNR's Ron Andrews said the exact number of new cygnets is hard to pin down but he estimates that there were about 75 new wild trumpeter cygnets in Iowa as of the fall of 2006.

Iowa launched its trumpeter swan program in 1995, and the first released trumpeters nested there in 1998, in Dubuque County. That pair hatched three cygnets—the first wild trumpeter swans hatched in the state since 1883. The same pair hatched and fledged several more cygnets in succeeding years.

As of early 2007, Iowa has released over 700 trumpeters into the wild, from its 50 or so trumpeter swan breeder pair partnership sites—the private landowners who keep flightless swans for the DNR. The state released about 80 new cygnets in 2006.

Andrews said trumpeters released in Iowa have nested in Ontario, Minnesota, Wisconsin, Illinois, and Missouri. At Savannah, Illinois, a pair of Iowa swans were the first trumpeters to nest in

---

[15] www.threeriversparkdistrict.org/nrm/wildlife_wildlife_swanlocations.cfm

Illinois in 160 years. At Dawn, Missouri, two Iowa swans built the first trumpeter nest in that state in 140 years—"a new dawn for trumpeters in Missouri," he said. One Iowa pair nested in Colorado.

"Our trumpeter swan population is on the verge of being self-sustaining," Andrews said. The state's goal was 15 nesting pairs in 2003. "We missed that by one year." The 2006 goal was 25 nesting pairs. "We reached that a year early." Wildlife populations do fluctuate naturally, he notes, and Iowa's trumpeters have been "riding the crest" of growth in recent years. "We might see a drop in numbers," he added, but he believes the swans are firmly established in Iowa. Conditions were very dry in Iowa through much of 2006, but winter rains bode well for the 2007 nesting season.

The breeder pair partnership sites continue to produce new cygnets; Andrews called those sites "a reproductive engine for trumpeter swans." Talks are underway to work with the Trumpeter Swan Society, to release up to 50 Iowa-hatched swans at sites farther south, possibly in Kansas, Oklahoma, southern Illinois, Kentucky, Tennessee, Missouri, and Arkansas. The birds would be released in winter, with wings clipped, in the hopes that they would establish new wintering grounds and migrate back to Iowa or adjacent states in the spring.

Swans congregate at three main wintering sites in Iowa and at a scattering of smaller sites. "None of them is on the scale of a Monticello [Minnesota]," Andrews said. The best site, at Webster City, hosts about 75 swans each winter. Atlantic, Mason City, and Wheatland, Iowa are also good winter sites for viewing the birds. Summer nesting sites are scattered throughout the state, and it is possible to see swans at some time of the year in just about every part of the state. "That's one of the great bonuses of all this effort," said Andrews, "the opportunity that people have, winter, summer, spring, and fall, to see trumpeter swans in Iowa, especially in flight."

EVERY YEAR IN ALASKA, THE US FISH & WILDLIFE SERVICE selects several species of the region's wildlife, including moose, bears, otters, and various migratory birds, and conducts a survey of those species. In August of 2005, USFWS pilots and observers conducted a month-long aerial survey of Alaska's trumpeter swan population. The project covered more than 50,000 square miles of trumpeter habitat, using up to 14 aircraft flying up to eight hours a day, through most of the month of August. The swan survey has been carried out every five years since 1975 and it is believed to be the largest wildlife survey of its kind anywhere in the world. At more than $225,000, the cost of the trumpeter swan survey is roughly equal to the cost of all the agency's other Alaskan wildlife surveys combined.

The 2005 swan survey used GPS (global positioning system), and computer mapping to plot the numbers and locations of trumpeter adults and cygnets throughout Alaska. The data will be used to influence a variety of decisions on land use policy and planning, including the creation or expansion of wildlife refuges, construction of power lines, and mining rights.

The survey counted 24,105 birds, nearly six times the number counted in 1975. Added to the 10,000 or so other wild trumpeters in the Lower 48 states and Canada, that puts the world's total at around 30,000 trumpeter swans. That is still a relatively small number, indicating a still-vulnerable species. But for the major flocks of trumpeter swans, the population numbers are clearly growing.

HOWEVER you measure it, trumpeter swan restoration in the Midwest Flyway has been a grand success. The Interior Population of trumpeter swans now numbers nearly 5,000 individuals, from the Dakotas to the Ohio Valley, from southern Canada, almost to the Gulf of

Photo: © *Marlene Sternberger*

Mexico. In 2005, estimates put the Rocky Mountain Population at 5,400 trumpeter swans.

According to Johnson, the states in the Midwest Flyway have a pretty good handle on productivity among trumpeters but not much data on mortality. However, he added, the growth in numbers throughout the region indicates that, overall, births are exceeding deaths. "And that's one of the measures of self-sustainability." Another indicator is "no more releases," he said. In the Midwest Flyway, "everyone is winding down" because trumpeter swan reintroduction has been such a success.

The Pacific population of trumpeters (including Alaska and part of the Canadian Yukon Territory) grew from 9,500 swans in 1985 to 13,500 in 1990, to 16,300 in 1995, and 17,000 in 2000. It looked as though the Pacific population had leveled off; then the 2005 USFWS survey counted more than 25,000 trumpeter swans. Johnson quipped: "All those Fish & Wildlife Service boys up there lost bets."

For a bird that hadn't been seen in Midwestern skies for more than 100 years, the current Interior population of trumpeters, with its rising number of birds and breeding pairs, is clearly a success story. Along the way, biologists and conservationists have gathered new information about the swans, themselves.

According to Ed Diebold, formerly of the Milwaukee County Zoo, the trumpeter swan project broke new ground in wildlife reintroduction techniques—decoy-raising, in particular—that can be applied to other waterfowl and adaptable to other species. He added:

> "The project also demonstrated how effectively North American zoos can contribute to the conservation of wild species, outside the zoo. And for me, as a zoo biologist, it has also been one of the most— no, the most professionally satisfying project I've been involved in."

One of the major lessons learned from the swan project, according to Matteson, is the value and the necessity of building partnerships and coalitions:

> "Partnerships and a diversity of partners are absolutely critical to the success of a program like this. The Trumpeter Swan Recovery Project included a wide range of partners, public and private. Most of the funding for the project came from the private sector, but state and federal funds were also important."[16]

All these factors have made Trumpeter Swan Recovery a model project for other species, other states, and other conservation challenges.

---

[16] Wisconsin taxpayers can donate to the DNR's Endangered Resources Fund through a line on the state income tax form. This is the single largest source of contributions to the Endangered Resources Fund, and the primary source of funding for the management and protection of hundreds of endangered plants, wildlife species and habitats in

Public education programs have reduced shooting of trumpeters by hunters who mistake them for other birds, and have built strong public support for this and other conservation efforts. Ongoing efforts by state DNRs and the USFWS are preserving and restoring swan habitats. They are steering migrating swans away from power lines and away from feeding sites that are heavily contaminated with lead. Serious obstacles remain to the trumpeter's long-term survival in the Midwest Flyway. Lead poisoning, illegal or careless hunting, habitat loss, power line collisions, competition from mute swans, and perhaps even the avian flu—all of these are still formidable obstacles to trumpeter swan restoration.

But the success of trumpeter swan recovery programs in several midwestern states has proven that long-term recovery of waterfowl species is at least possible. That knowledge and the lessons learned hold a wealth of promise for the trumpeter, for other threatened or displaced species, for other conservation projects, and for all of us who can once again hear the clear trumpet call of these magnificent birds.

In Michigan, as in other states, Johnson added, the trumpeters have helped raise public awareness of the need for preserving and restoring natural wetlands. "They have been real ambassadors for wildlife conservation, and symbols of high-quality wetlands."

the state. In 2005, the income tax "checkoff" added $630,000 to the Endangered Resources Fund.

Federal funds come through the 1937 Federal Aid in Wildlife Restoration Act, better known as the Pittman-Robertson Act.

Part II:
A Siberian Odyssey

Photo, © International Crane Foundation, Baraboo, WI.

"Saving an endangered species is like plugging a leaky bucket that's already nearly empty. You have to fix all the holes as soon as possible, before the water runs out."

—George Archibald

Chapter 5
Saving Siberian Cranes

GEORGE ARCHIBALD AND RON SAUEY MET AS GRADUATE students at Cornell University. They shared a passion for cranes and together they founded the International Crane Foundation in 1973, as a non-profit organization to research and conserve the world's 15 species of cranes. While he was still at Cornell, Archibald began traveling all over the world, studying the comparative biology of crane species, meeting with conservationists, pushing for protective legislation, and publicizing the plight of endangered or threatened cranes.

Meanwhile, Sauey devoted his time to one especially threatened crane species—the Siberian crane. Although this magnificent bird is revered by native Siberian people and is a central figure in their cultures, little was known about its biology, numbers, or ranges.

THE SIBERIAN CRANE (GRUS LEUCOGERANUS), known in Russia as the "white crane" or "Asiatic white crane," is a majestic, snow-white bird with black wing tips and "a silver voice." It is found in legends, art, traditions, and fairy tales throughout Russia and Central Asia—a symbol of faithfulness, purity, and hope. One Central Asian legend says that Siberian cranes are the souls of brave warriors killed in battle, heroes who "were never buried in a grave but as cranes with plumage white."

For the Khanty and Mansy people—reindeer herders of northern Siberia and Russia—the white crane occupies a prominent place in their oral histories and their rituals. According to George Archibald:

> "The Khanty live on the former breeding grounds of
> the central population of Sibes, and they consider
> the Siberian crane to be a sacred bird. They keep

> their domestic reindeer herds away from wetlands
> were cranes breed, for fear of disturbing the cranes
> and trampling nests and eggs."

Living off the land, much as they have for a thousand years, the Khanty hunt bears, among other animals. When a bear is killed, Archibald explained, "the Khanty wear crane costumes and perform a crane dance around the campfire. They hold that this ritual drives away the spirit of the bear."[1]

Standing five feet (140 centimeters) tall and weighing about 13 pounds (six kilograms), with a wing span of about 8 feet (2.4 meters), an adult Siberian crane looks almost identical to a Whooping crane. Its feathers are pure white, except for black wing tips. Its face, forehead, and the sides of its head are bare and brick-colored. Its cheeks are white—it lacks the black cheeks and "mustache" of the "Whooper." The Siberian crane's legs and toes are salmon-colored; its eyes are reddish or yellow. Its beak is serrated, which helps it to pull up slippery water plants. No other crane species has a serrated beak.

Of the world's 15 species of cranes, 7 nest in Russia. Siberian cranes (affectionately called "Sibes") were first described scientifically in 1773. For the next 200 years, ornithologists gathered little infor-

---

[1] The Khanty people once occupied a territory that reached from the mouth of the Ob River on the Arctic Sea to the confluence with the Irtysh River, and from the eastern foothills of the Ural Mountains, 400 miles eastward into the heart of Siberia. Together, the semi-nomadic Khanty and Mansi may have numbered about 16,000 individuals in the 19th century, when the population of Muscovite Russia was probably about 10 million. Never a unified people, the Khanty lived in separate clans, each with its own hereditary chief and shaman.

The TranSiberian Railroad, completed in 1905, brought Muscovite Russians to colonize the corridor along the railroad, and the Khanty people retreated north, living in isolation from the new colonists. The Soviets tried to "collectivize" the Khanty in the 1930s, shipping their men off to state-owned farms and their children to boarding schools, and killing their shamans and any chiefs who resisted the "reforms." By the 1960s, many of the Khanty had moved back to their ancestral lands in the taiga and taken up their traditional semi-nomadic life, herding reindeer, hunting, fishing, and gathering berries. Russian law that once persecuted them now protected them and their lands. The Kunovat Nature Reserve was established to protect both the endangered cranes and the endangered Khanty, reduced to a few hundred people living in traditional ways.

Today in post-Soviet Russia, oil exploration brings a new threat the Khanty and their lands. New land laws have stripped away protections, and widespread corruption cancels out the legal protections that remain.

mation about the birds' ranges, habitat, and ecology. Siberian cranes were not easy subjects for study; they live in some of the most inaccessible places on earth—the vast, trackless marshes of western and northern Siberia, a part of the world that was still closed to western scientists in 1973.

Siberian cranes were known to nest in a few remote, widely scattered areas in northern Siberia, but no one knew exactly where their summer ranges were located. The Russians knew that some of Siberia's cranes wintered in China, but China, too, was closed to westerners. Historically, one group of Siberian cranes had wintered in Iran, in the lowland marshes along western shore of the Caspian Sea, but by the 1970s, only twelve birds were spotted on the wintering grounds in Iran. Another group wintered in the Keoladeo Ghana Bird Sanctuary, a large wetland in north central India. Over ten years, Ron Sauey spent six winters at Keoladeo, studying the Siberian cranes there, and adding significantly to the collected knowledge of its diet and behavior.

In 1972, in the midst of the Cold War, the United States and the Soviet Union signed an agreement that allowed scientists and conservationists from the two countries to cooperate on conservation projects. Archibald and Sauey immediately wrote to Dr. Vladimir Flint, a Russian ornithologist who was one of Russia's leading experts on Siberian cranes. They began forging ties that would lead to international efforts to preserve the species in the wild.

In 1973, the year ICF was founded Russian ornithologists estimated that there were only about 400 wild Siberian cranes left in the world. Of those, 64 cranes were known to be wintering in India and an

Ron Sauey and George Archibald, co-founders of ICF, in 1979.
Photo, © International Crane Foundation, Baraboo, WI.

unknown number were wintering in China. Sauey and Archibald considered preservation of Siberian cranes to be among the organization's highest and most urgent priorities. The Siberian crane was named ICF's "Target Species" in 1975-76. They and the Russians desperately needed more information about the bird's numbers, ranges, and ecology The main summer nesting sites of the Siberian cranes were assumed to be somewhere in northern Siberia, a mostly trackless region with a land area larger than that of the United States. Flint and his colleagues had located a few Siberian crane nests in the Yakutia region, in northeastern Siberia. They were presumably part of the group that wintered somewhere in China. But what of the Siberian cranes that wintered in India and Iran? The Russians believed that they nested somewhere in western Siberia, but where? That was a mystery.

One of the long-term goals of ICF's founders was to create and maintain a species bank—a captive breeding program where scientists could study the bird and eventually reintroduce eggs and chicks back into the wild, to bolster declining crane populations. In 1974, ICF conducted a historic experiment to determine if it were possible to transport living crane eggs from one continent to another. In Sweden, crane conservator Dr. P.O. Swanberg collected six Eurasian crane[2] eggs from nests on the estate of camera manufacturer Victor Hasselblad. Tucked into a portable incubator, the eggs were shipped by air to Chicago and then to the ICF's newly established headquarters at Baraboo, Wisconsin. All six eggs hatched and all six chicks survived. That experiment opened the way for the transfer of the first Siberian crane eggs from ICF to Russia in 1977, three years later.

In 1976 George Archibald flew to Moscow at Vladimir Flint's invitation. He was joined by ICF volunteer and "Russia expert" Elizabeth ("Libby") Anderson. They discussed a plan to reintroduce Siberian cranes to wintering sites in Iran. Large numbers of Eurasian cranes winter in Iran. The biologists proposed placing fertile Siberian crane eggs, from captive birds, into the nests of Eurasian cranes in Western Siberia. The Eurasian cranes would incubate and raise these "foster children," eventually leading them on the annual migration to Iran, where more than a million migratory waterfowl winter in the

---

[2] Known in some parts of Europe and Asia as the "common crane," the Eurasian crane (Grus grus) is the third most abundant crane species, after Sandhill and Demoiselle cranes. There are an estimated 250,000 Eurasian cranes worldwide, and their numbers are believed to be increasing overall, though some local flocks are declining. The Eurasian crane is native to 80 countries from northern and western Europe to northern China and eastern Siberia. The species winters in France and the Iberian Peninsula, north and east Africa, the Middle East, India, and southern and eastern China.

South Caspian Lowlands.

The eggs of Siberian and Eurasian cranes are similar in size and color, so the foster parents would be unaware that their own eggs had been replaced by others. Eurasian cranes, themselves, do not resemble Siberian cranes. Averaging about four feet (115 cm) tall, Eurasian cranes are foot shorter than Sibes and slate gray in color. Their neck, cheeks, forehead, legs, and feet are black.

The Siberian crane foster chicks would imprint on their Eurasian crane parents, leaving them too confused to seek out their own kind for mating and breeding. Instead, the biologists hoped that these foster chicks would eventually become "guide birds" for whole new families of Siberian cranes. The new families would be created by releasing into the wild large numbers of young adult Siberian cranes that had been raised and fledged in isolation from humans, at the Oka Nature Reserve and other captive breeding sites around Siberia. It was a complex plan, perhaps a desperate one, to save two small flocks of Siberian cranes teetering on the edge of oblivion.

Before it could begin, the "cross fostering" plan faced a small obstacle: no one knew where in Western Siberia the Eurasian cranes nested and laid their eggs in the spring.

In Iran, in the winter of 1976-77, an Iranian team led by George Archibald attached bright green numbered banners to the wings of 91 of the grayish Eurasian cranes. Once attached, the banners caused no harm to the birds and were easily visible from a distance. As those bannered birds flew north in the spring, Russian ornithologists tracked several of them to nesting sites in western Siberia, just east of the Ural Mountains.

Now that ornithologists knew where the Eurasian cranes were nesting and laying their eggs, the next step was to remove Eurasian crane eggs from a few nests and replace them with Siberian crane eggs. It was a simple enough idea that immediately turned complicated.

Eurasian cranes nest much earlier in the spring than Siberian cranes. By the time the Siberian cranes lay their eggs, Eurasian crane chicks are already hatched. To solve that problem, ICF proposed to:

1. Gather a small number of Siberian crane eggs from Russia and send them to ICF Headquarters in Baraboo, Wisconsin.
2. Hatch and raise Siberian crane chicks as a captive breeding pair. Using artificial light to simulate the Siberian spring, induce the captive pair to lay eggs earlier than wild Siberian

cranes.

3. Return those eggs to Russia and place them in the nests of Eurasian cranes back in Siberia, before the wild Eurasian crane chicks hatched.

ICF staffers had already been threading their way through Russian and American red tape for two and a half years, to obtain Siberian crane eggs for captive breeding. Progress was slow, and the breeding program would take years to pull off—if it could be pulled off. Wild Sibes don't reach sexual maturity until five or six years of age, and no one had ever successfully bred Siberian cranes in captivity.

The Russians would launch their own captive breeding program for Siberian cranes at the Oka Nature Preserve 180 miles (300 km) from Moscow, in 1978, with the help of the ICF. But in 1977, ICF's "Crane City" at Baraboo had the staff, facilities, knowledge, and experience to begin a captive breeding program well ahead of the Russians. Crane eggs from ICF's birds would allow the Russians to begin reintroduction efforts before their captive breeding program was up and running.

By early 1977, when plans for ICF's breeding program were being finalized, the estimated world population of wild Siberian cranes was down to 350.

IN JUNE 1977, DR. FLINT flew with a colleague to the Indigirka River in eastern Siberia, to gather wild Siberian crane eggs for ICF. Believing that the cranes were about to begin laying their eggs, the team surveyed the nesting sites and found 40 nesting pairs over five days. They also located five nests with suitable helicopter landing sites close by.

Then fog and rain moved in for four days, grounding the helicopter. When the weather cleared on July 1, the team found that in all of the nests they had selected, the chicks had already hatched. Though they were disappointed at not finding any eggs for ICF, they were delighted to see the signs of a new generation of wild Siberian cranes.

The next day, the scientists pushed their survey farther out to other nesting areas in the region and finally found two nests, each containing two intact eggs. (Like most crane species, Siberians typically lay two eggs at a time, though usually only one chick will survive the summer.) They took all four eggs. The team would have collected more eggs, Flint said, but the helicopter was low on fuel.

Removed from their parents' nests, the four precious eggs faced the first hazard of their journey: the helicopter. ICF had built and sent an insulated wooden crate for transporting the eggs. But, upon inspecting it, Flint declared the transport crate "extremely unsuitable." It was not only cumbersome and difficult to handle, he said. Worst of all, the crate provided inadequate protection for the fragile eggs. Flint later wrote to Archibald:

> "With all that vibration in the helicopter, it would have been impossible to save the embryos by holding the crate on one's knees. We constructed a system of springs and elastic bands and then everything was just fine: The water in a glass which we placed on the lid of the crate did not even ripple, though the teeth of our men almost fell out from the vibration, particularly during the landings and lift-offs of the helicopter."[3]

By helicopter and airplane, the trip from the Indigirka River to Moscow took 27 hours. Inside their heavy wooden crate, the eggs were cushioned by foam rubber and Styrofoam, warmed by a hot water bottle, and insulated inside four heavy Russian wool socks. At the Moscow airport, Flint presented the crate to ICF volunteer Libby Anderson, who wrote that the handoff "had the drama and intrigue of a first-rate spy thriller," even though, "the whole proceeding was conducted openly and had the expressed and smiling approval of both the Soviet and U.S. governments." Occurring in the depth of the Cold War, more than a decade before the fall of the Soviet Union, this simple handoff had required:

- three years of negotiations between scientists and government officials in the U.S. and U.S.S.R.,
- a new international agreement between the two nations,
- two permits from the U.S. Department of the Interior,
- one permit from the U.S. Department of Agriculture, and
- a letter from the Soviet government agreeing that exporting Siberian crane eggs would not further endanger the threatened and much-revered Siberian crane.

Back in Baraboo, ICF staff had been on the phone for a month,

---

[3] ICF Brolga Bugle, Vol.3, #4.

ensuring that all the necessary permits and approvals were finally in place.

Anderson had been in Moscow since Tuesday June 28. Dr. Flint couldn't predict with certainty when the eggs would be collected and when they would arrive in Moscow, so the Russians reserved a seat for Anderson each day on the daily Aeroflot flight to Stockholm—and each day cancelled the previous day's reservation. At 6:30 a.m. on Saturday July 2, Flint called to say that he and the eggs were in Moscow, and Anderson raced to the airport. Her Stockholm flight had already departed. The Russians found her a flight to London and a connecting flight to Chicago.

While waiting for the London flight, Anderson and Flint inspected the eggs and took photographs of the event. When her flight to Chicago was called Anderson checked her baggage and prepared to board the airplane. She intended to carry the egg box with her, so she could monitor the temperature inside box throughout the flight.

"Nyet," said the Aeroflot agent. The box was too big; it would have to travel in the cargo hold with the rest of the baggage. Dr. Flint patiently explained to the agent that the box contained eggs of the endangered Siberian crane and that it had to ride with Anderson, so she could keep the eggs safe and warm. Perhaps, he said to her, she had seen him talking about this project on the popular Soviet television show "In the World of Animals." Flint's calm entreaty had the desired effect; the agent agreed to bend the rules and allow the egg case to travel in the passenger compartment. Anderson and the egg box boarded the plane for London. There and again in Chicago, Anderson would patiently repeat Dr. Flint's arguments, in order to convince airline agents to allow her to keep the egg box by her side. In London, she later wrote, she even threatened to remove the eggs from the box and carry them inside her blouse. Each time, the airline agents—at Aeroflot, British Airways, and Northwest—bent the rules for the sake of the precious eggs.

FROM CHICAGO, THE EGGS WENT TO MADISON, Wisconsin, to the University of Wisconsin's "Biotron" research facility—the perfect nursery for the Siberian crane eggs. Temperature, light, and humidity in the incubator and surrounding chamber could be precisely controlled to give the eggs—and hatchlings—the best possible chance of success.

Built in the 1960s, the UW's Biotron is one of only four such facilities in the United States. The one at Madison supports some of the most advanced research undertaken at a university renowned for cutting-edge science. Today there is a long waiting list of research projects for the Biotron's chambers, from smokehouse processes to plant, animal, and atmospheric studies, to possible environments on other planets.

The eggs arrived at the Biotron on the morning of July 3, 1977—two days and nearly 10,000 miles from their wild nests in eastern Siberia. Archibald and colleague Bill Gause placed them in the incubator and let them rest overnight before performing the "water test." An egg that contains a developed, living embryo will float high in water with the pointed end down, occasionally bobbing around as the chick moves within. An infertile egg or one that contains a dead embryo floats low and motionless in the water.

Carefully, Archibald and Gause lowered each pair of eggs into a container of water. The medium-sized eggs from one nest both floated high and bobbed around. They were alive. The two large eggs from the other nest floated low and motionless. When Archibald shook them gently, they sounded as though they were filled with liquid—a sure sign that they were infertile. Three long years of planning and effort had yielded just two fertile eggs.

Wild cranes turn their eggs every few hours. That prevents embryonic tissue from adhering to the inside of the egg. Archibald and Gause waited anxiously, turning the two fertile eggs and listening carefully for the first scratching signs of a chick about to hatch. Finally, on the fifth day, they heard the telltale rustling and cracking noises. The eggs were carefully moved from the incubator to the hatchery chamber, where a slightly lower temperature (98.75° F.) and much higher humidity mimicked the summer climate of eastern Siberia.

For crane chicks, hatching is an exhausting ordeal that lasts for several days. It took 41 hours for the first of the Siberian crane hatchlings to break free of its shell. Archibald named that chick "Vladimir," after Dr. Flint. "Kyta" emerged two days later. Within hours of hatching, each chick was dry, fluffy, beginning to stand, and begging for food. On August 2, the three-week-old Siberian crane chicks traveled the last leg of their long journey, to the ICF's "Crane City" near Baraboo, Wisconsin. There, they would join "Wolf" and "Philis," two Siberian cranes who came to the ICF as adults, from zoos. Philis came to Baraboo in 1976 from the Philadelphia Zoo. She was hatched in the central population of Siberian cranes, and captured for the Miami Rare Bird Farm, in Florida. She moved to the Philadelphia Zoo as an adult in 1954. Wolf came to Baraboo in 1976 from Vögelpark Walsrode in Germany. The Vögelpark had acquired him from the

Switzerland's Basel Zoo; keepers there said Wolf had hatched in the wild soon after the year 1900.[4] The Guinness Book of World Records once listed him as the oldest known bird. At Baraboo, Wolf lived to be more than 80 years old.

IN JUNE OF 1978, ICF co-founder Ron Sauey flew to Moscow to accept seven more Siberian crane eggs that Dr. Flint and his colleagues had collected from wild nests. As

A Siberian crane chick just out of its shell. Hatching is a prolonged and exhausting ordeal.

Photo, © International Crane Foundation, Baraboo, WI.

before, the eggs were collected by helicopter in late June. It was an exciting trip, not only for the number of eggs collected. Flint told Sauey:

> "We didn't have too much petrol after we had collected the last of the seven eggs. In Russian helicopters, there are three warning alarms that the aircraft is about to run out of fuel. The last one, a loud buzzer, occurs just before the helicopter drops out of the air. We landed at the small airport [in Siberia] just as that buzzer went off."[5]

---

[4] Over the past few decades, public zoos have increasingly become directly involved in efforts to save or restore wild species. Historically, zoos were seen simply as places for displaying "specimens" taken from the wild. For modern zoos, field research and conservation of wild species have become central parts of their mission.

[5] ICF Brolga Bugle, Vol. 4, No. 4

The suitcase Flint was carrying held another surprise. As he and Sauey opened it to check the eggs, one of the chicks was peeping and beginning to crack through its shell. Sauey carefully transferred the eggs to a plywood box lined with layers of Styrofoam© and foam rubber. In the bottom of the box was a chamber to hold hot water bottles. During Sauey's 13-hour flight to New York, the peeping coming from the box attracted lots of attention from other travelers on the Aeroflot jetliner.

In New York, an agent of the U.S. Department of Agriculture (USDA) inspected the eggs and cleared them to enter the country. Sauey's connecting flight to Chicago was at the other end of the airport—in just ten minutes. He had to make that flight, he told the USDA agent; it was July 4 and all other flights to Chicago were booked solid. The USDA agent dragged Sauey and the egg case outside, threw them into his own car, and announced that they were taking a "scenic route." They sped across the airport, racing down the edges of taxiways, beneath the wings of 747 Jumbo jets lined up for takeoff. On the other side of the airport, Sauey was led into the terminal through a locked door located beyond the passengers' security checkpoint. While the USDA agent argued with an irate security guard, Sauey dashed to the gate and down the jet way carrying the precious eggs. He was the last passenger to board the DC-10 before it departed for Chicago.

When the suitcase was opened again at Madison, it contained six eggs and a wet but healthy-looking Siberian crane chick sitting on a cashmere sweater lent to Sauey by a fellow passenger. The impatient chick was promptly christened "Aeroflot"—the only Siberian crane, and probably the only bird, ever to hatch 30,000 feet above sea level.

Of the remaining six eggs, two were infertile and four hatched at the Biotron, though one of the chicks died just a few days later. Despite these losses, ICF biologists considered the 1978 trip to be a success. Impatient "Aeroflot," plus the three chicks hatched at the Biotron meant four new Siberian cranes for the captive breeding program at Baraboo.

As yet, in early 1980, know one knew where the western flocks of Siberian cranes nested. That summer, the Russians made a lucky discovery. A group of Russian tourists canoeing on a branch of the Ob River in northwestern Siberia came across a bedraggled crane chick alone on a sandbar. Since the chick was too young to fly and was apparently abandoned, the canoeists took it with them, hoping to find someone to care for it. At the village of Gorki, a local woman, Tamara Soldatava, agreed to adopt the chick, adding it to her personal menagerie, which already included several huskies and a half-tame fox. Under Soldatava's care, the chick quickly outgrew its new home, and Soldatava wrote to the local newspaper, looking for someone else to adopt the crane. By chance, her letter was forwarded to the University of Moscow, where it came to Dr. Flint's attention. He dispatched fellow ornithologist Sasha Sorokin to find the crane and bring it back to Moscow.

In Gorki, Sorokin was the first person to recognize that the chick was in fact a Siberian crane. Since it was too young to fly when it was rescued, Sorokin knew that the nest where the young crane hatched had to be near the place where the bird was found. This was the first solid clue to where the Siberian cranes nested in western Siberia.

Sorokin took the crane chick back to Moscow, to Flint's apartment, where they gave it a much-needed bath before taking it to the new crane conservation center at the Oka Nature Preserve, 280 miles southeast of Moscow. In Gorki, the chick had lived under Soldatava's house with her dogs, subsisting on a diet of raw fish and covered in dirt and fat. (That the dogs did not eat the crane is a testimony to Soldatava's skill as a dog trainer—or the chick's unappetizing condition.) At Flint's apartment, it took three baths with baby soap to get the chick clean. The tame young Sibe endured it all without a fuss. Flint named the chick "Sauey," after ICF co-founder Ron Sauey.

A year later in 1981, Sorokin returned to Gorki. He spent several days searching the nearby marshes by helicopter and found eight breeding pairs of Siberian cranes on the Kunovat River, not far from where the chick Sauey had been rescued by the canoeists.

The "mystery of the missing Siberian cranes" was beginning to be solved.

WITH A TOTAL OF NINE CAPTIVE SIBERIAN CRANES AT BARABOO, ICF's efforts turned to breeding, to create a captive flock. Those captive cranes, it was hoped, would eventually produce eggs and chicks that could be returned to the wild. Two other captive breeding programs helped to ensure genetic diversity: the Soviets, with help from ICF, began a captive breeding program in 1978 at the Oka Nature Reserve southeast of Moscow. Another breeding program was established at Vögelpark Walsrude, an ornithological zoo in Germany. By 1980, there were a total of 25 captive Siberian cranes at the three breeding centers, but so far, most of their eggs had been infertile, and from the few Sibe eggs that hatched, no captive-bred chicks had survived.

Captive breeding of Siberian cranes presents some daunting obstacles. In captivity, the birds don't reach sexual maturity until they are seven or eight years old, compared with three to five years for some other crane species. Siberians are among the most aggressive of all the cranes, and that makes pair bonding difficult, with risks of injury to the birds and their handlers. Males and females look and act exactly alike until after pair bonding begins, though males might be slightly taller and have slightly longer beaks. Knowing the sex of the birds is essential if you want to pair them for breeding, but in captivity the sex of the each crane could only be determined conclusively through a procedure that required precise anesthesia—a delicate balancing act between putting the bird to sleep and killing it.[6]

When ICF's Siberian cranes finally managed to produce eggs, the Sibes were good incubators but there eggs were infertile. Cranes that lose their eggs early in the season will usually produce more to replace the lost ones. At ICF, the infertile eggs were removed from the nests to encourage more production. When the Sibes began producing fertile eggs, those eggs were put in the care of sandhill crane foster parents and then moved to the artificial incubators before they hatched.

After countless frustrations, and seemingly against all odds, a Siberian crane named "Duschenka" hatched and fledged at ICF in Baraboo in 1981. Her name means "Little Loved One" in Russian, and she was the world's very first captive-bred Siberian crane.

More successes followed. In 1983, ICF's captive Sibes produced four fertile eggs. Slated to be the first in the "restocking" program, these four captive-bred Siberian crane eggs would be placed in the nests of wild Eurasian cranes in western Siberia. There, if all went well, they would hatch, and the chicks would fledge and grow to adulthood. Upon their small, downy heads might rest hopes of pre-

---

[6] One might ask, why not put all the cranes together and let them sort out who's who? Sibes are among the most aggressive of all crane species and their courtship is part romance and part peace treaty. In the wild, cranes can avoid or break off risky confrontations by flying away. Captive birds don't have that option. Penning unpaired birds together in the hope that romance might blossom would often result in one or more injured birds. In captivity, courtship must always begin with a male and female in adjacent enclosures. The birds are placed in the same pen only after they display strong courtship behavior toward each other.

serving the rapidly dwindling wild flocks.

In 1981, Russian biologists and ornithologists, with support form the Soviet government, created "Project Sterkh" to study and protect Russia's Siberian cranes. "Sterkh" is the Russian word for Siberian crane.[7] In cooperation with the All-Russia Institute of Nature Protection and other organizations, including the International Crane Foundation, Project Sterkh studied the Siberian crane and developed new strategies for crane conservation.

According to the best estimates at the time, were about 200 Sibes nesting in eastern Siberia and one third as many in western Siberia, for a total wild population of just 275 Siberian cranes.

"Duschenka" two days old.
Photo, © International Crane Foundation,
Baraboo, WI.

IN MAY 1983, ICF CO-FOUNDER GEORGE ARCHIBALD flew to Moscow aboard a Deutsche Lufthansa airliner, carrying the four Siberian crane eggs from Baraboo. Since 1926, the trademark of the German-based airline, which appears on all of its aircraft, has been the stylized image of a crane. According to company literature, the Lufthansa crane symbolizes "stamina, strength, and power." In the early 1980s, Lufthansa began providing free international travel and other support to crane researchers from ICF and its European counterparts. The airline flew representatives to wildlife conferences in Europe and Asia, and transported people, equipment, and crane eggs around the world. Today, Lufthansa remains a major supporter and "the official airline" of the International Crane Foundation.[8]

---

[7] One of the mountains near the cranes' nesting area in western Siberia is called Sterkh Mountain, and among the native people in the area, the surname Sterkh is not uncommon.
[8] For more than three decades, Lufthansa has been an active supporter of efforts to save wild cranes, in Europe, the Mediterranean, Asia, and the Philippines. The company was a sponsor of the 1978 book, Rettet die Vögel ("Save the Birds"), which helped raise

From Moscow, Archibald took the four Sibe eggs 280 miles overland to the Oka Wildlife Reserve, where they would be placed in the nests of wild Eurasian crane foster parents. If all went well, the Sibe eggs would hatch, the chicks would fledge, and in the fall they would follow their foster parents on the long migration south.

Like most other cranes, Sibes and Eurasian cranes migrate by "flapping and gliding." They ride thermals—rising columns of warm air—flapping their wings as needed, but sparingly, and climbing to between 5,000 and 15,000 feet (1,500 to 4,500 meters)

Deutsche Lufthansa's crane logo

above sea level. Once they reach altitude, they glide away from the thermal, descending only very slowly and flapping their wings very rarely, if at all. When they encounter another thermal, they ride it back up and then glide again. This kind of flight is much more efficient than simply flapping along in level flight, as geese do. It allows the cranes to migrate long distances very quickly and very efficiently. Migrating cranes can cover several hundred miles in a day. Siberian cranes migrate farther than almost any other bird species—more than 5,000 miles (8,000 km) from northern Siberia to Central Asia and China.

Except when they land to rest or feed, cranes are rarely seen during these migratory flights, so high above the ground. But if atmospheric conditions are just right, they can be heard calling to each other as they pass overhead. And the Sibe's clear and high-pitched call—sometimes described as "clarinet-like"—is unique among cranes.

By 1983, the Russians were close to solving the mystery of the

public awareness of the plight of European bird species—including the cranes—and their habitats. In 1991, Germany's Nature Protection Association (Naturschutzbund NABU) and the World Wildlife Fund-Germany launched a work group called Crane Protection Germany. With significant support from Lufthansa, the group funds research on European crane species and preservation of crane habitats in Germany, Spain, and Israel. In 2001, the airline flew a cargo of 200 crane statues from South Africa to Europe. The two-foot-tall statues of African crowned cranes were fashioned of scrap metal by local craftsmen and transported free on a Lufthansa flight. The airline advertised the statues in its newsletter and on its Web site, and sold them all within two days, donating the proceeds to the South African Crane Working Group.

"missing" western flocks of Siberian cranes. Yuri Markin had found a few nests near Gorki in northwestern Siberia. Through banding of young birds, he found that these were Sibes that wintered in India. Other nests had been found farther south along the Ob River. These flocks of Siberian cranes migrated south through Afghanistan and Pakistan, to winter in Iran.[9] Both flocks migrated across dangerous routes. In southern Siberia, Afghanistan, and Pakistan, cranes were widely hunted for food or sport. Hunting along their migratory route was thought to be one of the principal causes of the western Sibes' decline.

The Eurasian cranes that nested at Oka Reserve migrated farther west and wintered in Turkey. That was one of the reasons they were chosen to be foster parents for the Sibe eggs from ICF. If the experiment went as the Russians hoped, the Siberian chicks would learn a new migration route from their foster parents—one that would keep them away from the hunting grounds.

There were 50 to 60 breeding pairs of Eurasian cranes living wild on the Oka Reserve, but finding their well camouflaged nests was a supreme challenge in the Oka's 223 square miles (577 sq km) of swamps and aspen thickets. By the time ICF's eggs arrived at Oka in May 1983, the Russians had located only one Eurasian crane nest in the reserve. One of the Sibe eggs was placed in that nest. The other three eggs from Baraboo were found to be infertile.

That trip highlighted the two overriding problems of restocking wild Siberian cranes: producing fertile eggs in sufficient numbers from captive Siberian cranes, and locating the same number of Eurasian crane nests in which to place the Siberian crane eggs. ICF and the Russians continued to make slow but encouraging progress on the egg production problem. And they hoped to find more nests by attaching radio transmitters to 20 Eurasian cranes during the winter, so their nests could be located the following spring.

In 1984, ICF's breeding program passed another benchmark. Vladimir and Bazov, two Siberian cranes who came from Russia as

---

[9] In the winter of 1995-96, Yuri Markin attached a satellite radio to a Siberian crane wintering in Iran. That crane led the Russians to a new nesting area 600 miles (1,000 km) south of the Kunovat Basin (the nesting area discovered in 1981), near the Irtysh River, a southern tributary of the Ob River. This is the nesting area of the Iran population of Sibes. The migration routes of the two western populations overlaps from the nesting grounds of the Iran population to the staging areas of both flocks on the Narzum wetlands of northwest Kazakhstan.

eggs in 1977 and 1978, successfully hatched the first chick from to come from ICF's Russian birds. Vladimir was also the world's first Siberian crane to successfully rear her own chick in captivity. As more captive birds reached sexual maturity, and as ICF and Oka staffs gained experience, more Sibe chicks hatched and fledged in captivity at both breeding centers. Russian-American cooperation was creating two viable captive species banks for Siberian cranes.

Captive birds cannot save a wild species from extinction. But the captive birds produced eggs that could be reintroduced into the wild flocks. And studying the captive birds gave scientists much needed information about the Siberian crane's biology and behavior.

Chapter 6
Good News, Bad News

"I DON'T GO ON JUST SIGHTSEEING TRIPS," Mary Kohler said. "But I love to go on a trip that has a mission—a dinosaur dig, a walking tour, lectures, that kind of stuff." In 1986, a notice in the ICF "Brolga Bugle" newsletter caught her attention; it called for volunteers to go to China in early 1987 to count cranes. It sounded interesting. Mary had never been to China, and she was going to be halfway around the world, anyway—in Australia for the America's Cup sail boat race. (Her husband Terry is the owner of North Sails Group, LLC, the world's leading maker of racing sails.) From Perth, Australia, she flew up to China and met the ICF group in Hong Kong. The Wisconsin DNR's Sumner Matteson was one of the leaders on the trip into China and it was on this trip that the friendship between Matteson and the Kohlers began.

The ICF's 1987 China expedition was concerned with counting the Siberian cranes of the flock that nested in eastern Siberia and wintered at Poyang Lake in China. At the time, ornithologists believed that there were about 250 cranes in that flock. Arriving in China, Mary learned that during the big count at Poyang Lake, she

Siberian cranes at Poyang Lake, China.
Photo, © International Crane Foundation, Baraboo, WI.

79

and all the other volunteers would be sent out in pairs with spotting scopes, to various locations around the reserve. They would all be counting at the same time, to avoid counting the same birds more than once. Mary's assigned partner was Ann Sands, another accomplished birder.

After reaching Poyang Lake, the volunteers spent several days learning to differentiate the four crane species that nest there. "We lived in a guesthouse," Mary said:

> "And they had tried to build it to sort of European standards. Each double room had a bathroom with a tub, a toilet, and a sink. In nobody's room did all of them work. In most of the rooms, two of them worked; some people had hot water in the tub—I don't think Ann and I did—and in some of the rooms, the toilets flushed."

On the day of the big count, the volunteers spread out to their assigned areas. Mary remembers:

> "They put Ann and me in the best place [for counting], I guess because they figured we were the best counters. We had to take a little bitty funny rowboat thing across the river, and they had to give us Chinese money for that.
>
> "Tourists don't get real Chinese money; they get 'tourist money'—this ratty little piece of paper. But they had to give us real Chinese money to pay the boatman to get us across the river, because he wouldn't accept tourist money.
>
> "Ann and I were very methodical and we counted these cranes very carefully. The cranes were very slowly moving in one direction. We moved slowly in the other direction so we would be careful not to recount any birds. And we counted close to 2,000 Siberian cranes, including adults and young.
>
> "Well, they flatly disbelieved us. They flatly disbelieved us for a whole year, until the next year when they went again and counted 2,000 Siberian cranes. And then I got a postcard from George

Archibald, saying, 'I'm eating crow.'"

Between the training and the count itself, the group stayed at Poyang Lake for about a week. On the way back from the count, four or five of the group members, including ICF's Jim Harrison, Ann Sands, and Mary, wanted to go hiking in the reserve. Mary recalled:

> "The Chinese wanted to send their park rangers with us, which seemed sensible. They also wanted to send a doctor. I don't know what they thought was going to happen, but the doctor and his bag had to come along."

During their hike through the wildlife reserve, the two women found some "unfortunate things," including an area where a local farmer had cut down a large woodlot in order to raise mushrooms. "The rangers obviously didn't know that this was going on; they'd never been back there," Mary said, adding, "These rangers didn't range very far."
She continued:

> "We were supposed to walk through [the reserve] and get picked up on the other side. It was getting to be late afternoon. The rangers didn't know where they were and the Americans finally said, 'Stop. Let's sit down and think about this, and we'll figure out how to get there.' Well, we did finally figure it out, but clearly, the rangers had never been back there. Things are better now, I am informed."

In 1990, three years after Mary's trip to China, a Japanese team counted more than 2,600 Siberian cranes wintering at Poyang Lake—members of the eastern flock that summered in the sub-arctic taiga[10] forests of far Eastern Siberia. The western flock that wintered in Iran and the central flock that wintered in India were still seriously threatened. But the latest counts brought renewed hope for the eastern flock and for the species as a whole. Still, the higher numbers were

---

[10] The taiga ("TIE-gah") is the boggy sub-arctic forest that grows in the climatic zone just south of the tundra. To the locals, summer is the "blue taiga," so-called for the blue-green needles of the predominant larch trees. Autumn is the "brown taiga," since the larches, though conifers, lose their needles each year. Winter is the "white taiga."

no guarantee of survival. The cranes' winter habitats on the Yangtze and Amur rivers in China were, and are, seriously threatened by human development. And as the western and central flocks continued to decline, crane biologists were deeply concerned that nearly all of the world's wild Siberian cranes were in one flock. An avian disease, or a natural or man-made disaster that struck the eastern flock could plunge the species into extinction almost overnight.

PLACING CAPTIVE-BRED SIBERIAN CRANE EGGS in the nests of wild Eurasian crane foster parents was one possible way of bolstering the rapidly diminishing western flock of Siberian cranes that nested along the Ob River, east of the Ural Mountains in northwestern Siberia. Perhaps Eurasian cranes nesting along the Ob River could also teach Siberian crane chicks to follow a new migration route, one that avoided the crane hunting grounds. Yuri Markin had studied the ecology of the Eurasian crane since the mid-1970s and knew that Eurasian cranes, like Siberian cranes, nested in the Ob River basin. But no one knew for sure where those particular Eurasian cranes spent their winters. It was not possible to follow the birds' migration over the vastness of western Siberia.

Tracking the birds by satellite was the only practical solution, and in 1989, ICF began pulling together the resources to fit several Eurasian cranes with radio-to-satellite transmitters. NASA (the United States' National Aeronautics and Space Administration) helped ICF obtain three of the $3,500 transmitters. NASA also provided a team to receive and process the tracking data. To mount the transmitters, biologists would first need to capture three cranes in the field, attach the transmitter harness to each bird, and then release the birds—all without injuring the cranes and as quickly as possible to avoid overstressing the birds. Staff and students at the University of Maryland helped to develop a four-barrel capture gun that would shoot a net over a crane. They successfully tested the capture gun at the crane colonies of the US Fish & Wildlife's Patuxent Wildlife Research Center, at nearby Patuxent, Maryland.

In May, 1990, Markin and American biologist David Ellis flew to northwestern Siberia to spend four weeks in the marshes along the Kunovat River, a tributary of the Ob and the nesting grounds of both Siberian and Eurasian cranes.[11] Ellis was a USFWS biologist based at the Patuxent facility. He had strong experience in field research on

---

[11] Ellis and Markin chronicled their adventures in the February 1991 issue of the Brolga Bugle.

cranes—especially relating to satellite transmitters.

Ellis and Markin planned to capture the cranes near their nests. They would fit the transmitters to male cranes, since the males are slightly larger than the females and could carry the 5.4-ounce (150-gram) backpack more easily.

The first difficulty in executing this plan (besides the obvious one of camping for four weeks on the half-frozen arctic bog of the Kunovat lowlands) was finding a Eurasian crane to capture. A Siberian crane nest lay very near their base camp on the Hoolyoogan River, but there were no Eurasian cranes to be found. Ellis and Markin hiked for days through the bog, looking for a few suitable nesting pairs. They followed a submerged "highway" of matted roots, wading through bogs from which the winter's ice had not entirely disappeared. At one point along the way, an unseen hole in their submerged path swallowed Ellis neck-deep in the freezing water. That forced the biologists to stop, build a fire, and dry out Ellis' clothes and equipment before moving on. After three days of splashing through the marsh, they had located just two suitable nesting pairs of Eurasian cranes. The nests were separated by a two-hour hike and were each several miles from the men's base camp.

The Kunovat Marshes.   *Photo: Kyoko Archibald, ICF, www.savingcranes.org.*

To cut their daily travel time, they moved from their base camp and set up a remote camp closer to the nests. By now, it was early June. They had been at Kunovat more than two weeks and they were finally ready to begin capturing cranes and fitting them with transmitters. The net guns developed at the University of Maryland had proven too bulky for hikers to carry around the marshes. Ellis and Markin would have to capture the birds by hand after doping them with anesthetic-laced bait.

Perched in a pine tree about 1,000 feet (300 m) from their first target nest, the two biologists waited for the opportune moment to place their bait near the nest, in hopes of capturing the male of the pair. After a long wait, they saw their chance. Markin slipped out of hiding, placed the first bait—a large piece of fish—near the nest and scurried back to the makeshift blind. But the finicky birds refused to eat their first bait and ignored the second—a sandpiper egg. Ellis and Markin decided to try their luck with the other pair of cranes.

A two-hour hike across the marshes brought them to the second nest. After observing the birds for two hours from a makeshift blind, Markin flushed the cranes away from the nest, placed the drug-laced sandpiper egg bait directly in the nest, and slogged back to the blind. Before the cranes could return to the nest, a large gull landed and settled itself on the sandpiper egg, apparently trying to incubate it, and possibly breaking the single crane egg in the process. The male crane returned, booted the gull out of the nest, and proceeded to eat what appeared from the blind to be the remains of the crane egg. The male then wandered away from the nest, leaving it unguarded and reinforcing the watchers' fears that the crane egg was broken.

Markin watched the bird intently and finally concluded that it was, indeed, showing the effects of the drug. It soon began to stagger, and Ellis and Markin began slowly stalking it, freezing in grotesque poses whenever the bird looked up. After several long minutes of stalking, Markin grabbed the bird and carried it back to the blind, while its mate circled overhead, crying out loud alarm calls. The crane egg in the nest was undamaged after all, and the female soon returned to guard it. But while Ellis and Markin were attaching the transmitter to the male, whom they named "Boris," crows attacked the nest, lured the female away, and destroyed the egg. If Boris had not been occupied with the two biologists, he could probably have foiled the crows' attack on the nest. This late in the season, it was unlikely that the pair would produce any more eggs that year. Both men were relieved that they had attached the transmitter but distraught that it had cost the cranes their only egg.

After sloshing back to camp, they tried once again to bait and capture the uncooperative male of the first pair, near the camp. As Markin placed the bait in their nest, he discovered two crane eggs, one of which was beginning to hatch. The parents soon returned to the nest but ignored the bait. At midnight, after several hours of watching the pair, Ellis and Markin turned in. Neither bird appeared groggy.

The next morning, the male stood sleeping near the nest, on wobbly legs. He was clearly drugged. The female was somewhere out of sight, along with the first chick, and a second chick was beginning to hatch. Fearful of leaving this nest and chick unprotected, Ellis and Markin quickly grabbed the male. An hour and a quarter later, they left him standing near the nest, still somewhat wobbly, and sporting a transmitter backpack and a new name, "Ivan." A few minutes later, Ivan was flying—a bit unsteadily—and Ellis and Markin moved quickly out of the area, to leave the crane family in peace.

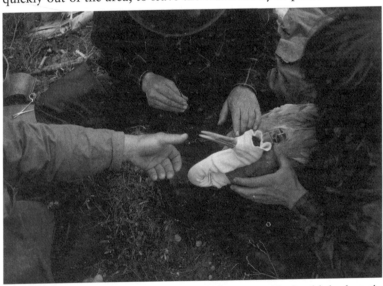

A "backpack" radio transmitter fitted to a Siberian crane. The hood helps keep the crane calm during the procedure.   Photo, © International Crane Foundation, Baraboo, WI.

The two men splashed back across the marshes to check on Boris and his mate, but in nearly eight hours of searching, they saw no sign of the cranes.

The spent the night camped near Boris' nest and waded back the next morning to check on Ivan. They found him wide awake and sitting on the nest, but the female and the chicks were nowhere in sight.

Was Ivan sitting on the second egg? Was the second chick alive? At least, they noted with relief, Ivan was completely ignoring his radio backpack.

Three days later, on June 17, Ellis and Markin spotted Ivan, his mate, and both chicks at the edge of a marsh. They all looked healthy and Ivan was still ignoring his backpack.

The next day, Russian crane expert Sasha Sorokin arrived in a helicopter to take Ellis and Markin back to base camp. They had one transmitter left, and before returning to base camp, they used the Mi-2 helicopter to search the marshes for another crane. They hoped to find a molting, flightless crane that would be relatively easy to catch, or a flying crane they could capture with the net gun, fired from the helicopter's wide side door.

Netting mammals and birds from hovering helicopters is not uncommon, but it usually involves small, maneuverable two- or four-passenger rotorcraft. The Russian-built Mil Mi-2 helicopter—a medium-sized cargo hauler—is far less agile than a crane, especially a crane flying evasive maneuvers. Still, they tried for three hours to get close enough (within 50 feet—15 meters) to net an airborne bird. Twice they came almost within range and twice the cranes' aerial dance put the big helicopter to shame.

Finally, Dr. Sorokin spotted a molting, flightless female, and the helicopter swooped in for a shot with the capture gun. But the frightened crane stuck to the woods, where the treetops kept the helicopter out of range. Ellis managed to fire two nets; one missed, the other brushed the bird with its edge and she slipped free. Finally, as the crane tired from the chase, Ellis, Markin, and Sorokin jumped from the helicopter and chased her on foot until Markin got close enough to pounce on her.

Now the biologists were in a race. The boggy ground offered no place for the helicopter to land; it could only hover or circle nearby. It was a contest to see whether the team could get the crane harnessed before the helicopter ran too low on fuel to continue loitering in the area. After a tense and busy 45 minutes, the female crane was released—harnessed and unharmed—and the two biologists clambered aboard the helicopter for the ride back to base camp. (The NASA tracking team later named this crane "Katya.")

Ellis arrived in Washington, D.C. a week later, on June 25, 1990, and learned that NASA was successfully tracking all three cranes with its TIROS satellites.[12] For a few months, the three cranes lingered in the Ob River Basin. Then they began moving steadily south in short hops, with Katya in the lead.

Ivan's signal vanished on October 10, about 600 miles (1,000 km) south of his nest. Boris' signal traveled about 500 miles south of the Kunovat marsh then stopped moving, though the signal could still be heard. It meant that either Ivan was dead or his transmitter had fallen off and been left behind.

NASA tracked Katya 2,000 miles to the Hari River, on the border between Iran and Afghanistan. Her signal became intermittent after mid-October, but NASA heard from her often enough to know that she was wintering on the Hari River. Katya thus became the first Eurasian crane from western Siberia whose wintering ground was known. Though the data gleaned from Katya's radio signal was limited, it nonetheless gave scientists and conservationists new and valuable information about the migration of Siberia's Eurasian cranes— information they hoped would aid efforts to preserve the region's wild Siberian cranes.

THE RUSSIANS WERE STILL WORKING ON PLANS TO PUT captive-bred Siberian crane eggs into wild Eurasian crane nests in the Ob River basin. By 1991, the breeding programs to produce those eggs were well established at Baraboo, Oka Reserve, and Walsrude. Having three geographically separate sites helped ensure genetic diversity for the captive birds and helped prevent a single infection from reaching all the captive birds. Ornithologists also hoped to preserve three separate flocks in the wild, where genetic diversity and geographic isolation would help insure against a single disease or environmental hazard wiping out the entire species.

In 1991, the eastern flock was known to number more than 2,500 Siberian cranes, but the central and western flocks of Sibes had been reduced to just 14 individuals. If those two flocks disappeared, that would leave the survival of the wild Siberian cranes dependent on a single threatened flock.

Soviet, American, German, and Indian researchers launched a "last-ditch effort" to save the desperately threatened western flock. In May, American ornithologist Jim Bland carried two Siberian crane

---

[12] NASA's TIROS (Television Infrared Observation Satellite) was first launched into polar orbit in 1960, as the world's first weather satellite. It was extremely successful and was followed by seven more TIROS and Improved TIROS (ITOS) satellites. Later satellites in the series could observe and measure cloud cover and type, sea surface temperature and currents, snow, ice, atmospheric temperature and moisture, atmospheric

eggs from ICF to Russia. At a stopover in Germany, he picked up four more eggs from the Vögelpark Walsrode, and then went on to Oka Nature Reserve. Bland traveled on scheduled Lufthansa flights, with the eggs in a portable incubator on the seat beside him.

Oka contributed two more eggs and the entire batch was flown north to the Siberian frontier village of Gorki, where Sasha Sorokin had first discovered the nests of the western flock ten years earlier, in 1981. In the interim, helicopter surveys had located the nesting area of some of the western Sibes in Kunovat Basin, a remote wilderness of bogs and forest, not far from where the Ob River meets the Arctic Sea. The area had until recently been closed to foreigners; in June 1991, Bland was only the third American ever to enter there. He wrote:

> "The most vivid impression I had from the helicop-
> ter was the huge expanse of forest as far as you can
> see, teeming with wildlife. Thunderstorms had just
> come through, and there was a forest fire burning on
> the horizon. On the vast Siberian plain, the huge fire
> looked like a little puff of smoke."[13]

The eight eggs Ellis carried were placed in an electric incubator in Gorki—the only settlement near the nesting area that had electricity. The two eggs from Oka failed to hatch. The other six eggs hatched but one of the chicks died of a respiratory infection. In June, the remaining five chicks were taken by helicopter to a wilderness camp near the nesting territory of a pair of wild Siberian cranes. There, led by ICF's Mimi Nagendran, a group of crane-costumed researchers taught the crane chicks to find natural foods and protected them from predators, including wolves, lynxes, otters, eagles, and bears. To keep them wild, the chicks were raised in isolation from human contact, using techniques developed at ICF by Kyoko Archibald and others. Whenever they were within sight of the chicks, the researchers wore white "crane costumes" and spoke as little as possible—and then only in whispers—to prevent the chicks from

chemistry, fires, pollution, and other environmental factors, day or night. The current satellite array can measure conditions at a given location anywhere in the world, every 12 hours.

TIROS satellites also receive and relay radio signals from Emergency Locator Transmitters (ELTs) carried by ships, aircraft, and individuals. ELT signals guide rescuers to the site of an emergency.

[13] ICF Bugle, August 1991

becoming accustomed to the sight and sound of humans.

Most cranes are born with the instinctive urge to migrate. But the routes they take, their wintering and summering grounds, and the places where they rest during the long migration are learned from their parents. The hope was that these five chicks would learn the western flock's migration route to Iran and pass it on to future chicks. If the western flock died out, the collective memory of its migration routes, and its nesting and wintering grounds, would be lost.

A costumed handler with a crane puppet teaches young cranes to forage. The tape player on her hip plays recorded crane calls. Photo, © International Crane Foundation, Baraboo, WI.

In August, as the wild Siberian cranes began their annual 5,000-mile migration to Caspian Lowlands in Iran, the researchers attached a tiny radio transmitter to one of the chicks, and then released the chicks near the wild Siberian crane nests. They hoped that the chicks would follow the wild birds as they flew to their wintering grounds. But the wild cranes departed early that fall, and the released chicks were left behind.

THROUGH THE 1990S, THE WESTERN FLOCK OF SIBERIAN cranes that wintered in Iran, and the central flock that wintered in India continued to dwindle in numbers despite the best efforts of ICF and Russia's Project Sterkh. New individuals introduced into the flocks as eggs or chicks either failed to make the migration or simply disappeared, victims of hunting, predation, exhaustion, weather, or disease. The phrase, "last-ditch effort" appears frequently during that decade in ICF reports on the western and central flocks of Siberian cranes.

By 1996, the central and western populations were nearly gone. The two flocks had totaled about 200 birds in the 1960s; in 1996, their numbers were estimated at fewer than ten individuals. Only seven Siberian cranes were sighted at the wintering grounds in Iran in 1996, in the lowlands bordering the Caspian Sea. In India, only one pair of Sibes was spotted, at Keoladeo National Park. (That pair was last seen in the winter of 2001-02.)

A historic 1995 meeting in Moscow brought together representatives of most of the countries that shared the western and central flocks of Siberian cranes—a part of the world not known for cross-border cooperation. Soon, there were new laws protecting the cranes in their summering grounds and along their migration routes. There were new international efforts to protect the birds, locate all of their nesting and staging grounds, and introduce new eggs or chicks into the wild from the three captive breeding programs. Still, the western and central flocks continued to shrink. Of the eastern flock that nested in Yakutia and wintered in China, estimates put the population at 2,500 to 3,000 birds. That was far more encouraging than earlier estimates in the hundreds. But in global terms, 3,000 Siberian cranes is a small and vulnerable group of survivors.

In the ICF Bugle newsletter, George Archibald wrote: "Saving an endangered species is like plugging a leaky bucket that's already nearly empty. You have to fix all the holes as soon as possible, before the water runs out."[14] For the central and western flocks of Sibes, the bucket was nearly dry.

---

[14] ICF Bugle, vol. 21, #3

Chapter 7
To Mother Russia

IN LATE 1996, GEORGE ARCHIBALD AND VLADIMIR FLINT began planning yet another "last-ditch effort"—a hopeful effort to hold off the looming extinction of the western and central flocks of Siberian Cranes. Once more they would place Sibe eggs from the captive breeding programs in the nests of wild Eurasian cranes in the desperate hope that new chicks would sustain those flocks a little longer, and keep the "bucket" from running dry.

Terry and Mary Kohler had been flying their Cessna Citation jet to Alaska each spring since June 1989 to bring trumpeter swan eggs to Wisconsin; and to Fort Smith, Alberta every year since 1990, to carry whooping crane eggs back to Baraboo. Archibald asked the Kohlers if they would consider flying their jet around the world—east to Russia, then across Siberia, and finally to Alaska and home. The route would take them to the Oka Nature Reserve, and to the nesting areas of the western and central flocks, to place Siberian crane eggs in the nests of wild Eurasian crane foster parents. From there, the team would fly to Katiya in northeastern Siberia, to observe the eastern flock in its nesting area. Covering the same route by commercial flights would be difficult, given the often-unreliable schedules and routes of the Russian airlines, especially in the more remote corners of Siberia.

The proposed flight appealed to the Kohlers' sense of adventure, and to their passion for the cranes, and they agreed to do it. Windway Chief Pilot Paul Jumes began planning for the flight with help from Universal Weather & Aviation, Inc.[15] Universal organized

---

[15] This Houston-based, worldwide company specializes in weather information, flight planning, flight support, and ground support services for business aircraft.

or obtained most of the logistical support needed for the trip, including travel visas and permits, official flight plans and flight permits, airport information, ground transportation, hotel reservations, security for the aircraft, and hundreds of other details that would help to ensure a safe, smooth, and successful flight across Russia.

EARLY ON THE MORNING OF TUESDAY, MAY 20, the sleek blue and white Windway Cessna Citation V was rolled out of its hangar at the Sheboygan County Airport (43° 46' N; 87° 51' W),[16] a few miles west of the city of Sheboygan, Wisconsin. Paul Jumes and Terry Kohler began their preflight inspections and checklists. Passengers Mary Kohler and Jenni Blackledge loaded luggage and then settled into the cabin. Jenni, one of Windway Aviation's aircraft mechanics, would accompany the airplane as far as Brussels, Belgium, the last stop before Moscow. She was along to handle any "squawks" or "gremlins" (malfunctions) that might occur during that part of the trip, and to ensure that the Citation was in top shape before it headed across Russia.

One critical piece of equipment for the trip was the Vollrath egg carrier. Designed and built to transport swan eggs from Alaska, it would serve as an onboard, climate-controlled portable incubator for Siberian crane eggs during the long flight to Russia. In the air, the egg carrier's temperature control system could draw power from the Citation's electrical system. On the ground, it could operate on 110-volt house current, or on a 12-volt motorcycle battery. The Kohlers purchased and brought along an assortment of power converters for use with standard 220v European house current.

After a brief delay, caused by a missing piece of hardware from the egg carrier, the Citation departed Sheboygan just after 9:00 a.m. for the 85-mile (136-km), 20-minute flight to Baraboo-Dells Airport, where it would pick up George and Kyoko Archibald and the eggs from ICF.

---

[16] For the Siberian flight, locations are given in standard latitude and longitude. 43° 46' N; 87° 51' W means Latitude, 43 degrees, 46 minutes north of the Equator, and Longitude, 87 degrees, 51 minutes west of Greenwich, England. Sixty minutes of latitude or longitude equals one degree. One degree of Latitude is about 70 miles (112 km). A degree of longitude varies in distance depending on the latitude, since the longitude lines are not parallel, but meet at the earth's poles. At Baraboo, Wisconsin (43° 30' N), a little less than halfway between the Equator and the North Pole, one degree of longitude is about 50 miles (80 km).

At Baraboo, the Kohlers were greeted by a large send-off party of ICF staff. The Archibalds' gear was loaded, along with six Siberian crane eggs in a field carrying case. At 10 a.m. on Tuesday, May 20, the Citation was positioned at the "starting line," on the runway at Baraboo-Dells Airport (43° 31' N, 89° 46' W). Terry advanced the throttles and released the parking brake, and the aircraft began to roll—the official start of the round-the world odyssey.

Forty-five minutes later, they landed at Chicago's busy Midway Airport (41° 47' N; 87° 45' W), where they were greeted by the cameras and microphones of a local television news crew. ICF staff had tipped off a Chicago TV station that the eggs and their chaperones would be passing through Midway. While George Archibald did an interview for the news crew, U.S. Fish & Wildlife Service (USFWS) inspectors put their stamp of approval on the CITES[17] paperwork that was required for moving Siberian crane eggs out of the country. After the eggs were cleared for export, they were placed in the onboard Vollrath incubator, the Citation's fuel tanks were topped off, and the wheels left the runway at 11:15 a.m., en route to Stephenville, Newfoundland.

NEWFOUNDLAND IS A RUGGED AND BEAUTIFUL PLACE—the 15th largest island in the world—on the northeastern edge of the North American continent. It is the more populous portion of the Canadian province of Newfoundland/Labrador. Thrust into the North Atlantic at about the same latitude as Duluth, Minnesota, Newfoundland endures long winters and heavy snows, punctuated by cool summers. Ruled by the sea that surrounds it, the island's climate is one of the most variable in North America. Newfoundlanders refer to their weather as "character-building" and "invigorating."

Commercial fishing is the island's main industry, while hunting and sport fishing are popular tourist attractions. With roughly the same land area (43,007 square miles—111,400 sq. km.) as Louisiana, the island of Newfoundland features nearly 6,000 miles (9,700 km) of rugged coast, and the vast majority of the population lives within a few miles of its coastline. Stephenville (48° 32' N; 58° 33' W), where the Citation would stop overnight, is on the island's southwest

---

[17] CITES (the Convention on International Trade in Endangered Species of Wild Fauna and Flora) was adopted in 1973 and became effective in 1975. It is an international agreement designed to ensure that international trade in wild animals or plants does not threaten the survival of their species. As of 2005, 169 countries have joined in the treaty.

side, on St. George's Bay, off the Gulf of St. Lawrence. The airport was built as a military base during World War Two.[18]

The Citation landed at Stephenville at 5:15 local time, three and a half hours and three time zones from Chicago. Newfoundland has its own time zone, with its clocks set one half-hour later than those in adjacent Labrador and Quebec.

The eggs presented a problem in Stephenville. They were not cleared for import into Canada, so regulations required that they would have to stay in the airplane during the team's overnight stop. That meant one of the travelers would also have to spend the night on the airplane, to monitor the temperature inside the egg carrier and to turn the eggs every few hours. But after a brief parlay with a Canadian wildlife inspector, George Archibald was allowed to take the eggs to his on-airport hotel room for the night. Similar negotiations, with similar results would be repeated at Reykjavik, Iceland and Brussels, Belgium.

The evening was spent in a brief bird watching tour and a dinner with George's brothers, Sandy and Peter Archibald. The next morning, the Citation headed north on a one-hour, 280-mile (450 km) hop to Goose Bay, Labrador (53° 19' N; 60° 25' W), the jumping-off point for the North Atlantic crossing. There, the crew would top off the fuel tanks and stretch their legs before the long over-water flight to Reykjavik, Iceland.

As the Cessna Citation approached Goose Bay on Wednesday morning, the weather was "marginal"—overcast with a 300-foot ceiling and visibility of just half a mile. In instrument conditions like these, the normal procedure is to use ILS (Instrument Landing System) for the approach and landing. ILS is a ground-based radio system that provides precise guidance to the pilot in both horizontal

---

[18] Newfoundland's provincial capital, St. Johns, on the southeast tip of the island, is the oldest European settlement in North America, founded in 1497 by John Cabot, an Italian sailing under the English flag. Cape Spear, just south of the capital, is the easternmost point of Canada. L'Anse aux Meadows, at the northern tip of Newfoundland, is the site of the first known European settlement in the New World, and the only authenticated Viking settlement in North America, outside of Greenland. Around 1000 A.D., Vikings from Scandinavia tried to establish permanent settlements along Newfoundland's coast. Some historians believe that this was the "Vinland" that was settled, according to legend, by the Viking explorer Leif Ericson. The Norse Sagas tell us that the natives (probably members of the extinct Beothuk tribe) put up such a fierce welcome that the Norsemen gave up their settlements and sailed back to Greenland. The remains of a Viking village were discovered at L'Anse aux Meadows in 1960.

and vertical planes, using focused radio signals. In the cockpit, the ILS receiver has two needles, a "localizer" needle for guidance in the horizontal plane and a "glide slope" needle for guidance in the vertical plane. When both needles are centered, the aircraft is properly positioned for the approach and landing. If the pilot keeps both needles centered, the aircraft will arrive at the landing end of the runway, lined up with the runway centerline.

But that morning at Goose Bay, the airport's ILS was inoperative. Fortunately, lots of military aircraft land at Goose Bay and the airport is equipped with a military Precision Approach Radar (PAR) system. PAR is a ground-based radar that locates an aircraft precisely in three dimensions. Using a radar screen in the approach control center, the air traffic controller gives verbal instructions

A typical ILS aircraft gauge: the horizontal needle is the glide slope; the vertical needle is the localizer. The needles here indicate that the aircraft is lined up on the runway (the localizer) but flying above the glide slope for this approach.   Author's photo.

to the pilot, to guide the aircraft to a safe landing even when visibility is zero. Terry had not flown a PAR to a landing since he left the Air Force in 1959. But the lady operating the radar gave him a quick refresher course over the radio, and with Paul Jumes sitting back, listening, and watching the show, Terry flew an uneventful PAR approach and landing into Goose Bay.

While the ground crew topped off the airplane's fuel tanks, Terry and Paul checked the weather to the east, over the North Atlantic. Though skies over Labrador and Greenland were "socked in" with a thick overcast, the Citation would soon be flying at 35,000 feet (10,700 m)—well above the clouds. Nearer to Iceland, the weather was better and the passengers and crew might actually get to see the North Atlantic Ocean, instead of just cloud tops, before they reached Reykjavik. They lifted off from Goose Bay at 11:05 local time, and pointed the Citation toward Iceland, three hours and 1,300 miles across the Atlantic. Terry noted in his log, "None of us had ever crossed either major ocean in a corporate jet before, so we all set personal records on the way to the ex-Danish island." On that long leg across the ice-strewn cold of the North Atlantic, the team experienced the only aircraft malfunction of the entire trip: The light bulb in the "Autopilot Engaged" indicator burned out.

From Labrador, across the North Atlantic, the Citation followed a historic route. In January 1942, barely a month after the United States entered World War Two, airline pilots flying Douglas DC-3 airliners pioneered a route from Presque Isle, Maine to Gander, Labrador, the first leg of a proposed aerial lifeline to Great Britain. Over the next few months, they pushed the route to Greenland and Iceland, and finally to Scotland.

These pathfinders flew overloaded airplanes across unmapped terrain and trackless ocean, through thick fog and blinding snowstorms, and in temperatures well below 0°F. (-18°C.), to establish routes, airbases, and navigation aids along the way. Pilots dubbed it "the Pine Tree Route," for the vast evergreen forests of the Maritime states and provinces. By the war's end, the airway navigation aids along the route were better than any over the United States. At the height of the war, planes of the US Army Air Transport Command, North Atlantic Division were flying back and forth, at the rate of one every four minutes. Terry Kohler served in the US Air Force as a bomber pilot in the late 1950s, and tracing the historic Pine Tree Route held a special meaning for him.

After a smooth landing at Reykjavik (64° 7' N; 21° 56' W), at 5:50 p.m. local time, the Kohlers and their passengers lugged baggage and incubator through the airport gate and across the street to their hotel. Earlier, reports from Universal Aviation stated that the incubator and eggs would be allowed no farther than the on-airport flight services lounge, and that "the egg specialist can overnight with the eggs on the lounge sofa." By the time the team landed, they had secured permission to carry the incubator to the hotel, 50 yards (45 m) from the flight service lounge.

As quickly as possible, they settled the incubator into George and Kyoko's room, and plugged it into the room's 220v current, using one of the power converters they had brought along. Then they jumped into their rental car and set off toward the coast for an evening of birding. To their delight, they discovered that they had arrived in Iceland right in the middle of the spring migration; the beaches and fields were awash with migratory birds. A long evening of birding ended with a late supper, and the Kohlers and Archibalds rose the next morning for a five o'clock breakfast and another trip to the southwest shore to see the island's native puffins and other cliff-dwelling birds. By the time they departed from Reykjavik at noon, en route to Brussels, Belgium, the birders had logged 36 out of about 95 bird species native to the island. Their birding success was well worth the delayed departure, and they could still make the 1,100-mile flight to Brussels and arrive in good time on this, the third day of the trip.

Still following the Pine Tree Route, they made landfall over Scotland, in honor of Mary Kohler's Stewart ancestors. They crossed the North Sea, with its oil rigs standing like strange water birds, and descended to Brussels, Belgium (50° 27' N; 4° 27' East), arriving at 6:15 p.m. local time, after 3 hours, 15 minutes in flight.

At Brussels, George was met by an official from the Belgian Ministry of Agriculture, who inspected the eggs and their paperwork. With that, the eggs were hustled off the airport and into the Archibald's hotel room. That evening, Jenni Blackledge replaced the burned-out light bulb on the autopilot indicator, and gave Terry a short course on operating the Magellan Satellite Communications (SATCOM) System—a satellite telephone that would be the team's principal voice link with the rest of the world during their trip across Russia. This would be Jenni's last night traveling with the team. After a few days' vacation, she flew home to Sheboygan.

To say that Cessna Citation parts and mechanics were scarce in

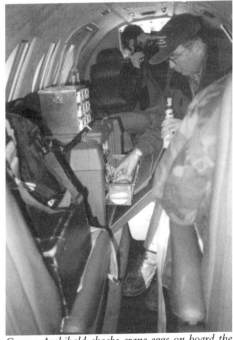

George Archibald checks crane eggs on board the Kohlers' Citation business jet.

Photo: Kyoko Archibald, ICF, www.savingcranes.org.

Russia in 1997, is certainly an understatement. If the Kohler's airplane needed service in Russia, they would have to import it, themselves. There was no way of knowing what sort of mechanics they would find along the way, and expensive aircraft parts shipped into the country by normal channels had a way of disappearing into the Black Market. To provide maintenance backup in case anything "decided to come unglued" from the airplane during its trip across Russia and Siberia, Kohlers contracted with an aircraft maintenance service company—one of several that will fly mechanics and parts anywhere in the world to repair a sick airplane. As it turned out, the airplane made the entire round-the-world trip with only one squawk—the burned-out autopilot indicator light. The egg carriers presented a different, more troublesome story.

On Friday, Day Four, the team awoke to problems with the incubator system. The battery charger was overheating the battery and causing the entire system to crash. The whole apparatus worked fine when it was drawing onboard power from the airplane. But when it was plugged into the standard 220-volt wall sockets in European and Russian hotel rooms, it crashed. The problem first appeared in Reykjavik and, as the trip progressed, it recurred with distressing frequency, putting the eggs and the mission at risk. It would take several days of fiddling, head scratching, and tweaking to find a solution.

At 10 a.m. local time, the Citation departed Brussels for Moscow, 1,250 miles away.

IN THE UNITED STATES, PRIVATE AVIATION is heavily regulated, but pilots flying in U.S. air space still have a relatively high degree of autonomy. By comparison, flying in Russian air space is tightly bound up in regulations, restrictions, and red tape. Five and one half years after the December 1991 collapse of the Soviet government, the Russian Federation was the principal power in the region. And though it had made huge strides in opening its borders to foreign travel and commerce, many vestiges remained of the old labyrinthine Soviet bureaucracy. Any civil aircraft flying in Russia was required to adhere strictly to assigned routes and timetables. Deviations from either one could result in heavy fines or worse.

For all domestic flights (flights beginning and ending within the Russian Federation) the Kohlers were required to carry a Russian navigator. Joining the crew in Moscow, Sergei Klementiev rode in the cabin seat nearest the cockpit, and handled all navigation duties and all communications with Russian air traffic controllers (ATC). He also filed all domestic flight plans with air traffic control and then read the navigation coordinates to the flight crew. Universal Aviation cautioned that, while the Russian navigator would provide metric conversions as required, the flight crew should be sure to "check the figures." Terry recalled that having the Russian navigator along was "comforting:"

> "Sergei was not a pilot at all. He was probably a part-timer with the KGB, but he worked for a civilian outfit that did the handling of foreign aircraft in Russia. It was clear that he knew what he was doing, that he'd been around airplanes a long time. His English was not perfect but it was certainly good enough to get the job done. And he handled all the radio communications because it was all in Russian in the back country. The air traffic controllers in Moscow and Vladivostok—our arrival and departure airports—spoke English; everywhere else they spoke Russian. Sergei didn't do any of the actual navigating, although he knew where we were going and why."

Terry Kohler, Sergei Klementiev, Paul Jumes Photo: Kyoko Archibald, ICF, *www.savingcranes.org.*

For flights within Russia, all routes and all departure times had to be submitted and approved in advance by the Russian Civil Aviation Authority (CAA). Optional schedules were not allowed; and an aircraft could depart no more than 30 minutes earlier or later than its approved schedule, unless it first applied for and received a new clearance from CAA. (While enforcement of this rule might be spotty in the hinterlands, Universal Aviation advised that it was strictly enforced in Moscow.) Each takeoff or landing required a clearance; each clearance required a permit, obtained in advance; and each permit required a fee. Last minute changes in schedules were unwelcome and, for three or more schedule changes, CAA could levy double fees.

Most airports also imposed stiff landing fees, sometimes as high as $1,000, payable only in cash. Airports also collected navigation fees. After you landed, each airport would levy a navigation fee for the route you had just flown and another fee for the route you were about to fly. And at the end of your trip, as you departed Russia, you might be required to pay navigation fees for your entire trip through the country, unless you could produce your receipts from the airports you had visited.

Passengers and flight crew could be required to show Russian visas at any airport, even for stops during which none of the travelers left the airport.

Vnukovo International Airport (55° 46' N; 37° 40' E) is on the southwest edge of Moscow in the "suburban zone" about 15 miles (24 km) from the heart of the city. It is one of the largest air transportation hubs in Russia, ranking fourth in the number of passengers. Built before World War II, it was a crucial link in the Russian's defense of Moscow against German forces in the winter of 1941-42. It was the Citation's first stop in Russia.

Everyone on board the Citation was excited as the airplane descended for landing at Vnukovo. They were flying a privately owned American aircraft into Moscow—a rare event—and they were carrying a precious cargo of six Siberian crane eggs. It was definitely a flight for the record books.

As instructed, Terry flew an ILS (Instrument Landing System) approach to Vnukovo Airport. The Citation's autopilot was coupled to its navigation systems, and for most ILS approaches, Terry would allow the autoflight system to fly the approach to the proper decision height (the point at which the pilot decides whether to continue the landing or go around for another attempt). At that point he would take over manual control and complete a normal landing. But the ILS signal at Vnukovo was "the most unstable ILS approach I had ever experienced," Terry wrote.[19] All ILS signals have some instability, and the Citation's ILS receiver and autopilot have a "smoothing" function that averages the signal's normal instability and keeps the airplane on a smooth track. The extreme instability of the Vnukovo ILS was too much for the autoflight system to handle and the Citation bobbed and weaved, trying to follow the signal. "I punched off the autopilot to prevent air sickness among the passengers, and flew a manual approach to the airport," he said. "That allowed a manual smoothing of the signals that just could not exist in the autopilot. That ILS was a doozy!"

On the ground, they were met by Vladimir Flint, the Russian expert on Siberian cranes. Flint was accompanied by his colleague Dr. Sasha Sorokin, an ornithologist at the All-Russian Institute for Nature Conservation and the leader of Russia's effort to sustain the Siberian crane. Flint and Sorokin were old friends to the Archibalds, and had met the Kohlers earlier in the U.S.

FERAS—East Russia Aircraft Services—provided an armed guard and perimeter security for the airplane at Vnukovo, as recommended by Universal Aviation. At all other stops, Universal lined up private security firms to guard the airplane. Universal also cautioned the flight crew and passengers not to go anywhere alone:

> "Crime against foreigners is a problem, especially in major cities. Pickpocketing, assaults, and robberies occur day and night, most frequently on city streets, in underground walkways and the subway, on intercity trains, in train stations and at airports, at markets, tourist attractions, and restaurants, and even in hotel rooms. Groups of children are known to assault and rob foreigners."[20]

The team's Russian "ground handler" hustled them off to the Metropol Hotel in downtown Moscow, where the crane eggs were safely tucked into the Archibalds' room for the night and the following day. That evening, the Russian scientists joined the Americans for

---

[19] Terry Kohler's unpublished notes on the trip
[20] Universal Aviation, memo to Paul Jumes, 05/14/97

dinner at the hotel, just off Red Square. "It was," Terry wrote, "a fine reunion, with appropriate amounts of wine and frigid vodka."

Over dinner that evening, Archibald and the Russians reviewed the plan for the team's trip to the crane nesting grounds. They would first visit the nesting grounds of the Iran flock of Siberian cranes east of the Ural Mountains on the Ob River, in western Siberia. Then they would head north, 1000 miles (1,600 km) down the Ob River to the nesting grounds of the India flock, near the Arctic Circle. At both sites, they would place Siberian crane eggs in the nests of Eurasian cranes that shared the same nesting areas. The Americans brought six eggs; the Russians would contribute another three from the captive breeding program at the Oka Nature Reserve.

The Sibe eggs would be placed in Eurasian crane nests because wild Siberian cranes are very finicky eaters. They eat shallow water plants almost exclusively. Their migrations to India or Iran follow Central Asian wetlands, where their favorite foods are found. Eurasian cranes' diet is more varied and more plentiful than that of the Sibes. They prefer to feed in agricultural fields, especially in the fall when recently harvested hay and grain fields offer a bounty of insects and gleanings. The Russian biologists hoped that the Eurasian crane parents would teach the Sibe chicks to savor a new, more abundant diet and to become less dependent on wetlands during the long migrations.

The oldest of the six eggs from ICF was due to hatch in just three days. Dr. Sorokin was afraid it might hatch before it could be placed in a wild Eurasian crane nest. He suggested that it be taken south, to be added to the captive "species bank" of Siberian cranes at the Oka Nature Reserve

Early on Saturday morning, the fifth day of their journey, the travelers and their Russian hosts journeyed southeast by bus. The trip took six and a half hours, through the gently rolling hills and deciduous forests of the Meschera lowlands, to the Oka Reserve, along the Oka River. As the bus left Moscow, the single Oka-bound egg rode in George Archibald's lap, in a portable incubator heated by a hot water bottle.

They arrived at the reserve's headquarters around 1:30 p.m. and placed the ICF egg in an electric incubator with a dozen other Siberian crane eggs. They spent the afternoon touring the complex and meeting the reserve's captive cranes. The visitors were treated to a boat trip on the Oka River and lots of warm Russian hospitality, before departing around 6 p.m. for the 6-hour bus ride back to Moscow. They took with them three eggs from Oka's incubators, making a total of eight Siberian crane eggs to be placed in wild Eurasian crane nests.

On Sunday, May 25th, a noon departure from Moscow allowed the Americans a chance to sleep in and recover somewhat from the previous day's adventures. At the airport, they met Sergei Klementiev, the Russian navigator who would accompany them all the way to Petropavlovsk on the far east coast of Siberia. With two Russians—Flint and Sorokin—added to the passenger list, and with the additional three eggs from Oka Reserve tucked

Tending young cranes at the Oka Nature Reserve.
Photo: Kyoko Archibald, ICF, www.savingcranes.org

away safely in the Vollrath egg carrier, the Citation left Moscow and headed east across the Ural Mountains, the dividing line between Europe and Asia. Their destination was Tyumen' (57° 10' N; 65° 28' E), the capital city of Tyumen' Oblast ("district") of western Siberia.

TYUMEN' IS AMONG THE OLDEST RUSSIAN settlements in all of Siberia. Founded in 1586 as a Cossack fortress on the Tura River just east of the Ural Mountains, it became an important stop on the Trans-Siberian Railroad. Today, it is an industrial city of half a million people, and a major transshipment point between the river and the railroad.

The vast wetlands complex northeast of the city is the summer nesting ground for the western flock of Siberian cranes, as well as Eurasian and Common cranes, and other waterfowl.

The two-and-a-half-hour flight from Moscow to Tyumen' covered a thousand miles[21] and two time zones. Landing at 4:30 p.m. local time, the Americans were startled to find a World War Two vintage C-47 "Gooney Bird" cargo plane standing "gate guard"— mounted on a pedestal at the airport.

During World War Two (known in Russia as "the Great Patriotic War"), the United States sent more than 700 C-47s, the military version of the famed Douglas DC-3 airliner, to the Soviet Union, along with parts and tooling for building the plane. Under license from Douglas Aircraft Company in California, the Soviets' Lisunov aircraft works built an estimated 2,000 of the rugged, versatile transports, designated Li-2. After the war, the Lisunov PS-84 (the civilian version of the Li-2) became the backbone of Soviet civil aviation, much as the DC-3 had done a decade earlier in the U.S. Curiously, the Soviets never acknowledged the American origins of the aircraft, nor paid any of the royalties due to Douglas Aircraft. Officially for the Russians, the Li-2 and PS-84 were "Soviet" designs.

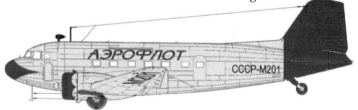

Lisunov Li-2 / PS-84, bare aluminum with scarlet nose, cowls, and tail.[22]

IN JULY 1996, THREE PAIRS OF SIBERIAN CRANES that wintered in Iran were discovered nesting in the wetlands near Tyumen'. Now, one year later, Archibald and Flint expected to plant four of their captive-raised eggs in Eurasian crane nests there. In Tyumen', as in Moscow, Terry wrote, "the entertainment department was of major proportions, and as we returned to our hotel that evening we

---

[21] The flight distances given are only approximate, straight-line distances. The actual lines of flight were often longer, since the airway routes dictated by Russia's CAR rarely follow straight lines east of the Ural Mountains.
[22] Image by Erik A. Pilawskii, from his <u>Soviet Air Force Fighter Colours 1941-45</u>, Classic Publications, Ltd., UK, 1994-2005. Reprinted with permission.

were beginning to think of our mission in different terms!"—as one of diplomacy and conviviality, in which the travelers were treated like old friends. Their hotel was the "Quality Hotel," built two years earlier. The Americans found it quite modern, but not very busy, certainly not as busy as Moscow's Metropol.

Monday May 26 was the seventh day of the journey. The plan for the morning was to drive north by van to Uvat, a small settlement about 25 miles (40 km) east of where one of the radio-banded Siberian cranes from Iran had been located by satellite tracking. From there, the team would fly by helicopter to the nesting grounds, planting the eggs in Eurasian crane nests and trying to spot any Siberian cranes. Everyone was up and ready for an early start but they were delayed by the infamous Russian bureaucracy. After visa stamps and more paperwork, plus official visits from local apparatchiks, they departed Tyumen' far behind schedule. At Uvat, the bureaucrats in charge of helicopter flight operations announced that it was too late in the day for the helicopter mission. It would have to wait until the following morning.

Mary and Terry Kohler, and Kyoko Archibald drove back to Tyumen' to deal with the next day's packing and flight planning. Flint, Sorokin, and George Archibald spent the night in Uvat. On Tuesday morning, the helicopter took them to the Eurasian cranes' breeding area. They conducted the water test on each of the four Siberian crane eggs, and all four were alive. One Siberian crane egg was placed in each of four Eurasian crane nests. With luck, the eggs would hatch, the chicks would fledge, and in the fall the young Sibes would migrate with their Eurasian crane foster parents. The Eurasian crane eggs that displaced from the nests were later taken back to the Oka Reserve, to hatch in captivity.

Back at the Tyumen' airport, the rest of the team was waiting tensely. They intended to take off from Tyumen' at noon—as late as possible under their approved flight plan. Any further delay would mean spending another night in Tyumen', and applying to the Civil Aviation Authority (CAR) for new permits and clearances for the rest of the trip. And the CAR was not fond of last-minute changes.

Kyoko and the Kohlers packed and went to the airport after lunch, then waited and waited, tending the remaining eggs and the ailing converter/charger combination on the egg carrier. Later, back at the Vollrath Company, they would learn that their difficulties were not with the incubator system itself. The power converters they carried along for the standard 220-volt European current were not up to the task. That caused the charger problem that overheated the incubator's battery and repeatedly caused the system to crash and the converters to fail. When all of the power converters purchased for the trip had died, Mary Kohler pulled out of her luggage a tiny converter that she had used for ten years to boil water for morning tea in hotel rooms around the world. It worked better than all the other "heavy duty" converters and saved the day.

One half hour before the final deadline for takeoff imposed by the flight plan and Russian regulations, the field team arrived at the airport, back from Uvat. As quickly as possible, everyone climbed into the airplane. Terry and Paul completed their detailed pre-flight checklists, and taxied the Citation out to the runway. The clock had run out on their flight plan, and they were gambling that taxiing was as good as taking off, from the bureaucrats' point of view. If so, they might still get off the ground before the Russians shut down their clearance and flight plan.

The gamble worked, and just after noon, the Kohlers' jet lifted off the runway at Tyumen', bound for Salekhard and the nesting grounds of the central flock of Siberian cranes, nearly 1,000 miles (1,600 km) to the north.

Chapter 8
The Land of Eternal Frost

PERMAFROST UNDERLIES 20% OF THE EARTH'S land surface
and 75% of Siberia. In Yakutia, the "eternal frost"—frozen rock,
gravel, sand, and bog—is nearly a mile thick. In northern Siberia,
summer thaws the ground to a depth of a few inches, creating a thin
bog with the consistency of jelly. Below that, the permafrost is imper-
vious to water, so most of the melt water either runs off into streams
and rivers, or collects in countless ponds and lakes. Rainfall and
snowfall are light in this region and these natural catch basins preserve the taiga forests and the moss and lichen carpet by holding
much of the ground water in place. Without its "bedrock" of eternal
frost, vast areas of Siberia would probably be desert.

Humans have so far had only limited impact over most of this
area, but near the cities and towns, mining, reindeer herding, small-
scale logging, and burning threaten the natural ecosystem. Clear-cut
or burned-over taiga forests are rarely replanted, but are instead
replaced by treeless tundra. In summer the moss/lichen carpet is fragile—a tracked vehicle, like a Snow Cat, leaves deep, barren ruts that
will persist for centuries.[23]

Virtually the only navigation aids available in sub-arctic Siberia

---

[23] In some parts of the Russian Arctic, permafrost has been melting to a greater-than-
usual depth in recent summers, creating an unexpected bounty for paleontologists.
Melting permafrost is unearthing buried, frozen, and well-preserved carcasses of mam-
moths, woolly rhinos, Siberian tigers, steppe lions, giant deer, ancient foxes, and ancestors of the Siberian horse.

According to newspaper reports published in late 2005, a joint Russian and
Japanese team of scientists hopes to recover intact DNA from these ancient carcasses,
clone it, and repopulate the sub-Arctic steppe with extinct species in a proposed
Siberian game park the size of Japan. Some species, like the Siberian tiger, disappeared

are non-directional beacons (NDBs) and the satellite-based Global Positioning System (GPS). Each stationary, ground-based NDB has its own frequency. In the aircraft, pilots tune to the frequency of an NDB, and an aircraft instrument called an Automatic Direction Finder (ADF) points directly toward the beacon. If an aircraft can pick up signals from two or more NDBs, and the pilot or navigator knows (from a map) where those beacons are located, he can use those signals to triangulate the aircraft's position on the map.

GPS uses signals from three or more satellites to triangulate the aircraft's position and altitude. There are more than two dozen GPS satellites in orbit, offering worldwide coverage that no ground-based system can provide. With positioning data from the satellites, an onboard GPS receiver can calculate lots of other information for the pilot, including the aircraft's heading and speed over the ground, and the distance and estimated flight time to his destination.

Using its own internal database and information entered by the pilot or navigator, a sophisticated GPS receiver, like the two in the Kohlers' Citation,[24] displays a "moving map" showing the airplane's position, speed, altitude, heading, and intended track, plus airports and airport information, navigation aids, special or restricted airspace, and terrain features such as roads, rivers, mountain peaks, cities, towers, smokestacks, and other visual landmarks. With good satellite signals, civilian GPS receivers provide real-time position data accurate to 30 to 50 feet (9 to 15 m) in all three dimensions, almost anywhere in the world. Military GPS may be more accurate; its exact capabilities are classified.

For the Kohlers' Citation, GPS provided very accurate navigation, as well as precise instrument approaches and landings. At Salekhard airport (66° 33' N; 66° 34' E), the air traffic controller instructed Kohler to cross the airfield's radio beacon at low altitude, and then loop around for a six-mile instrument approach using GPS. "It could just as well have been an ILS approach, in terms of its precision," Kohler wrote in his log. "Actually, it was more stable and accurate than most ILS approaches in the U.S. I would go anywhere with [GPS] after this trip."

---

only recently. Others, like the mammoth and woolly rhinoceros, have been extinct for 20,000 years. In 2002, the scientists focused their search for ancient animals at a site near Chokurdakh, where local people reported many animal remains buried in the permafrost.

[24] The Kohlers' Citation was equipped with an Allied Signal GNS-X LS Flight Management System and a Trimble TNL-2000 GPS.

As they taxied to the parking area behind a "Follow Me" truck, the crew was surprised to see another reminder of World War Two. Part of the airport was paved with pierced steel planking.[25] It was the first time Terry had seen this type of airport surface since his Air Force tour of duty on the island of Guam in 1957.

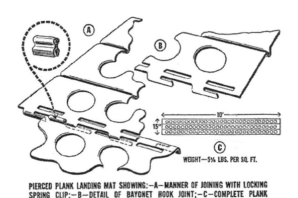

PIERCED PLANK LANDING MAT SHOWING:—A—MANNER OF JOINING WITH LOCKING SPRING CLIP;—B—DETAIL OF BAYONET HOOK JOINT;—C—COMPLETE PLANK

Pierced steel planking (PSP), from a US Army Field Manual.

They declined to follow the airport's "Follow Me" truck through a snow and mud bank, and parked the Citation next to a line of "truly forlorn" airplanes on the "far out end of nowhere." Throughout Russia, Terry was struck by the apparently "terrible quality of maintenance on aircraft." By 1997, the Russian economy had been in decline for many years. Still, Terry said, "it was amazing to see so many aircraft with worn tires, with engines removed, with tail sections missing—lots of planes that were clearly inoperable, just sitting on the ramp."

Leaving the airport for their hotel, they passed another C-47 gate

[25] Pierced steel planking (PSP), also known as "Marston Mat," was developed during World War II as a way of quickly laying down a smooth, stable surface for a runway, taxiway, or parking area on soft or unstable ground. When laid on a stabilized subsurface, PSP could provide a semi permanent runway. It was used in every theater of operations in World War II and again in the Korean War, and remains in use at remote airports in the Pacific islands, Asia, and parts of Europe. A PSP surface was constructed of interlocking steel planks, each 15 inches by 10 feet. A typical 150-foot by 5,000 foot runway required 60,000 steel planks, weighing nearly 2,000 tons, and requiring 35,000 cubic feet of cargo space to deliver. A PSP runway that size could be assembled in 175 hours by 100 unskilled men.

guard. "I saluted this Grand Dame, as well," Terry wrote. Salekhard is located directly on the Arctic Circle—a fact that is commemorated by a huge 30-35 meter aluminum archway at the airport near the on-field hotel. As was becoming standard procedure, they trooped off to the hotel and then to another party—this one on a boat on the Ob River that took them down to the sea, to a seaside village "at the end of everywhere," and back again. Terry described the excursion as fascinating but primitive. "And as usual," he wrote, "the vodka and wine and frozen fish and sausage and smoked fish and cheese and fried fish and hospitality were all part of the scene." It was well after midnight when they returned to the hotel, where George had stayed to tend the eggs and the incubator, which was powered now by a truck battery.

WEDNESDAY, MAY 28, DAY 10: A MIL MI-8 HELICOPTER took the team from Salekhard, south for about an hour to the "Sauey Hotel"—a crane research field camp named for ICF co-founder Ron Sauey. Russian ornithologist Yuri Markin and his field crew had been out in the taiga of the Kunovat lowlands for a couple of weeks, searching for Siberian cranes and for enough nesting Eurasian cranes to accommodate the last five captive-raised Siberian crane eggs.

On that trip Mary Kohler rode in the flight engineer's seat, between the Russian pilots. She noticed that, compared to the Kohlers' Citation, the helicopter had a rather old-fashioned instrument panel, but she also discovered a tiny Garmin handheld GPS

"Craniacs" disembark from Mi-8 Helicopter in the taiga
Photo: Kyoko Archibald, ICF, www.savingcranes.org

taped under the instrument panel, with an antenna leading up the windshield center post to a spot high on the windshield—a kind of seat-of-the-pants upgrade to the helicopter's Soviet-era technology.

At the Sauey Hotel, the helicopter picked up Markin, several of his field crew, and a Russian television crew that had been working with them. The helicopter handled the crowd of 20 or so people without a fuss; The Mi-8 is a large machine built to carry up to 36 combat soldiers, and it is widely used in commercial service throughout Eastern Europe and Asia.

With Markin giving directions to the pilots, the helicopter took off again for the nesting areas. As it approached the first nest, the helicopter dropped down over the marsh to hover just above the water, next to the Eurasian crane's nest platform, a typically huge mound of sticks, reeds, and grasses. As the whine of the helicopter's two turbine engines and the wash from its huge five-blade main rotor flushed the startled crane from her nest, Markin and Sasha Sorokin leapt out the door of the helicopter, followed quickly by the television crew, all splashing into the water, a meter below. Terry opened the egg box on his lap; Mary removed one of the four Siberian crane eggs and handed it to George, who was lying on his stomach next to the open door. George passed the egg down to one of the Russians and two Eurasian crane eggs were handed back up to George, to be snuggled into the egg box. Then Markin, Sorokin, and finally the TV crew clambered back onto the helicopter, which moved off to the next nest. All the while, Kyoko was moving in and out of the action, and firing away with her camera. This seemingly chaotic performance was repeated two more times, at two more nests.

With two eggs left to place, a fruitless half-hour search turned up no more nests. As large as they are—up to four feet across—Eurasian crane nests are almost impossible to spot from the air, because they are so well camouflaged. Markin and Sorokin assured the group that they would have an easier time finding the nests from the ground, on foot or by boat in the swamps, because the Eurasian cranes stay on their nests much longer when approached quietly at ground level. The helicopter dropped its passengers at the Sauey Hotel, then went to look for a sandbar where it could safely land and shut down for a couple of hours. The two remaining Sibe eggs were tucked away in a hastily improvised field incubator for their overnight stay at the camp. These two eggs were successfully placed in Eurasian crane nests a few days later.

Sauey Hotel is a primitive tundra camp and crane rearing station not far from the Arctic Circle, isolated in the trackless marshes of the Kunovat lowlands. The visitors were given a walking tour of the camp, including the pens for rearing crane chicks near the wild nesting sites and in isolation from human contact. They saw an untamed taiga landscape of marsh and small willowy brush, punctuated by groups of small trees huddled tightly where the ground rose above the permafrost. While the visitors carefully stuck to the pathways, the TV crew plunged headlong through the brush and marsh, to get their best shots.

Inevitably, the visit ended with a party. Even in this isolated tundra camp the hosts laid out a bounty of all the customary fishes, cheeses, and sausages, washed down with vodka and wine in an endless round of toasts.

The helicopter returned and ferried them to the nearby camp of a family of reindeer herders. The family's two teepees housed two kids, two dogs, parents, and grandparents. There was also a covered "smoke room" that the reindeer could enter to get away from the region's clouds of mosquitoes and flies. Most of the year, this family lived out on the vast taiga/tundra, in absolute isolation from anywhere and anyone.

The return to Salekhard by helicopter seemed anti-climactic after a long and busy day in the field. Most of the group begged off of the

Reindeer herders' camp, Northeastern Siberia.
Photo: Kyoko Archibald, ICF, www.savingcranes.org

nightly party. George had missed the previous night's revels, so they sent him alone to the Russians for the standard treatment of fish, cheese, sausage, wine, and vodka. A few members of the group visited the local museum, which offered exhibits on natural history and local cultures. During World War Two, slave laborers, including prisoners of war, toiled to build a railroad through Salekhard—a line that was never completed. At the museum, Mary and Terry were struck by the "terrible isolation of the slave labor camps." Returning early to their hotel, Mary, Terry, and Kyoko dropped into their beds for a long night's sleep.

NEXT MORNING, THE GROUP AWOKE TO RAIN and thick fog. After breakfast, Dr. Flint spoke with Russian officials and learned that the airport was closed to all traffic because of the weather. The visibility appeared to be at least half a mile and the ceiling (the base of the clouds) was at least 200 to 300 feet. In the U.S. such conditions are scarcely a problem for an instrument take-off, although they would be marginal for the non-precision approach one would have to make to return to the same airport, in case of a mechanical or other problem. An hour later, either the weather or the bureaucracy shifted, and the airport was declared open for the Citation. After quick farewells to Sasha Sorokin, who was bound for his home in Moscow, the group hustled their luggage and egg crate into waiting vans for the trip to the airport and the inevitable hurry-up-and-wait—the seemingly endless bureaucratic process required to depart a Russian airport by airplane. Terry noted in his log:

> "We are incredibly spoiled in the United States by the comparative lack of such processes, and yet we wail endlessly about [U.S. Federal Aviation Regulations]—which may be why it really isn't too bad to live in our free society."

Loaded at last, the Citation taxied back out across the steel mat to the runway and took off into the "clag" (fog & drizzle).[26] Their immediate destination was Noril'sk, 600 miles (1,000 km) to the east,

---

[26] Among bush pilots, "clag" refers to calm, typically coastal weather of low clouds, fog, and drizzle, which is unflyable under Visual Flight Rules (VFR). The British word for this kind of weather is "duff."

a fuel stop before the longer leg to Chokurdakh, in northeastern Siberia. The clouds thinned out and, after an hour and a half of flying over a seemingly endless and nearly featureless landscape of snow and ice, the Citation landed at Noril'sk (69° 21' N; 88° 01' E), in north central Siberia.[27]

The team's itinerary estimated one hour for this fuel stop, but here the bureaucracy was in full swing. The pilots and passengers trooped into the administration building to stretch their legs and use the restrooms, then returned to the airplane, and waited . . . and waited . . . and waited some more. Just fifty yards from where they were parked, a front-end loader was working on a 50-foot snow bank; that provided some entertainment. The fuel truck showed up eventually, offering some hope of progress. And then they waited . . . and waited . . . and waited some more.

According to the Russians, Noril'sk is a "very busy" airport, despite its location in the far north of Siberia. The Kohlers and their passengers surmised that "very busy" was another bureaucratic code word used to justify endless delays. At Chicago's O'Hare Airport, one can see four aircraft movements (a takeoff or a landing) every two to four minutes. At the Experimental Aircraft Association's annual "AirVenture Oshkosh"—the largest aviation gathering in the world—controllers often handle three or four aircraft movements every 15 seconds. In two hours of waiting on the ramp at Noril'sk, the Americans saw just three or four aircraft movements on this very busy and very northern airport.

After more than two and a half hours on the ground, the Citation's pilots were given the documents accepting their flight plan and clearing them for departure. Everyone rushed into the airplane and they taxied out to the runway just in time to—not quite—make their appointed takeoff time. The Citation lifted into an almost clear blue sky and turned northeast from Noril'sk, on a heading that would take it 1,200 miles (1,900 km) to Chokurdakh, (70° 22' N, 148° 11' E), the closest airfield to the breeding grounds of the eastern flock of Siberian cranes.

About 15 minutes out of Noril'sk, the Citation crossed Longitude 91° 46' East—halfway around the world from Baraboo, Wisconsin (89°46'W).

---

[27] Noril'sk, with a population of around 130,000, is Siberia's northernmost city and the world's second largest city (after Murmansk) above the Arctic Circle.

The weather at Chokurdakh was, in aviation parlance, "severe clear" and the sun was still high at 8:30 in the evening, local time. Terry could have landed the Citation entirely by visual references; instead the control tower cleared the airplane for a complicated NDB instrument approach and landing. Terry flew the approach using the GPS and, although it meant a lot more work than a visual landing, it worked out fine, until the Citation turned to Final Approach, the last leg of the landing pattern, in which the aircraft lines up with the runway centerline and makes its final descent. As Terry lowered the airplane's nose and throttled back on Final Approach, Sergei, the Russian navigator relayed the message from the tower, "Cleared to land." No sooner had those words left Sergei's mouth, than a jeep-like vehicle surged onto the runway halfway down its length and its occupants fired a flare toward the Citation. At that instant, Terry's US Air Force training kicked into gear, especially the part that said, "a flare on the runway during approach means 'Abort the landing; go around—NOW!'" As he pushed the throttles full forward and pulled back on the control yoke, Terry quickly said to Sergei, "That means 'go around,'" and Sergei shouted back, "No, no, cleared to land! They're just welcoming us!" The Kohlers' Citation was the first American private aircraft ever to land at Chokurdakh. And it was the first American aircraft of any kind to land there since World War Two.

Terry and copilot Paul Jumes never did understand any of the Russian language they heard continuously on the aircraft's communication radios—except the occasional "nyet." At Chokurdakh, as elsewhere in Siberia, there was much radio chatter from a very few aircraft, but Terry and Paul couldn't sort any of it into coherent messages or sources. On Final Approach at Chokurdakh, there were no other aircraft in the air or the landing pattern but the airport was tower-controlled, and all of Terry's training said that a flare on the runway meant trouble.

With some trepidation, Terry again throttled back, lowered the Citation's nose again, and completed a routine landing, touching down with plenty of runway to spare, despite the near-abort. The touchdown brought a second surprise. Terry wrote in his log:

> "And the quality of the [runway] surface came to smite us mightily. In ALL of our previous flying experience, NO paved surface in memory was so

rough, undulating, arched, and hollowed as our landing end of choice. Sergei then told me that this was the GOOD end! We finally understood with a certainty why all the Russian aircraft we saw in-country had very large balloon tires and very large trailing-link landing gear suspension."

Like the runway, the ever-present Russian bureaucracy at Chokurdakh was worse than most, due to the city's isolation and the recent appointment of a new regional military administrator. After appeasing the bureaucracy and attending the inevitable hospitality party, the group fell into their beds.

FRIDAY, MAY 30, DAY 11: BREAKFAST AT CHOKURDAKH was excellent—the now-familiar fish and other fare, along with a delicious and fattening local fried bread. After breakfast, the group toured the local history museum. Terry noted that it was almost as interesting as the museum at Salekhard, but conspicuously absent was any mention of the history of the local airfield. During World War Two, the field was built as a refueling stop for American Bell P-39 Airacobra fighters supplied to Russia under the Lend-Lease Program. Again, it seemed, the Russians had chosen not to recognize an American contribution to Soviet aviation or to the Soviet victory in the Great Patriotic War. Today, Chokurdakh is an air defense base for the Russian Federation Air Force.

The nesting grounds of the eastern flock of Siberian cranes,

Bell P-39 Airacobra fighter in WWII Soviet markings. The U.S. sent 4,600 P-39s to Russia under the "Lend-Lease program. Unpopular with American pilots because of its poor performance at high altitudes, the P-39 was well liked by Russian pilots, who used it to deadly effect in low-level air combat and ground support roles.

Photo: U.S. Army Air Force, author's collection.

which numbers between 2,500 and 3,000 birds, stretch along the far northern edge of the Siberian Republic of Sakha, formerly Yakutia, along the shore of the East Siberian Sea. Most of the known nesting sites are in a 600-mile (1,000-km) wide swath running west to east from the Yana River to the Kolyma River. Chokurdakh, on the Indigirka River, is in the center of the nesting range. Located 300 miles (500 km) north of the Arctic Circle, this is a sparsely-populated region of taiga forest. Permafrost limits the growth of trees here. On the far northern taiga, small stands of trees—mostly larch—are widely spaced; most of the ground is carpeted with mosses and lichens, when it is not covered with snow during the long arctic winter. Some of the world's coldest temperatures have been recorded here, as low as −94° F (-70° C).

The region is home to about 200 species of birds. Owls, hawks, hazel grouse, woodpeckers, jays, nutcrackers, and capercaillies are among the most common. Native mammals include elk, brown bears, wolverines, lynx, ermines, sables, weasels, arctic hares, red squirrels, and Siberian chipmunks. Fifteen species of fish inhabit the region's rivers, lakes, and coastal waters. All of these animals, including the critically endangered Siberian cranes that summer here, are well adapted to this extreme permafrost environment.

THE TRAVELERS' PLAN FOR THE DAY—Day 11 of their odyssey, was to fly north by helicopter to a newly-created nature reserve, owned and operated by the native Yakut people, and located within the nesting grounds of the eastern flock of Siberian cranes. The journey's serious work—delivering Siberian crane eggs to Eurasian crane nests in western Siberia—was done. This stop on their journey offered the travelers a chance to visit the nesting grounds of the larger eastern flock of Sibes, and to see first-hand the wild, trackless land that had hidden these cranes so long from outsiders.

Their host was Dr. Nikolo Germoganov, along with several other Russian ornithologists from Yakutia. Before boarding the Russian Mi-8 helicopter, the team was subjected to a thorough and lengthy check of their passports and visas, and electronic surveillance of their bodies and possessions. The Russian powers-that-be require these things to be done, and so they are done in meticulous detail, even at 71° North latitude, for a local flight in a chartered aircraft that is chartered by the passengers, who are no doubt accompanied by a stringer for the KGB or its local affiliate. In such situations,

Terry noted, a sense of humor is invaluable.

During the helicopter ride, George Archibald recalled, "Terry shouted 'SIBES!' He had seen a pair through the tiny round window." At the nesting grounds, there were birds aplenty, but no other sightings of Siberian cranes. There were, however, many pairs of sandhill cranes to be seen. These birds migrate each year from Texas, to Alaska, and across the Bering Straits to Yakutia—more than 4,500 miles (7,200 km).

At the nesting grounds, the travelers found themselves at a research camp in a snowy taiga wasteland where temperatures hovered just below freezing. Terry noted in his log that the birds really seemed to think that spring had come to the North. The humans, on the other hand, considered that a snowball fight might be the best diversion this "spring" had to offer.

"After the helicopter landed," said George Archibald,

> "we walked to the top of a nearby hill and surveyed the vast expanse of surrounding frozen and snow-covered landscapes. Pairs of Sandhills were calling from several distant locations but there were no signs of Siberian cranes. But then, how can one spot a snow-white crane against snow!"

While the rest of the travelers returned to the camp, George Archibald and Mary Kohler hiked to the end of that long narrow hill, where they found a Peregrine falcon and several sandhill cranes.

They returned to Chokurdakh in early evening, to a very pleasant goodbye celebration dinner. This was farewell to Dr. Flint. He would remain at Chokurdakh for a few days before returning to the Oka Reserve with his clutch of Eurasian crane eggs taken from the nests in the Ob River Basin. "After another lavish dinner of fresh fish and bread, we all fell into deep sleep," said George. "Time changes and our packed schedule had caught up with us."

SATURDAY MORNING, MAY 31—DAY 12—was the start of the long trip home. This day's planned flight would take the Americans from Chokurdakh, south to Petropavlovsk, then east to Cold Bay, Alaska, and finally to Anchorage. Sunday, they would be back at Baraboo, completing their circumnavigation.

Contrasting with the meticulous inspection of documents, bodies, and baggage before the previous day's helicopter flight, the Russian bureaucracy was conspicuously low-key on Saturday morning. With freshly-filled fuel tanks, the Kohlers' Citation taxied out at nine o'clock. The takeoff from Chokurdakh was even more of a roller coaster ride than the landing, though Sergei was still adamant that the other end of the runway was worse.

Flying at 31,000 feet (9,400 m), through mostly clear skies, the pilots and passengers could see the vast Siberian interior spread out beneath them. Their course took them 1,200 miles (1,900 km) almost due south to Petropavlovsk, the regional capital and the famous Russian submarine and naval base and international airport of entry on the Kamchatka Peninsula. Below them, the flat, snow-covered plains began to darken in spots, then in streaks, revealing the brown landscape of a Siberian spring. The taiga plains gave way to ridges, brown grasslands to dark conifers. Ridges in turn gave way to mountains as the Citation flew southward.

Near 55° N latitude, a left turn took them out over the sea and the rugged 13,000-foot (4,000-m) peaks of the Kamchatka Peninsula. Approaching Petropavlovsk, they could see Russian Navy ships and submarines—dark, menacing "boats of war"—arrayed in the harbor. As they turned northwest for a visual final approach, the aircraft was bathed in brilliant glare from the snow-capped volcanoes that form a stunning backdrop to this storied outpost of Russian Imperial might.

The airport at Petropavlovsk (52° 53' N; 158° 42' E) was larger than anything the team had seen anywhere in the rest of Siberia. There were dozens of military aircraft of all types parked around the field, and lots of airliners landing and departing. For the first time since leaving Moscow, they saw U.S.-registered business jets and airliners. (At the time, Air Alaska offered scheduled flights for passengers and freight between Petropavlovsk and Anchorage; that service has been discontinued.)

On the ground at Petropavlovsk, Sergei, the Russian navigator, got the Americans connected with their ground handlers, said goodbye and dashed off to catch the next plane leaving for Moscow. He had been told earlier that he would have to wait nearly three weeks for a passenger seat to take him home. Luckily, he managed to find a ride with a pilot friend who needed a navigator-to-go. During the trip across Russia, Sergei had helped the team in all kinds of ways. He and the Americans parted as newfound friends.

Checking out of Russia gave the bureaucracy one last opportuni-

The Kohlers' Russian navigator, Sergei Klementiev (2nd from left) parlays with Russian officials, while Windway Chief Pilot Paul Jumes (l.) looks on.

Photo: Kyoko Archibald, ICF, www.savingcranes.org

ty to do its stuff, and the apparatchiks at Petropavlovsk were at the top of their game. The travelers hand carried all their luggage from the plane to a waiting bus. The bus drove to a building located on the flight line. They lugged the luggage 50 meters from the bus, into the customs department—each bag with its owner, each bag opened and inspected by at least one customs official, each bag through an X-ray machine, and each person through a metal detector. Each American filled out a customs declaration and gave declaration and passport to a customs official. Everyone carried their bags and passports to the immigration department, where their Russian visas were examined, then taken. Finally, luggage in hand, the Americans headed out the other end of the building to the waiting bus, which had moved a few yards to meet them. The entire process took more than two hours, and the team wasn't carrying any eggs that would have involved even more complicated inspections and permits. Depending on how one counted the crew around the aircraft (including an assigned security guard), there were five, six, or seven people doing the job of processing the Americans to leave the country—a job that American officialdom would have done with two people, in one quarter of the time. All in all, it was a splendid grand finale performance by Russia's legendary corps of paper shufflers, document checkers, and inefficiency experts.

THE PILOTS AND PASSENGERS FINALLY got all their baggage gear back in the airplane, climbed in behind it, and closed the door. Suddenly it was all their own little world again, with a long taxi, a smooth takeoff, and the familiar sound of air traffic controllers barking at the pilots in English, just as they had barked in Russian as the plane flew into Petropavlovsk. The Citation threaded its way up between the snowy peaks to cruise altitude. The Russian weather service gave them a favorable forecast for their next destination, a fuel stop at Cold Bay, 1,400 miles (2,250 km) to the east, near the western tip of Alaska's Aleutian Peninsula.

At "Checkpoint Charley" Outbound, still in sight of the Kamchatka coastline, the pilots said goodbye to Russian air traffic control and hello to the controllers at Honolulu Center, using the Citation's single-sideband HF radio. American-ese boomed back at them reassuringly over 2,000 miles (3,200 km) of ocean. An hour later, as they neared Alaska's Pribilof Islands (57° 24 N; 170° 15' W), northwest of Cold Bay, Honolulu handed them off to Anchorage Center in Anchorage, Alaska.

They asked Anchorage for an update on the weather there and at Cold Bay, and a very cold bucket of water hit them in the face. The latest news looked nothing at all like the earlier weather report they had received. Cold Bay, Anchorage told them, was now reporting visibility of half a mile and with the ceiling obscured—marginal conditions even for an instrument approach.

They had planned a fuel stop at Cold Bay (55° 12' N; 162° 43' W) because the Citation didn't have the range to make it all the way to Anchorage non-stop from Petropavlovsk. U.S. Customs officials had given them special permission to refuel in Cold Bay before clearing through Customs in Anchorage.

But if they attempted an instrument landing approach at Cold Bay, and missed it, forcing them to go around, they would have just two choices left: shoot a second approach and land successfully; or ditch the Citation in the cold Bering Sea. Their fuel reserves would not permit a third landing attempt.

They immediately ruled out any shot at Cold Bay and alerted Anchorage to their fuel situation.

The nearby Pribilof Islands offered one option. There was fuel at the airport there, just minutes away, and Terry had landed there once before, on a sightseeing visit during one of the trumpeter swan egg collecting missions to Alaska. From the Islands, Anchorage was well within range.

But the runways and taxiways at the Pribilof Islands airport are made of compacted black volcanic ash. And the ash that a moving airplane kicks up from the runway does terrible things to composite (foam and fiberglass) flaps and ailerons, like those on the Citation.[28] Pribilof, the pilots decided, would be their emergency backup. They continued to look for a better option. So did Anchorage Center.

Several years of flying to Alaska for Trumpeter swan eggs had left Terry with a deep respect and appreciation for the personnel at Anchorage Air Traffic Control. Now those same folks went into high gear at midnight local time, to identify and examine as many alternatives as they could. Two possibilities stood out: the Air Force's fighter base at King Salmon, Alaska (58° 40' N; 156° 38' W), at the foot of the Aleutian Peninsula, and Bethel, Alaska (60° 46' N; 161°50' W), well to the north and a little west of King Salmon, on the Kuskokwim River in the Alaskan interior. The pilots changed course to a heading that split the difference between the two possible destinations.

Whichever airport they chose, someone would have to get out of bed to refuel the airplane, so they could proceed to Anchorage to clear Customs, as required. Anchorage Center made a phone call to Bethel and found a refueler willing and able to meet the Citation at the airport. The Citation turned toward Bethel. They landed in the wee hours of the *morning* of May 31, after departing Petropavlovsk early on the *afternoon* of May 31st. Somewhere west of the Pribilof Islands, they had crossed the International Date Line.[29] The Citation was quickly refueled and took off in the sub-Arctic twilight. At Anchorage (61° 10' N; 149° 59' W), a very easy-going group of American officials cleared them quickly through Customs—the passengers and crew didn't even have to leave the airplane. At 3 a.m. Anchorage Time, they cut the engines and climbed down for a few short hours of sleep before the last two legs home. In his log, Terry wrote:

---

[28] When he landed the Citation at Pribilof on that earlier trip, Terry recalled, "I made the mistake of hitting the [thrust] reversers [to brake the airplane], and the billowing clouds of black dust completely enveloped the plane instantly, causing me to pull the throttles out of reverse just as fast. But the whole underbody of the aircraft carried all that black ash back to Wisconsin, where I had to endure the wrath of my whole engineering team and the laughing of my pilot staff! It's always something when you fly."

[29] The International Date Line runs mostly through open Pacific Ocean. It lies on 180° Longitude, except at the northern end, where it zigs west to capture the Aleutian Islands in the Hawaii-Aluetian Time Zone, and then zags east to keep the eastern tip of Siberia on Siberian time. South of the Equator, it makes another side trip east of Australia to pull several British-owned islands into the New Zealand time system.

> "It was a warm and pleasant feeling to return, par-
> ticularly to Alaska where the frontier spirit of the
> United States of America still is spread broadly
> across the land: Help your neighbor; you'll need it
> soon enough yourself."

IN ANCHORAGE, IN MAY, THE SUN SETS LATE AND RISES
EARLY. The travelers awoke to their first American breakfast in
nearly two weeks, and all agreed that it is amazing how much one
can miss such ordinary things far away from home.

With full fuel, they departed Anchorage at midmorning, bound
for Kalispell, Montana, the airport of the great Glacier National
Park. It was a beautiful day and the mountains of the Alaska
Panhandle and British Columbia offered a breathtaking panorama.
The travelers were now on a familiar route and over friendly territory (George Archibald's native Canada). The tensions and concerns of
traveling into unknown regions melted away. They landed at
Kalispell (48° 10' N; 114° 18' W), three and a half hours out of
Anchorage, with stunning views of Glacier Park during their
approach. While the plane was refueled, they made a passel of phone
calls home to assure everyone that they were fine and would arrive
soon. They loaded box lunches onboard and took off for the final leg
of the circumnavigation, from Kalispell to Baraboo. Below them, the
western mountains gave way to the Great Plains, then to the farms
and woods of Minnesota and Wisconsin. The weather was clear,
except for a few big "Cumulo-Bumpus" clouds scattered around the
horizon. Nearer to Baraboo, the familiar haze of Wisconsin summer
reappeared. It was a great day for flying and the weather gave them
a fine welcome home. The Archibalds' reception committee at
Baraboo was smaller than the sendoff party had been, and it was less
boisterous and less fattening than Russian and Siberian hospitality,
but the world travelers pronounced it to be a more than adequate
homecoming celebration.

After a scant hour at Baraboo, Mary, Terry, and Paul flew the last
85 miles to Sheboygan.

"We touched down," Terry wrote in his log,

> "with the absolutely amazed realization that we had
> no aircraft squawks to log, and only the single
> burned out light bulb of the autopilot to even talk

Whoopers take a break during an ultralight-led migration.

Whoopers at Chassahowitzka National Wildlife Reserve, the end point for the Wisconsin-to-Florida ultralight-led migrations.

The last Siberian crane in India, Keoladeo National Park, 2001-02.

Reindeer herders' camp, Yakutia, Northeastern Siberia.

Trumpeter swans at Monticello, MN.   Photo: Harry B. Burns

Whooping Crane.   Photo, © *www.operationmigration.org*

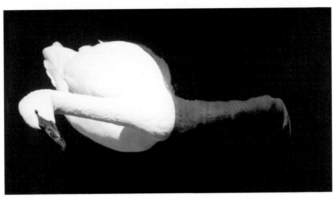

Left and center: Trumpeter Swans.
Right: Siberian Crane, Ob River, Siberia.

Whooping Cranes.

Young Whoopers explpore the world.

Photo, © International Crane Foundation, Baraboo, WI

Kent Clegg leads a flock of sandhill cranes on migration over Utah.

Photo: © Kent & Peter Clegg

Dr. Richard Urbanek, USFWS, collects sandhill crane eggs; Terry Kohler pilots his Bell 406 helicopter. Right, Adult sandhill crane.

Photos, © International Crane Foundation, Baraboo Wisconsin

about. The airplane behaved flawlessly, as well as honestly, and we could not have been happier with its performance. It was never lacking. Nor was our aircraft umbilical incubator system ever a problem. The only oversight we had was the 220-volt input to our inadequate converters, a problem easily solved by a quality check for the next mission . . . and we are ready."

At the end, they had logged 39.2 hours of flight time and traveled nearly 13,000 miles (20,900 km).[30]

A few months earlier, George Archibald had written to Terry Kohler, "I believe this will be the first time a private plane has flown around the world across the Russian land mass." He was almost right. In July 1992, a group of 14 private airplanes, carrying 37 pilots and passengers, crossed the Russian land mass on a flight around the world. Their "World Flight Over Russia Rally" was billed as a goodwill tour and a grand adventure, and it was both. That flight was officially recognized as the first round-the-world flight by aircraft traversing Europe, North America, and Russia.[31]

The Kohlers' Citation was the first private jet ever to circle the globe across Russia. But for the Kohlers and Archibalds, the flight

---

[30] At the equator, the earth's circumference is 24,859 miles (40,008 km). But at 45° Latitude (Baraboo), it is only 17,700 miles (28,500 km), and at 70° Latitude (Yakutia) it is just 8,500 miles (13,600 km) around the world. Baraboo, at 43° N, was the southernmost point on the Kohlers' route. Chokurdakh in Yakutia, at 70° 22' N was the northernmost point on their route.

[31] Ten of the World Flight aircraft started and finished in Santa Monica, CA; four others started and ended near London, England. The French organizers, Marcel Large and Eric Vercesi, encountered logistical and bureaucratic obstacles far worse than those faced by the Kohlers and their companions. In 1992, five years prior to the Kohlers' flight, the ex-Soviet government was in such a state of collapse that the U.S. Embassy in Moscow couldn't tell the World Flight planners who was in charge of what. World Flight had to provide its own fuel, carried in a chartered Aeroflot IL-76 freighter, and pumped by hand from 50-gallon drums into the planes. A Beech King Air support plane carried a mechanic and spare parts. Planning for the 20-day flight took 18 months, and the last clearances from the Russians weren't granted until ten days after the group returned to Santa Monica. Large and Vercesi wanted to make the World Flight an annual event, but the cost, complexity, and risks—there were some narrow escapes from tragedy during the 1992 flight— proved too daunting. An American group tried to organize a similar flight in 1996 and again in 1997. Both times, the Russians denied permission, "because of the danger involved." Brad Butler's book, A World Flight Over Russia, documents the 1992 flight.

wasn't about setting aviation records. There were plenty of "firsts," to be sure (all unofficial), but it was the eggs and the cranes and the international effort that mattered. The mission was a huge pleasure, an unforgettable adventure, and great success for the entire international team.

Two weeks later, on the 13th of June, a message from western Siberia dispelled any worries about bad luck on that particular Friday the Thirteenth. Dr. Flint reported from the Kunovat Lowlands south of Salekhard that all five Siberian crane eggs that the team had placed there had hatched successfully under Eurasian crane foster mothers. The first two to hatch were named "Mary" and "Terry."

Chapter 9
Siberian Epilogue

SIBERIAN CRANES FACE A DISHEARTENING array of threats to their survival as a species. In part, this is because they are the most finicky of all the cranes in their choice of habitats and foods. They nest only in marshes, bogs, and other wetlands, most often in wide expanses of shallow fresh water that offer good visibility and ample warning of an approaching predator. During migration, they rest and feed in large isolated wetland areas. Their favorite foods, almost to the exclusion of any others, are the roots, tubers, sprouts, and stems of sedges and other wetland plants.

In recent years, sweeping changes in the politics and economics of Russia and the former Soviet republics have had a profound impact on the conservation of wild species and habitats there. The newly autonomous republics are recognizing and promoting the social and economic value of preserving and restoring wild spaces within their borders, after decades of environmental exploitation and damage by the Soviets. At the same time, the fall of Russian communism gave rise to a new class of entrepreneurs who are eager to exploit the natural resources of the region, with little regard for their environmental impacts. Uncontrolled logging, mining, and farming are polluting or destroying large areas of wetlands and other fragile habitats throughout Siberia and Central Asia. The national and regional governments in the former Soviet Union are desperately short of funds for the research, protection, conservation, and education, and . pervasive corruption undermines what progress they make.

In the far north, gold mining and drilling for gas and oil are polluting rivers in the Yakutia region of northeastern Siberia—nesting grounds of more than 95% of the world's remaining Siberian cranes. Mining and farming threaten the wetlands in the Ob River basin in northwestern Siberia, where the dwindling central and western flocks of Siberian cranes build their summer nests.

In the Baikal region, lumbering feeds the region's enormous pulp and paper mills. Huge areas of taiga have been clear-cut, polluting wetlands and watersheds. The immense hydroelectric dam at Bratsk on the Angara River has disrupted large areas of wetlands that are stopovers on the Siberian cranes' migration route.

The Amur River, which divides Russia and China, is one of the most important stopovers on the cranes' eastern migration route. A proposed hydroelectric project, to be built jointly by Russia and China, would damage or destroy vast areas of Amur wetlands. When that project is completed, China plans to relocate 100 million of its people to the area to farm and develop the sparsely populated region along the Amur. That can only increase the pressure on the shy and sensitive Siberian cranes.

In China, the eastern population of Siberian cranes winters in wetlands along the Yangtze River, including those in the Poyang Lake Nature Reserve. Those wetlands harbor more than 100,000 waterfowl. Farther up the Yangtze , the world's largest hydroelectric dam is under construction on the river. The "Three Gorges Dam," will change the way the river's floodwaters replenish Poyang Lake, putting new pressure on several threatened species, including the Siberian crane. The dam will also bring more than a million new human inhabitants to this largely rural area.

Another of the cranes' migration and wintering areas, China's Heilongjiang Province, contains huge areas of wetlands and the country's largest remaining tracts of hardwood forest. Plans call for large scale clear-cutting of the forests and draining of wetlands, to turn this region into China's "northern bread basket."

If the wetlands disappear, the Siberian cranes will disappear with them.

Poaching of wild birds is a growing problem at Poyang Lake. It has been estimated that as many as 300,000 birds, including some Siberian cranes, are killed there each year by poachers using poisoned grain. In the Poyang Lake Nature Reserve, the number of birds lost to poachers from has risen sharply in recent years as restaurants in the area have added the birds to their menus.

The tiny western flock of Siberian cranes migrates through

Central Asia to winter in Iran's Caspian lowlands on the western shore of the Caspian Sea. Along that route, the wetlands of Azerbaijan are important stopovers for the cranes. When the Soviet Union collapsed in 1991, Azerbaijan became a free nation; it was also a bankrupt nation. Locals hunted cranes and other waterfowl for food in areas where the birds had been protected under Soviet rule. The western flock of Sibes crashed, dwindling to a handful of birds in the 1990s.

The central flock of Sibes migrated to India through Russia, Kazakhstan, Uzbekistan, Afghanistan, Pakistan, and India. Most of the countries through which the cranes migrate have banned the hunting of Siberian cranes but illegal hunting continues. In Afghanistan, where it is still legal to hunt the cranes, and where decades of war have ruined the economy, cranes are widely hunted for food.

In Pakistan, the central Indus River and its wetlands are an important migration stop for waterfowl. But the Indus watershed is also home to most of Pakistan's 122 million people. With the human population growing at three percent per year, grazing, farming, and irrigation put rising pressures on the Indus' wetlands. Hunting of cranes continues in Pakistan. Farther south in Iran, the cranes wintering grounds are also disappearing under pressure from the growing human population and growing land use.

In India, where the Siberian crane is known as the "lily-bird," the last known breeding pair to winter there has disappeared. Prime Minister Indira Gandhi created Keoladeo Ghana National Park in 1981, in part to preserve the Siberian crane's wintering grounds. But the park's wetlands, which recently covered 11 square kilometers (4.25 sq. mi.), are now reduced to 1 sq. km (0.38 sq. mi.). This wildlife sanctuary usually attracts nearly 400 species of birds each winter. It is one of the five most important wetland ecosystems in India, and the nesting area for many of India's native waterfowl. But the flow of water through the park has been reduced to a trickle by the new Panchana Dam, 60 miles (100 km) up the Gambhir River. Under intense political pressure from farmers in the Karauli District, the Indian government diverted the water for irrigation, water that was supposed to be reserved for the park's wetlands. In 2004, the government released from the dam less than four percent of the 500 million cubic feet (14.2 million cu. meters) of water promised under the original agreement forged before the dam was built. As a result, the numbers of birds in the park were drastically reduced and fewer than half of the nesting species were able to breed.

Though the farmers have greater political clout, park supporters are determined to fight for their promised share of water. The park and the tourists it attracts are crucial to the economy of the depressed Bharatpur District.

By early 2005, the Indian government had put in five wells to provide much-needed water, to maintain the park's remaining wetland area. But the wells are seen only as a stopgap measure—one that could have serious consequences for the water table in the park and in the surrounding agricultural fields.

IN 2006, THE WORLD CONSERVATION UNION[32] listed the Siberian crane as "critically endangered." As their wetlands disappear, the listing states, the cranes are "expected to go undergo an extremely rapid decline in the near future." The Union estimates the eastern population at somewhere around 3,000 birds, and declining. The western population is estimated to contain about ten birds—not enough to be self-sustaining. According to Union's 2006 report, the central population of Siberian cranes is "biologically extinct."[33]

Since the late 1980s, the International Crane Foundation has been working to foster cooperation among crane biologists and governments, and to promote protective legislation and the creation of waterfowl preserves in most of the countries that share the Siberian cranes' summer, winter, and migration areas. It hasn't been easy. This part of the world is rife with old quarrels and suspicions. According to ICF co-founder George Archibald, "from the tundra to the subtropics, few endangered species involve so many complex problems in so many countries as the Siberian Crane."

In 1993, the International Convention on the Conservation of

---

[32] The World Conservation Union, headquartered in Switzerland, is the world's largest conservation network. It was founded in 1948 as the International Union for the Conservation of Nature and Natural Resources. Though its name was changed to World Conservation Union in 1990, the organization is still known by its original acronym, IUCN. Today, 82 countries, 111 government agencies, and more than 800 non-governmental organizations (NGOs), are members of the Union, along with some 10,000 scientists and experts from 181 nations. Its stated mission is to "influence, encourage and assist societies throughout the world to conserve the integrity and diversity of nature and to ensure that any use of natural resources is equitable and ecologically sustainable."

To learn more, visit www.iucn.org.

[33] The IUCN Red List of Threatened Species, www.iucnredlist.org.

Migratory Species (CMS) developed a Memorandum of Understanding (MoU) that was signed by 12 nations—most of the countries that lie within the range of the Siberian crane.[34] The MoU originally focused on the disappearing western and central populations. In 1999, it was expanded to include the larger eastern population of Siberian cranes. The MoU's overall goals are to preserve remaining crane populations, increase the numbers and genetic diversity of the western and central flocks, protect and manage the habitats on which the cranes depend, and foster better cooperation between the nations in the range.

Together, the range nations that signed the MoU agreed to a set of Siberian Crane Conservation Plans in 2001. As of 2005, there were signs that those Conservation Plans and other efforts under the MoU were starting to produce some results—mainly in new research, better information about important sites within the range, and more cross-border coordination of crane conservation efforts. But the number of wild Siberian cranes continues to fall.

The Siberian Crane Wetland Project (SCWP) is an eight-year, $10 million international initiative funded by the United Nations Environmental Programme under the auspices of the MoU, to study and preserve 16 wetland sites critical to the Siberian crane and other Asian migratory birds, including more than 30 threatened waterfowl species. In Russia, China, Kazakhstan, and Iran, the SCWP is working on managing crane habitats, regulating ecotourism, and promoting consistent federal and provincial conservation laws. Working from its headquarters in Yakutia and

Yuri Markin (l.) and Vladimir Flint place Siberian crane eggs in a common crane nest.
Photo, © *International Crane Foundation, Baraboo, WI*

---

[34] Afghanistan, Azerbaijan, China, India, Islamic Republic of Iran, Japan, Kazakhstan, Mongolia, Pakistan, Russian Federation, Turkmenistan and Uzbekistan

Salekhard, SCWP has recently been fighting two new threats to the western cranes: Hunting lodges are proliferating in the Tyumen' District, an important migratory staging area. And oil exploration is encroaching on the western population's main breeding area in the central Ob River Basin.

In sharp contrast, efforts to create a captive species bank of Siberian cranes have been very successful. Three captive flocks are thriving—at the ICF in Baraboo, Wisconsin, at the Cracid Foundation in Belgium, and at Russia's Oka Nature Reserve. These three flocks total about 125 birds, and successful captive breeding is producing a growing number of eggs and chicks. But captive Siberian cranes cannot save a wild species.

Each year since 1991, Russia's Project Sterkh has been rearing captive-raised Siberian crane chicks and releasing them into wild flocks just before the fall migration. So far, all efforts to reintroduce captive-raised birds into the wild western and central flocks have apparently failed. These Siberian cranes migrate up to 5,000 miles, from northern Siberia to the southern shore of the Caspian Sea. Not one of the captive-raised Siberian cranes has been seen to complete the long migration south.

Of the captive-bred Siberian crane eggs placed in wild nests in the Ob River Basin, several have hatched and been banded for identification, and several of these foster-chicks have begun the long southward migration. Since then, a few banded birds have been sighted at the wintering grounds. But the area is vast and inaccessible, and the Russians lack the funds for satellite tracking. As a result, little is known about the fate of the released birds.

In 2002, the Russian Research Institute for Nature and Protection launched a new effort inspired by the successful ultralight-led whooping crane migrations in the United States.[34] Sasha Sorokin, director of the Oka Nature Reserve, contacted Angelo d'Arrigo, a world hang-gliding champion who had been working with soaring birds. D'Arrigo agreed to work with Sorokin in Russia to teach a group of captive-raised Sibes to follow his hang glider. Unlike an ultralight, a hang glider can use thermals to gain altitude and then glide for long distances, just as cranes do when they migrate. D'Arrigo's Stratos® hang glider, specially modified for the crane project, was equipped with solar-powered GPS, wingtip speakers for recorded crane calls, and a tiny engine with a folding propeller for launching from flat ground.

The ambitious plan was to lead a flock of six captive-raised Siberian cranes from the crane nesting grounds near the Arctic Circle, down the eastern flank of the Urals, through Central Asia, to the cranes' summering grounds on the Caspian lowlands in Iran. A ground support crew would follow by boat up the Ob River, and then switch to trucks at the southern Russian steppe, following D'Arrigo and the cranes all way to Iran. Had the plan succeeded, it would have been the world's longest human-led migration and longest hang glider flight. Capricious Siberian weather was the project's nemesis.

In the spring of 2002, a group of Siberian crane chicks was hatched at the Oka Reserve and flown north by helicopter to the cranes' nesting grounds in the Yamal region near Salekhard on the Ob River Estuary. (In the language of the local Nenets people, "Yamal" means "end of the earth.")

Rainy weather kept D'Arrigo and the birds in the Yamal region longer than expected. After a few weeks of local flights behind the hang glider, the birds were transported by boat to the Belozerki Nature Reserve 900 miles (1500 km) south, in southern Russia. At several stops along the way, they made local flights with D'Arrigo, in the hope that the birds would learn enough of the migration route in stage-by-stage fashion to repeat it on their own. The weather remained uncooperative and from Belozerki, three birds were released. From there, the Russians lost track of them. The other three birds were returned to Oka for the winter. Next winter, two of these birds were transported to Iran for release on the wintering grounds. One of them migrated as far as Dagestan, Russia in the spring. The other bird was kept in captivity in Iran.

In 2005, two captive-raised Sibes, along with a pair of captive-raised Eurasian cranes, were led by ultralight on the 900-mile (1,500-km) migration from Yamal south to the Belozerki Reserve. Alexander Ermakov was the chief pilot for the project. As a bush pilot, Ermakov had flown Sasha Sorokin around the marshes near Gorki in 1980, when Sorokin located the first known nesting grounds of the western population of Sibes. Ermakov was captivated by the cranes and went on to establish the Sterkh Foundation, which supports and promotes crane conservation and education projects in Russia.

For the ultralight project, Ermakov, with help from George Archibald, obtained funding from ITERA, a Moscow-based oil and gas company. With three ultralights purchased and modified for the project by ITERA, Ermakov and his team hope to lead captive-raised

Siberian cranes from Yamal to newly discovered Eurasian crane wintering grounds in Uzbekistan. That migration will follow the Siberian cranes' historic migration route but will stop short of the dangerous passage through Afghanistan and Pakistan. Ermakov and his team have been assisted by the ICF and by Canadian Joe Duff of Operation Migration, the organization that is conducting ultralight-led migrations of whooping cranes between Wisconsin and Florida in the United States.

CRANES HAVE LONG BEEN REVERED IN CHINA, RUSSIA, and other cultures as a symbol of peace. In the 1970s, as the United States and the Soviet Union stood wary of each other on opposite sides of the Iron Curtain, international friendships were formed and international cooperation forged between the two adversaries, in the name of the Siberian crane.

In 1978, Ron Sauey was returning to the United States from Soviet Russia on an Aeroflot airliner, with a box of Siberian crane eggs, bound for the captive breeding program at Baraboo. One of the eggs was already hatching and the chick's peeping attracted the curiosity of other passengers on the plane. After Sauey described the project with his typical enthusiasm, one passenger asked why it was so important to Sauey to save the Siberian cranes. He replied:

> "Because they are so beautiful; because I get excited
> when I see them; because there is no reason for them
> to become extinct."[35]

---

[35] ICF Brolga Bugle, 1979, Vol. 5, #1

Part III
Whoopers & We

"[The crane] is the symbol of our untamable past, of that incredible sweep of millennia which underlies and conditions the daily affairs of birds and men. When we hear his call, we hear no mere bird."

—Aldo Leopold

Chapter 10
So Near the Precipice

". . . [T]HE WHOOPING CRANE IS SO NEAR THE PRECIPICE of extinction that it is apt to topple over any moment." So wrote Arthur A. Allen, an ornithologist and professor at Cornell University, in 1937, in the August issue of National Geographic Magazine. That was the year that Texas' Aransas Migratory Waterfowl Refuge was purchased (and later became the Aransas National Wildlife Refuge) by an act of Congress that was intended, in part, to protect the world's few remaining whooping cranes.

In the 1930s, conservationists recognized that the whooping crane had become extremely rare. In 1937, the year Allen's article appeared, there was one small flock of whoopers wintering at Aransas. So far as anyone knew, they were the last surviving whooping cranes on earth. That tiny flock included a few youngsters, which meant the whoopers were nesting somewhere. No one knew where.

The first official count of the Aransas flock, in the winter 1938-39, counted 14 adults and 4 young whoopers.[1]

Around the same time, biologists stumbled on a small non-migratory flock whooping cranes living year-round near White Lake, Louisiana. Thirteen whoopers were counted there in 1939. While that was a significant increase in the known world population of whoopers, no one breathed a sigh of relief. There were 22 whoopers counted at Aransas NWR that same year, including seven juveniles.

---

[1] The official flock size is always the peak population at Aransas in any given winter. Before the whoopers' nesting grounds were located in the mid-1950s, these numbers left out any birds that didn't survive to the midwinter count or that might have wintered somewhere else. And during World War II (1941-45), there were few aircraft available for wildlife surveys, so counts were probably less accurate than later surveys.

The presence of the young birds was encouraging but a total of 35 birds in two tiny isolated flocks still put the whoopers perilously "near the precipice."

Most endangered of the world's crane species, the whooping crane (Grus americana) is named for its unique "whooping" unison call.[2] Whoopers were probably never abundant. Early explorers and settlers rarely reported seeing whoopers. The first scientific description of whooping cranes appeared in 1722, when an Iroquois Indian presented a whooper's complete skin to Mark Catesby, an English naturalist and artist. The large white bird that Catesby described was, he said, entirely new to science. Around 1770, when Samuel Hearn explored the Great Slave Lake region in northern Canada, he saw whoopers "only in pairs and that not very often." The Lewis and Clark Expedition, which traversed the whoopers' historic range, recorded seeing migrating whooping cranes at the mouth of the Little Missouri River in 1805, but made no other mention of whoopers in their journals.

Fossil evidence suggests that the whooper might have been a relatively uncommon bird all the way back to the Pleistocene Epoch, 1.5 million years ago, when it ranged from central Canada to Mexico and from Utah to the Atlantic coast. Based on the whoopers' known winter distribution and current population densities, biologists have estimated that there might have been as many as 10,000 whooping cranes before Europeans began settling the New World. After that, the number of whoopers fell rapidly. By around 1870, it is estimated that there were between 500 and 1,400 of the birds in North America. The whoopers' range and its numbers continued to decline sharply during the latter half of the 19th century, until the species all but disappeared.

Thomas Nuttall, an English botanist who was touring the young United States in 1811, wrote that he saw "a mighty host" of whooping cranes migrating along the Mississippi River flyway, and many later authorities took (and repeated) Nuttall's report at face value. Today, most ornithologists say that a careful reading of Nuttall's journal and other contemporary sources reveals that the birds he saw were almost certainly sandhill cranes.

Somewhat smaller than whoopers and pewter-colored, sandhill cranes have been very successful as a species, currently numbering

---

[2] To hear the whooper's call, visit the International Crane Foundation's Web site at www.savingcranes.org.

close to 650,000 in North America. Mike Putnam, ICF's Curator of Birds explains:

> "Sandhill cranes were always more abundant than whooping cranes, and occupied a much wider range in North America than whoopers. In Wisconsin, the sandhills may have been reduced to as few as 25 mating pairs [in the early 1900s], but it turns out there were lots of other sandhill crane populations that survived.
>
> Sandhills may be less aquatic than whoopers, using smaller wetlands. As the large wetlands were drained, sandhill cranes were able to hold on and use the smaller remaining wetlands that were not suitable for whooping cranes. It may be that sandhill cranes are tolerant of more varied habitats than whoopers."[3]

Before European settlers ventured into the North American Interior, whooping cranes nested mainly in Illinois, Iowa, Wisconsin, Minnesota, and eastern North Dakota. As the immigrants pushed out across the fertile prairies of the upper Mississippi watershed, they drained the marshes and sloughs for cultivation, robbing the whoopers of nesting habitat. Without nests, the birds' numbers began to dwindle rapidly and, for all anyone knew, to die out. The last recorded whooping crane nest in this entire range was abandoned after 1894. A few whoopers nested farther north in Alberta, Saskatchewan, and Manitoba. But as the great Canadian prairies yielded to the plow, the whoopers were pushed aside. A nest near Muddy Lake in western Saskatchewan—the last known whooper nest in Canada at the time—was vacant after 1922. When Aransas refuge manager Jim Stevenson counted 22 whoopers in Texas in 1940, no one knew where they nested—or much else about them, for that matter.

Fortunately for the whoopers and many other critters, public support for the idea of conservation was on the rise through the

---

[3] Putnam also notes that not all sandhill crane populations have been successful. Non-migratory sandhill populations in Mississippi and in Cuba are small and "very fragile," due in part to habitat loss and the effects of recent hurricanes.

1930s and 1940s. The federally funded Civilian Conservation Corps (CCC) provided desperately needed jobs for more than 3 million young men between 1933 and 1942. CCC was the New Deal's[4] most popular program by far, improving and reclaiming millions of acres of state and federal parks and other public lands, and planting an estimated 3 billion trees to restore forests decimated by unregulated or poorly regulated logging, mining, and other commercial activities. The $30-a-month wages paid to CCC laborers (with an extra $25 a month to men with families) saved an untold number of small American towns from economic oblivion. The CCC also fostered a widespread public awareness of the value and the urgency of preserving America's wild places and wild creatures. World War Two brought an end to the Great Depression and the Civilian Conservation Corps. But the growing American conservation movement only paused until the war was over, and then continued gaining strength.

In 1946, the U.S. Fish & Wildlife Service (USFWS) and the National Audubon Society established the Cooperative Whooping Crane Project to study the cranes and, it was hoped, find a way to preserve them from extinction. Audubon biologist Robert Porter Allen led the study and became the world's leading expert on whooping cranes. Allen spent two winters, 1946-47 and 1947-48, studying the birds at Aransas, adding volumes to what little was known about them. Meanwhile, the Audubon Society printed and distributed thousands of leaflets to hunters in the central U.S. and Canada, describing the whooping cranes and cautioning hunters that the birds were a federally protected species. The publicity campaign effectively ended the shooting of whooping cranes and the bird became a widely recognized symbol of wildlife conservation in the United States. The Audubon Society continued to support the search for the whoopers' nesting grounds, in order to ensure that the birds' habitats would be protected.

During the summers of 1945 and 1946, U.S. and Canadian

---

[4] "The New Deal" was a series of government programs created under President Franklin Roosevelt, during the Great Depression of the 1930s. The programs provided direct relief to individuals and families, helped spur economic recovery, and imposed reforms on the US financial system. Most of the New Deal programs ended in the late 1930s or early 1940s. A few are still important government programs, including Social Security, the Federal Deposit Insurance Corporation (FDIC), the Securities & Exchange Commission (SEC), and the Tennessee Valley Authority (TVA).

wildlife staff working with Allen searched for the whoopers' nesting areas in northern Saskatchewan and eastern Alberta. They covered thousands of miles on the ground and in the air, but came up empty-handed. During the next two summers, 1947 and 1948, Allen and USFWS biologist Bob Smith flew 20,000 miles, searching more than 65,000 square miles of northern Canadian wilderness, without finding a single whooping crane.

In 1952, Smith spotted two whooping cranes north of Great Slave Lake,[5] in Canada's Northwest Territories. They were not a nesting pair—in fact, they were 30 miles (50 km) apart when Smith found them, and there were no nests in sight. Was this a nesting ground or were these two birds lost or wandering, far from the hatchery? A year later, in 1953, another lone whooper was spotted in the same neighborhood. And in 1954, searchers reported eight whoopers along the Great Slave River that flows northward into Great Slave Lake. The nests had yet to be found, but the clues were starting to add up. The answer, when it came, came almost by accident.

Photo, © International Crane Foundation, Baraboo, WI

---

[5] Great Slave Lake is the deepest lake (2,020 ft/615 m) in North America, and one of the largest. It is 298 miles (480 km) long and 62 miles (100 km) wide, with a surface area of 10,980 square miles (28,450 sq km), making it slightly larger than Lake Erie. The first Europeans reached Great Slave Lake in 1771. Gold was discovered there in 1930. The lake forms the headwaters of the Mackenzie River, which is, at 1,100 miles (1,800 km), Canada's longest river.

WOOD BUFFALO NATIONAL PARK IS in Alberta's extreme north and spills over into the Northwest Territories. The park's northern boundary is less than 20 miles (30 km) from the south shore of Great Slave Lake. The Slave River forms the park's eastern boundary. Covering 17,300 square miles (44,800 sq km), Wood Buffalo is Canada's largest national park—more than five times the size of Yellowstone National Park—and home to the world's largest wild bison herd.

Located at the western edge of the Canadian Shield—a huge continental formation of exposed Precambrian crystalline rocks—Wood Buffalo National Park includes four primary geological areas. The largest is the Alberta Plateau, a wild plain covered with forest, muskeg, bogs, slow-moving streams, and huge silt-laden rivers. The plateau's gypsum bedrock is riddled with caves and sinkholes, connected by underground streams that bring fish to countless seemingly landlocked ponds. In the southeast corner of the park the Peace, Athabasca, Birch, and Slave Rivers flow together to form the Peace-Athabasca Delta—one of the world's largest fresh-water deltas. To the southwest, the Caribou and Birch Uplands rise 4,900 feet (1,500 m) above the delta. The uplands are covered with spruce and lichen tundra and their sedimentary rocks are rich with Cretaceous age fossils. The Slave River Lowlands form the eastern boundary of the park. Just east of the park, the land rises to the plain that marks the western reach of the Canadian Shield.

Whoopers nest in the far northeastern corner of the park, along the Slave River and its tributaries. Farther south in the park, minerals leaching out of the Canadian Shield are brought to the surface by lowland springs and deposited in a 95-square mile (250 sq km) salt plain—the only one of its kind in Canada. Several plant species normally found in coastal salt marshes thrive here, and the whoopers often come here to feed.

Wood Buffalo National Park's vast wetland areas provide nesting and staging areas for millions of waterfowl, including geese, ducks, swans, and pelicans. Sandhill cranes, bald eagles and peregrine falcons are also found in the park. Other residents include wolves, bear, moose, caribou, beaver, muskrat, and red fox. Humans have lived in the park and its environs for at least 9,000 years, and the local Micasaw-Cree people still hunt and trap here. A few native families live in the traditional way at Peace Point, a wilderness settlement within the park.

In June of 1954, a fire swept the northeast corner of the park. On June 30th, a forester was returning from the fire by helicopter to the park headquarters at Fort Smith, Alberta. Along the way, he called Fort Smith by radio with an urgent message for the park biologist. In one of the remotest, least accessible corners of the park, he had spotted three whooping cranes—two adults and a chick. It was too early in the year for the chick to fledge. This had to be a nesting ground.

To avoid disturbing the crane family, aerial searches of the area were cut back and a ground search was postponed until the following spring. Searching by airplane a year later in the spring of 1955, park biologists found a whooping crane nest along the Sass River in the far northeastern corner of the park.

Searching for whooper nests on the ground proved difficult. The first attempt, by motorboat and canoe, was frustrated "roadblocks" on the narrow winding creeks that led into the crane's nesting area. A seemingly endless number of downed trees made the creeks impassable, even by canoe. In the second attempt, a team of searchers was ferried into the lowlands by helicopter, but to the wrong place. It took them two days to get their bearings and realize they were lost. Getting back to civilization took another two weeks of weary slogging through the muskeg and bogs, and the thickets of dwarf tamarack, spruce, and birch. On one particularly hard day, traveling just a mile and a half as the crow flies required 13 hours of hard work. For all their trouble, the team found no cranes' nests on that trip.

On the third search attempt, a helicopter dropped Allen and his team half a mile from a known whooper nest. Over the next week and a half, they located several more nests. The birds were evasive, disappearing into the tall grass, but the nests were there to see and fresh whooper tracks were everywhere. By the end of the summer of 1955, nearly two thirds of the Aransas flock of whoopers had been accounted for in the Sass River area.

IN 1937, THERE WERE JUST 15 WHOOPING CRANES AT Aransas National Wildlife Refuge and just six whoopers remaining in the nonmigratory flock in Louisiana, for a total world population of 21 whooping cranes. In 1958 Allen and noted wildlife photographer Fred Truslow[6] counted 32 cranes in the Aransas flock, including nine new fledglings, up from the 14 whoopers found in the refuge 20 years

---

[6] Truslow's stunning color photographs, published in the November 1959 issue of National Geographic, were some of the first close-up photographs ever taken of wild whoopers.

earlier. Another juvenile from the flock wandered off during migration and spent the summer of 1958 in Missouri—the first time a whooper had been sighted in that state since 1913.

Though the Aransas flock had more than doubled in size in two decades, it was still perilously small. And threats to the whoopers' survival were many. Droughts and diseases such as avian cholera and avian tuberculosis took their toll. During migration, whoopers were caught in storms, collided with power lines, or were illegally hunted.

Whoopers rarely breed successfully before age four or five and each breeding pair typically raises only one chick each season, though twins sometimes survive. Their slow maturity and low reproductive rate make this species especially vulnerable and slow to recover.

The Migratory Bird Treaty Act of 1918 gave whoopers and certain other birds "protected" status. In 1967, Congress declared the whooper an "endangered" species—a precursor to the historic Endangered Species Act of 1973. The U.S. Fish & Wildlife Service began a whooping crane recovery program in 1967, based at the U.S. Geological Survey's Patuxent Wildlife Research Center (WRC) in Laurel, Maryland.

THE PATUXENT WILDLIFE RESEARCH CENTER was established During the Great Depression of the 1930s, when large tracts of abandoned farmland were turned over to the federal government. Two biologists in the Department of Interior's Bureau of Biological Survey lobbied Congress to set aside a piece of that land near Washington, D.C. as a permanent wildlife research station—the first of its kind. After looking at several possibilities, J.N. Darling, Director of the Bureau of Biological Survey, and Ira Gabrielson, the bureau's Chief of Wildlife Research, chose a 2,700-acre tract on the Patuxent River, near Laurel, Maryland. The land was transferred to the bureau in late 1936 and officially dedicated as a "wildlife experiment and research refuge" in 1939. Three new laboratory buildings were constructed and the Civilian Conservation Corps built roads, trails, and wetland catchments on the site. During World War II, Patuxent was a work camp for Conscientious Objectors, who helped with various conservation and research projects.

One of the main areas of study during the center's early years was the eating habits of various wildlife. Biologists all over the U.S. sent animals' stomachs and gizzards to Patuxent, where their contents were cataloged and then preserved.

After the War, the center undertook a comparative study of farming techniques to determine their effect on wildlife. Researchers established two farms on the property. One farm made maximum use of all its tillable land. With no cover and no food for wildlife, that farm soon had no wild furred or feathered tenants. On the other farm, hedgerows grew between the fields and natural boundaries were left between fields and neighboring woods. Hunting and trapping were allowed on both farms and both were surveyed for wildlife. Where habitats were preserved and improved at the boundaries of the fields, wildlife thrived.

In experiments and studies in Patuxent's wetlands, new techniques were developed for restoring and managing wild wetlands, and the lessons learned were widely used by federal, state, local, and private conservationists around the country. Some of the studies at Patuxent after World War II focused on the insecticide DDT and its effects on wildlife. Rachel Carson's seminal book, Silent Spring, published in 1962, warned of harm from pesticides to humans and wildlife, and helped launch a powerful grass-roots environmental movement. Much of the book was based on research conducted by biologists at Patuxent. Carson's book spurred increased research at Patuxent, and in 1969 Patuxent biologists issued a report confirming that DDT and other pesticides in the food chain caused birds to lay eggs with thin, fragile shells—too fragile to survive incubation. That report led to a federal ban on the sale of DDT and other chlorinated hydrocarbons in 1973.[7] Biologists at Patuxent continue to study the effects on wildlife of pesticides and other chemicals and pollutants.

The USFWS whooping crane recovery program, started at

---

[7] DDT (dichloro-diphenyl-trichloroethane), the first organic chlorinated pesticide, was created in 1939 and earned its Swiss creator a 1948 Nobel Prize for medicine and physiology. Used during World War II to kill malaria-bearing mosquitoes and typhus-bearing lice, it saw a rapid increase in use worldwide after the war. It was cheap to produce and seemed relatively safe for mammals, and the World Health Organization estimated that in the early years of its use, DDT saved 25 million lives worldwide by helping to prevent insect-borne diseases. But problems emerged: Some insects quickly became DDT-resistant. DDT was highly toxic to fish, it was linked to thin eggshells in birds, and there were signs of long-term toxicity for mammals. DDT is metabolized very slowly by mammals, with a metabolic half-life of eight years. If it remains in the food chain, it will build up in mammals' fatty tissues over time, with adverse effects. In humans and other mammals, DDT has been linked to a higher incidence of miscarriages, birth defects, premature births, and low birth weight.

Although its sale was banned in the U.S. in 1973, it remains in use elsewhere

Patuxent in 1967, involved several concurrent approaches and became a prototype for other endangered species recovery programs. The first approach was to study whoopers in the wild, to answer basic questions about their eating habits, behavior, biology, reproduction, migration, adaptations, and requirements for survival. The second approach was to study whoopers in captivity at Patuxent, with the aim of establishing a successful captive breeding program. The third approach was to develop tools and techniques for hatching and rearing captive chicks, imprinting them on adult whoopers, and releasing them successfully into the wild. Among other challenges, the captive-rearing approach included designing and building an improved mechanical incubator, improving puppet-rearing techniques for raising chicks in isolation from humans, and experimenting with artificial insemination of captive birds.

Much of the work on whoopers at Patuxent has involved comparative studies—painstaking trial-and-error experiments and analysis of results to determine the best way to manage a wild population of whoopers, and to push the species back from the precipice of extinction.

The first whooper for Patuxent's captive flock arrived in 1966. Originally from Wood Buffalo, the bird had injured its wing and had been captured and placed in a zoo. Patuxent's flock grew as biologists from the U.S. and Canada gathered whooper eggs from wild nests in Wood Buffalo National Park, to be hatched and raised in captivity.

Between 1967 and 1996, 174 eggs were taken to Patuxent. Most breeding pairs of whoopers produce two eggs but raise only one chick each season. Since one egg from each nest is virtually "wasted" each year, biologists proposed snitching one egg from each wild nest and leaving one viable egg for the parents to raise. Initially, there was some strong and vocal opposition to the proposal, from individuals and conservation groups. But the biologists made their case and in 1967 began gathering eggs for the captive breeding program. Those purloined eggs produced a captive flock of 19 whooping cranes, living at the Patuxent Wildlife Research Center and producing more

around the world, especially in Asia. By 1978, five years after the U.S. ban, DDT concentrations in Lake Michigan waters had diminished to ten percent of their peak levels. DDT continues to be a problem in the Great Lakes however, where it remains concentrated in the flesh of the lakes' fish and fish eaters. DDT and other chemical contaminants accumulate up the food chain as plankton and smaller fish are eaten by larger fish. The highest concentrations end up in the largest and oldest predator fish, which are also the top game fish.

whooping crane eggs. Gathering eggs at Wood Buffalo National Park did not adversely affect the whoopers' productivity, as critics had predicted. In fact, the Wood Buffalo flock actually raised more chicks in years when eggs were gathered. In 1973, when no eggs were gathered, the flock produced only two chicks. In 1975, when 14 eggs were gathered by the biologists, eight chicks successfully fledged in the wild.

Eventually, three captive flocks would be established—at Patuxent, at ICF in Baraboo, and at the Calgary Zoo in Alberta.

In May 1975, a whooping crane chick named "Dawn" emerged "healthy and vigorous" from her egg at the Patuxent Wildlife Research Center. She was the first chick to hatch from an egg produced by Patuxent's captive flock of whoopers, and the world's first whooper produced through artificial insemination. Her mother had also hatched at Patuxent, from an egg brought to Maryland from Wood Buffalo National Park. Dawn survived only a few days, apparently dying of congenital defects. Nonetheless, her hatching, and the artificial insemination that made it happen, were important steps forward in the efforts to save the whooping crane.

The number of whoopers was growing but the species was still perilously close to oblivion. In the fall of 1975, 49 wild whoopers made the annual 2,500-mile (4,025-km) migration from Canada's Wood Buffalo Park to Aransas NWR. Among that flock were eight youngsters born that spring and spotted by biologists at Wood Buffalo. Amazingly, all eight chicks completed the long flight. Chicks are often lost during the fall migration, possibly to predators, disease, or collisions with power lines.

HAVING THREE SEPARATE CAPTIVE FLOCKS encourages diversity in the management of those flocks, which can lead to better practices for managing the species. Having separate flocks also helps prevent a single disease, disaster, storm, or vandalism from decimating the entire captive breeding stock.

For the same reasons, the U.S. Fish & Wildlife Service sought to establish a new wild migratory flock, geographically isolated from the Wood Buffalo/Aransas flock. The risks facing a single flock were brought home to crane conservationists in the mid-1970s, when avian cholera broke out among sandhill cranes and other waterfowl along the Platte River, a migration stop for some of the whoopers from the Wood Buffalo/Aransas flock. Biologists waiting along the

Platte chased away several whoopers that tried to stop there, and avian cholera did not strike the whooping cranes. The biologists' actions may have saved the tiny flock of wild whoopers from a potentially disastrous epidemic.

In 1975, with Patuxent's captive flock well established, USFWS biologists took the next step toward the creation of a new wild flock of whoopers. They began placing whooper eggs from Patuxent into greater sandhill crane nests in the Grays Lake National Wildlife Refuge in southeastern Idaho. Raised by sandhill cranes, the whoopers would (the biologists hoped) grow up just as wild as their sandhill foster parents. They would learn new feeding habits and, most important, a new migration route from the nesting grounds in Idaho to the Bosque Del Apache National Wildlife Refuge in New Mexico.

Grays Lake NWR had much to recommend it as the starting point for a new flock of whoopers. Its shallow wetlands provide excellent breeding grounds for the resident sandhill cranes. The sandhills that nest there migrate each fall to the Bosque del Apache NWR in south central New Mexico and to protected sites along the Rio Grand River farther south. The main stop along the route is the Monte Vista NWR in southwestern Colorado; that and some of the flock's other migration stops are on protected land. The migration route is over relatively isolated and unsettled territory, so contacts with humans and associated risks are minimal. And the Rocky Mountains isolate the Grays Lake sandhills' range from the Wood Buffalo/Aransas whoopers' range.

Wild whoopers and sandhills have similar diets and prefer similar habitats on their nesting grounds, though the rest of the year sandhill cranes forage for seeds in upland areas while whoopers prefer more aquatic habitats. From experiments with captive cranes, Sandhill cranes were known to be good foster parents and were fairly tolerant of pesky biologists poking around their territories. The cross-fostering experi-

A pair of sandhill cranes engage in a courtship dance.

Photo, © International Crane Foundation, Baraboo, WI.

ment still presented plenty of obstacles and unknowns, but Grays Lake looked like the right place to give the method a try.

Sandhill cranes range from Alaska to Hudson Bay and California to Florida. If the foster parenting plan worked, biologists reasoned, wild sandhills could be used to introduce new and separate populations of whooping cranes throughout North America. The specific goal set by the USFWS for whooping introduction was to establish at least three self-sustaining flocks of whoopers—one of them non-migratory.

In May 1975, 14 whooping crane eggs from wild nests in Wood Buffalo Park were flown to Grays Lake NWR in Idaho and placed in the nests of greater sandhill cranes. Nine of those eggs hatched and six chicks survived to fledge that fall. In mid-October, when the sandhills began heading south, the six young whoopers accompanied their foster parents on the migration to New Mexico. Most of the birds made the 850-mile (1,360 km) migration to the area around Bosque Del Apache NWR in less than a week. By the end of October, four young whooping cranes were wintering in the refuge with their sandhill foster parents in refuge corn and alfalfa fields. A fifth whooper was sighted briefly and then disappeared. The whereabouts of the sixth young whooper from Grays Lake was unknown.

For a few weeks in the summer of 1976, the total number of whooping cranes in the world, wild and captive, topped 100—the highest number ever recorded since accurate counts began early in the century. By early winter, that total had declined to 89, due to chick mortality, mainly in the captive breeding programs. That was still a higher total than the previous year, and the numbers gave crane biologists and enthusiasts renewed hope that the whooping crane was indeed on the flight path to recovery.

From 1975 through 1989, 287 whooping crane eggs from Wood Buffalo and Patuxent were placed in the nests of sandhill crane foster parents at Grays Lake. Of those eggs, 210 hatched and 85 chicks successfully fledged. But chick mortality was high, due in part to a sustained drought in the region. There were never more than 33 adult whoopers in the Grays Lake flock at any one time.

All the surviving Grays Lake whoopers—chicks and adults—migrated to New Mexico and back with their sandhill crane foster parents. A few wandered down to wintering grounds in old Mexico. So far, the cross-fostering experiment looked like a qualified success. The next hurdle was reproduction. As the Grays Lake whoopers reached sexual maturity around age four, some of the males began building nests and defending territories at Grays Lake. They occasionally engaged in courtship displays—aimed at sandhill females—but both sides quickly lost interest. While the courtship dances of whoopers and sandhills might look pretty much the same to us, to the birds they are a world (and a species) apart.

The male whoopers at Grays Lake seemed to have the right nesting instincts. Several of them helped sandhill pairs raise their chicks—protecting the chicks and patrolling the territory. At least one male whooper became a stepparent, helping a male sandhill crane to raise its chick after its sandhill mate was killed.

The female whoopers at Grays Lake presented a different story. With no males of either species courting them, they showed no interest in nesting. They spent their time apart, defending no territories and avoiding male whoopers who had established territories or were sharing the territories of nesting sandhill cranes.

In 1989, the Whooping Crane Recovery Team decided to stop placing whooper eggs at Grays Lake. USFWS Whooping Crane Coordinator Tom Stehn explained that flock mortality was too high to justify any more releases. Water levels in the nesting marshes at Grays Lake could not be controlled and that made it much easier for predators to take the chicks in drought years when water levels were low. Mortality among Grays Lake adult birds was also on the rise. Stehn explained that center-point irrigation systems had begun to dominate the lowlands in Colorado's San Luis Valley, an important migration staging point for the cranes. Each new irrigation system required a new power line, and more and more cranes were colliding with the lines. Also, said Stehn, there was strong biological evidence that the whoopers were improperly imprinted by their sandhill foster parents.

IN 1992, CRANE BIOLOGISTS PROPOSED using some of the surviving Grays Lake whoopers as guide birds, to raise new whooper chicks (from eggs provided by Patuxent) and teach them the migration route to New Mexico. Two of the Grays Lake whoopers, a male and a female, were captured at Bosque del Apache NWR in January 1993 and moved to a pen near Grace, Idaho, about 80 miles (135 km) from the Grays Lake nesting area. The pen was located on a ranch owned by Kent Clegg, a rancher and crane biologist.[8]

In May 1993, four whooper eggs from Wood Buffalo National

---

[8] Kent Clegg later became the first person to teach cranes to fly behind an ultralight aircraft. That story is told in Part IV.

Park hatched at ICF and the chicks were raised in isolation from human contact. In June, one of Terry Kohler's aircraft flew the four whooping crane chicks to Idaho. The chicks were placed in a pen adjacent to the two adult whoopers from New Mexico. After a short time, they were placed in the same pen with the adults. The chicks and adults seemed to develop family bonds. The adults spent lots of time feeding the chicks or pointing out tasty foods, and the chicks and adults often danced together.

After the chicks fledged in August, the two adult guide birds and three chicks were taken back to Grays Lake where they were placed in pens for a day (to acclimate them to the new location) and then released. (The fourth chick had an injured wing and was held back.) Over the next two months, the chicks stuck together as a group, the female divided her attention between the chicks and the male, and the male more or less ignored the chicks. In October the adults left on their migration to New Mexico; the chicks stayed behind, near the release pen.

The plan was to capture the three chicks, fly them to the New Mexico wintering site, and release them there. But during transport back to the Clegg ranch, the chicks became extremely agitated. One died en route and a second died a few days later.

In November, the surviving chick was given a tranquilizer and flown to New Mexico. It slept most of the way and arrived sleepy but healthy. After its release, it spent some of its time with the adults from the Clegg ranch. Surrounded by thousands of pewter-colored sandhill cranes, the young whooper was attracted to white birds and spent some time associating with trumpeter swans. It was often harassed by sandhills and ignored by the whooper guide birds. In late winter, the chick died of avian cholera.

In February 1994, seven attempts to capture more adult whoopers in New Mexico netted only one male, who was flown to the Clegg ranch in Idaho. In May, Kohler flew four whooper eggs (originally from wild nests in Canada) from Baraboo to Idaho. The chicks were raised in isolation using methods similar but somewhat simpler than those used at Baraboo. Three of them died within ten days of hatching. The surviving chick was introduced to the adult guide bird when it was about three weeks old. The adult male offered or pointed out food to the chick and the two danced together over the summer. After the chick fledged in September, the two were transported to Grays Lake and released. The chick was limping and eventually sat down.

The male approached the chick several times but was ignored. Handlers captured the chick and took it to a veterinarian, who diagnosed a bruised ligament.

After eight days of "R & R" at the Clegg ranch, the chick was again released near the guide male at Grays Lake. The chick approached the male several times but was ignored. Harassed by sandhills, the chick spent most of its time foraging alone. In late September, the chick was attacked by a coyote. Rescued by human handlers, it was flown to New Mexico for treatment, but its injuries were too severe and it was euthanized. Researchers concluded that, ignored by its foster-parent, the chick had failed to learn some of the basic lessons of survival.

The deaths of the chicks made it difficult to evaluate the guide bird idea. What data the team had acquired were not encouraging. The 1993 chicks failed to migrate with their guide birds, and the 1994 chick was ignored by its guide bird. The 1994 U.S. Whooping Recovery Plan had called for releasing captive-raised whooper chicks into wild sandhill flocks, to see if the chicks could learn survival techniques and migration routes from the sandhills. But at Grays Lake and Bosque del Apache, wild sandhill cranes harassed and chased away the whooper chicks released in the guide-bird experiments.

One important lesson from the project was that chicks needed special care during transport. Adult cranes, even wild cranes, seemed to tolerate crating and transport fairly well. But the chicks proved unexpectedly difficult to handle and transport.

BY 1999 THE WHOOPERS THAT HAD BEEN FOSTER-RAISED by wild sandhill cranes at Grays Lake NWR were nearly gone; only four remained. That was the last reported sighting of whooping cranes at Grays Lake. A year later, there was only a single survivor, summering at Red Rocks Lake in western Montana. By the spring of 2002, the last cross-fostered whooping crane was gone.

The foster-parenting experiment did produce one, possibly two, unusual offspring. In the spring of 1975, as biologists began collecting whooper eggs to put in sandhill nests, U.S. Fish & Wildlife researchers at Patuxent cross-bred a whooper and a sandhill crane. It was possible that whoopers and sandhills would crossbreed at Grays Lake, and the biologists wanted to learn what sort of crane a hybrid would be. A captive sandhill hen was artificially inseminated with semen collected from "CAN-US," a wild-captured whooping crane who was part of the captive breeding flock at Patuxent. The hen produced one fertile egg, which was successfully incubated and hatched. The world's first "whoophill" chick was strong and sturdy. George Archibald described the chick as "beautifully patterned with brown and white." Three more whoophill hybrids were hatched at Patuxent but didn't survive to maturity.

"Ghostbird," the world's first whoophill crane, lives on at Patuxent. In his appearance and behavior he has both whooper and sandhill characteristics, according to the staff, and "his call is kind of a mix." In his pen at Patuxent, Ghostbird is paired with a greater sandhill crane. And although he is sterile, he and his companion are "excellent incubators and parents." Together they have reared several whooper chicks.

In the fall of 1992, observers at Colorado's Monte Vista NWR spotted an odd-looking bird among the migrating sandhill cranes. Its wings and back were pearl gray, like an adult sandhill, but its coloring was broken with uncharacteristic white splotches, and its neck was almost completely white. At the time, biologists concluded that it was the product of a male whooping crane and a female sandhill crane, and that it had hatched and fledged in Yellowstone National Park. Kelli Stone, wildlife biologist for the Monte Vista and Alamosa NWRs, said the bird was spotted for a year or two, and then disappeared. No one was ever able to capture the supposed whoophill to confirm that it was in fact a hybrid.

Chapter 11
Rära Avis

THE WHOOPING CRANE IS NORTH AMERICA'S tallest bird. Males can reach five feet (1.5 m) in height and have wingspans of seven to eight feet (2.4 m). Females are slightly smaller but, as with most crane species, males and females appear identical. An adult whooper weighs, on average, only about 15 pounds (6.8 kg). In comparison, a trumpeter swan with a similar wingspan weighs 25 to 30 pounds (11-13.5 kg). With their long wings and light weight, whoopers are excellent flyers and gliders, well adapted for long migrations.

Adult whoopers' feathers are snowy white, except for jet-black wingtips and a black "mustache." The black primary feathers make the whooper easy to recognize and may have a practical use, as well. Black pigment adds a bit of strength to the feathers that take the heaviest beating during flight.

On top of their heads is a fleshy red crown, sparsely covered with black hair-like feathers. Their beaks are a dark olive-gray, and their legs and feet are black. Most whoopers have yellow eyes.

Whooper chicks are cinnamon-colored. During their first summer, their wingtips turn black as flight feathers replace the hatchlings' down. Their body feathers are mix of cinnamon and white, turning all white by the time the birds are about 15 months old.

All paired cranes engage in unison calling to mark and defend their territories and to strengthen their pair bond. The whoopers' unison call is its distinctive "whoop."

The female often initiates the call, standing erect with her head thrown back and her wings at her sides. She makes two higher-pitched calls, which the male answers with one lower-pitched call. He also stands erect, pointing his beak skyward and lifting his wings over his back, or lowering them at his sides, so that his black wing tips are visible. The coordinated unison calling can last for more than a minute with a complex series of calls.

Unison calling is an important part of the whoopers' pair bonding. ICF's George Archibald explained that either sex can begin the courtship display, but more often it is the female who makes the first call. That suggests that the female is more able than the male to choose a particular suitor, Archibald said. And it is consistent with the fact that whoopers' sexual imprinting is more pronounced in females than in males. "She is the one to make the choice [of a mate]. He is the one to get the territory."

The duration of the unison calling display is usually determined by the male. The female keeps responding for as long as the male keeps calling. That, said Archibald, could give the impression that "the female has the last word, but she is actually responding to the last call of the male." And that fits with the male's role as the primary defender of the territory. "It's such a sophisticated and absolutely beautiful system."

A long loop in the whooping crane's trachea (wind pipe) gives its voice the distinctive "whoop."[9] USFWS, the Canadian Wildlife Service, the Platte River Trust, and a German volunteer and crane vocalization expert, Dr. Bernard Wessling, are cooperating in a research project to determine whether each pair of whoopers has a unique unison call, and whether those calls might be used to identify each pair. The project biologists have been successful in using voiceprints—computer-generated graphs of the frequencies and modulations of whooper calls—to identify individual birds. But ICF biologists at Baraboo say that, with a few rare exceptions, they cannot identify individual birds simply by listening to their unison calls. Mike Putnam, ICF's curator of birds, explained that one of the male whoopers at Baraboo could be identified by the unusual "braying" sound he interposes into his unison calls. "He sounds a lot like a mule," Putnam said.

Whoopers, themselves, have no trouble telling the boy cranes from the girl cranes. Not so for biologists. Like other birds, cranes'

---

[9] Stretched full-length, an adult whooper's trachea is nearly five feet (150 cm) long. You hear whooping crane calls on the ICF Web site: www.savingcranes.org (click on "Species Field Guide"), and on the Operation Migration Web site: www.operationmigration.org (click on "Our Work").

sexual organs are inside their bodies. You can't just lift their tails to find out who is who. And poking around inside to determine sex is an uncomfortable procedure for the crane and a dangerous one, since it requires anesthesia. There are ways for observers to tell who is who in a mated pair; in most cases, males are a bit larger than their mates. A more reliable indicator is that during the unison call, the male usually drops his wings so his black wing tips are visible, while the female keeps her wings folded. But unmated cranes do not make unison calls.

When whooping cranes are disturbed, they make "guard calls" to warn each other of possible danger. In 1991, Glen Carlson, a graduate student at Idaho State University, analyzed whoopers' guard calls and found that the female's whoop is distinctively higher pitched than the male's. But, Stehn notes, the two birds answer each other's guard calls so quickly that, among wild cranes, it can hard for an observer to tell which whoop is coming from which bird.

If appearance, size, and behavior don't separate the boys from the girls, what's left? At Hokkaido University in Japan, biologist Motomichi Sasaki used genetics to determine the sex of crane chicks. Each cell in a crane's body carries a set of chromosome pairs, half of which are inherited from each parent. In a male crane, the chromosomes in each pair look alike. In female cranes, the chromosomes in each pair look alike, except for one odd pair—the one that determines the bird's sex. One of the chromosomes in this pair is only about one third the size of the other. Dr. Sasaki looked for the odd unmatched pair that indicated a female bird. But the procedure, developed in the 1960s, was complicated, time-consuming, and expensive. It involved culturing cells, allowing them to divide, isolating the chromosomes, and then matching each chromosome with its mate to look for an oddly matched pair.

In the late 1970s, Dr. Ellen Rasch, an ICF research affiliate, looked at Dr. Sasaki's method and wondered if the female crane's genetic material might weigh less than the male's, because of that oddly matched chromosome pair. At Marquette University in Milwaukee, Wisconsin, where Rasch was then a professor of biology, she brought together blood samples from every crane of known sex at ICF, from every whooping crane of known sex at Patuxent, and from a Siberian crane of known sex at the Philadelphia Zoo. She used an integrated-scanning microdensitometer to weigh the genetic material in a single cell from each of her samples. She found that the males' genetic material did indeed weigh more than the females'—by an average of about one 20-millionth of a gram. That was pretty close to the limits of precision for her instruments, so Rasch concluded that this method would only be correct about 95 percent of the time. But, compared to Dr. Sasaki's complex procedure, this method was quick and simple. Biologists at ICF could put one drop of blood on a slide, send it to Rasch, and have an answer overnight.

Advances in biochemistry and DNA analysis have eclipsed Dr. Rasch's method. Birds can now be sexed by molecular analysis of their DNA. A small blood or tissue sample is analyzed for distinctive genetic markers that are unique to each sex. The test is quick (24 hours for results), inexpensive (about $20 per test), and accurate. The leading laboratories claim 99 percent accuracy with blood or tissue. And there is minimal trauma for the birds because the samples required are very small—a few drops of blood from a clipped toenail or tissue from four or five feather shafts plucked from the bird's chest or wing. (The feathers grow back in four to six weeks.)

Dr. Ken Jones is a research associate with the Division of Biology at Kansas State University, and he has been the genetics advisor to the International Whooping Crane Recovery Team since 1996. "In addition to blood and feathers," he said, "we are now using egg shell membranes from newly hatched chicks for sexing and paternity analyses. That way we do not have to pull feathers or draw blood on the young ones. With Whoopers, we are trying for the most noninvasive procedures possible."

IN THE WILD, WHOOPERS PAIR OFF and can begin exhibiting breeding behaviors at two years of age, though they don't reach sexual maturity until they are three years old. In an elaborate mating ritual, paired birds call, flap their wings, bow to each other, throw sticks in the air, and make soaring leaps that often carry one bird completely over the other.[10]

Whoopers can mate for life, performing the courtship dance each spring as the mating season begins. The dance triggers hormonal changes that prepare the birds for successful mating. A pair might also dance after successfully driving off an intruder or predator, or

---

[10] Crane species are found all around the world, except in South America and Antarctica, and were once far more common than they are today. All cranes dance. And costumed crane dances are an almost universal element of human culture, from funerals to harvest dances—from South Africa to northern Siberia. Even Greek

simply to release tension. Mated pairs dance year-round, though most of their dancing takes place in the spring.

When an intruder approaches, one or both of the pair (usually the male) will make threat displays, beginning with a slow, stiff-legged walk toward the intruder. A male defending his mate will try to put himself between the intruder and the female. The defender may preen its feathers as part of the display, all the time keeping an alert eye on the intruder. If the intruder isn't impressed, the crane will raise itself to its full height facing the intruder, fluff its feathers, and spread its wings with wingtips drooping, to make itself appear as large and imposing as possible. It will sound alarm calls audible more than two miles (3 km) away. In close quarters, it may "growl" at the intruder. The crane may also arch its neck to display a larger area of its red fleshy crown to the intruder. If the alarm calls and threat display fail to discourage the intruder, the defending crane may charge with wings spread and neck arched. A whooper's six-inch (15-cm) pointed beak can be a formidable weapon.

If the intruder is another crane—most often an unattached subadult—it might flee or it might assume a submissive posture, bending its legs, lowering its head and neck, holding its wings close to its body, and generally making itself look as small and unthreatening as possible.

A pair of whoopers tends a pair of chicks.
Photo, © International Crane Foundation, Baraboo, WI.

After the intruder is sent packing, the defending pair often unison call to announce victory and blow off the tension built up during the encounter.

mythology mentions the crane dance. Plutarch, the Greek priest and author (c. 45-125 A.D.) wrote that after the mythic hero Theseus killed the Minotaur at Crete, he and his companions sailed off to Delos, where they celebrated by performing a crane dance.

A 2003 essay by two Cornell University scientists, an anthropologist and an ornithologist, poses some interesting questions about the origins and antiquity of human crane dances, as suggested by recent archaeological finds. In ancient Anatolia (Turkey) 8,500 years ago, dancers appear to have made crane costumes from crane feathers laced to crane bones. (See: Russell, N. & McGowan, K., "Dance of the Cranes: Crane Symbolism at Catalhoyuk and Beyond," Antiquity, Vol., 77, #297, Sept 2003, pp 445+)

IN THE WILD, ALL CRANES can be extremely aggressive in pro-tecting their territories, especially during nesting season. Whooper pairs sometimes appear to tolerate an unpaired subadult on their winter feeding territories, after they have shown the intruder that they are dominant. But nesting territories are jealously guarded.

In the captive breeding programs at ICF, Patuxent, and else-where, the breeding cranes are allowed to imprint on other cranes but are raised in close contact with humans, so that they will be more comfortable breeding in the presence (and with the occasional assis-tance) of humans. Cranes raised around humans lose their fear of humans, but not their aggression, and that creates challenges for the cranes' human keepers. Routine tasks like feeding the birds and cleaning their enclosures require a mix of creativity, subterfuge, and "crane diplomacy." At Baraboo, ICF aviculturists use a variety of tac-tics and techniques to avoid confrontations with aggressively territo-rial birds. The specific tactics used depend on the personality of the individual bird. Some of ICF's cranes are content as long as the avi-culturists don't approach too closely. Keeping a reasonable distance from those birds usually keeps things peaceful.

Still, working with the captive cranes can be dangerous. Standing at eye level with a person, most cranes will try to attack the person's eyes with its beak. Some cranes will attack by leaping into the air and slashing with their feet. Such attacks carry the risk of serious injuries to the humans and the cranes.

For aviculturists at ICF in Baraboo, knowing the personalities and fighting styles of the individual cranes is essential. Aviculturalists then use that knowledge to avoid or ward off confrontations.

Sometimes, a little trickery helps. Throwing some grain into a far corner of a crane's pen might distract the bird long enough for chores to be completed. Mimicking a crane's threat display or simply shout-ing at the bird might keep the crane calling and displaying, instead of attacking. If an attack comes, a bit of water flicked into the bird's face from a brush can make the bird pause enough to allow the avi-culturist to get away. Staff members sometimes arm themselves with a broom to distract or gently fend off the cranes. For the most aggres-sive cranes, a sliding door operated remotely by ropes allows the avi-culturist to isolate the crane in one part of the enclosure while chores are completed in another part.

Wisconsin winters can be harsh. Long stretches of temperatures below 0°F. (-17°C.) are not uncommon and wind chills can drop to

–60° or –75° F. (-50° to –60° C.). In the wild, cranes migrate to warmer climates each winter. But at Baraboo, Wisconsin, ICF's captive cranes cope rather well with the winter weather. Arctic-nesting cranes—Siberian, Eurasian, and Hooded cranes among them—are actually quite cold hardy. At Baraboo, all the cranes' pens have shelters from the weather but the shelter doors are typically left open all winter to allow the birds greater freedom of movement. The arctic-nesting cranes can often be found outdoors and content in cold weather, with no more shelter than a windbreak and with their heads tucked snugly under a wing.

Crowned cranes, which live year-round in tropical Africa, don't tolerate the cold well. They are typically kept indoors at ICF with electrically heated floor pads (called "pig pads") for warmth. A winter diet of corn, which is rich in carbohydrates, helps all of ICF's captive cranes stay warmer during the cold months.

The crane population at ICF includes a number of older[11] and injured cranes. They receive special care and attention to keep them comfortable and healthy in the winter months.

Cold winters offer at least one advantage to the breeding programs at ICF and Calgary Zoo: the cold and snow cleanse the outdoor pens of disease microbes that naturally accumulate in the soil during warmer months. (Cold winters on the wild cranes' nesting grounds may have the same effect.) Crane eggs are vulnerable to infections from pathogens in the soil. Winter temperatures kill many of those pathogens and give the eggs a better chance in the spring.

WHOOPERS EAT A WIDE VARIETY OF FOODS in the wetlands they inhabit. Animal matter makes up much of their diet. They will eat clams, shrimp, crayfish, eels, minnows and other fish, snakes, frogs, snails, grasshoppers and other insects, and even mice and voles. They also eat seeds, fruits, and tubers from water plants. During migration, when they are not feeding in wetlands, the whoopers' diet switches mainly to agricultural grains—especially corn. At their wintering grounds in Texas, whoopers' favorite food is the nutrient-rich blue crab.

---

[11] At ICF, it is not unusual for captive cranes to live 30 to 40 years. In general, older cranes tolerate the cold as well as younger cranes. It is not uncommon for cranes to develop arthritis as they age. At ICF, birds as young as 18 have had arthritis, but the disease is more prevalent in the older cranes. Arthritic cranes get supplement heat, to help ease their symptoms.

The sweet meat of the blue crab is high in protein, fat, vitamins, and minerals. If there are enough crabs to go around, an adult whooper might eat as many as 75 to 80 blue crabs a day—80 to 90 percent of the birds' diet. Blue crabs live in the brackish, nutrient-laden waters of coastal estuaries, from Chesapeake Bay to the Gulf of Mexico. Like any wild species, blue crabs endure ups and downs in their numbers. Water levels in the fresh water rivers that feed their estuaries, natural ocean cycles, and other environmental factors affect the populations of blue crabs in any season and location. These natural cycles have little effect on the crabs overall, but have a profound effect on the whoopers. An eight-year study at Aransas NWR revealed that when blue crabs were in short supply, there was a sharp rise in the number of whooping cranes that died during the winter. Clearly, the blue crab is the whooping cranes most important winter food.

They may also be the whoopers' most challenging food. An adult male blue crab can measure 10 inches across. Adult females are a bit smaller. Their name comes from the bright blue coloring on the underside of the male's large claws. (The female's claws are brown or tan.) Those claws can inflict serious injury. The crab's hard shell body also has lateral spines to discourage predators and to clear obstacles as the crab walks sideways.

When the weather is cool and the crabs are dormant, adult whoopers probe in the mud with their bills to locate crabs. Small juvenile crabs are eaten whole. Whoopers carry larger crabs to the shore and break them up. First the crane flips the crab on its back and pulls off its large claws. With the crab "disarmed" and on its back, the bird pulls off the crab's legs and eats them whole. Then it will peck repeatedly at the crab's softer underside to break it up. Pieces of the soft undershell are swallowed along with the contents of the shell, leaving only the crab's hard upper shell (carapace). Whooper chicks learn the technique from their parents.

EACH YEAR THE WHOOPERS BEGIN LEAVING ARANSAS NWR in late March, on the long 2,500-mile (4,000-km) migration to Wood Buffalo Park. By mid-April, the last of the adult whoopers has left Aransas. They head north in small groups of two or three birds, following a migration corridor through central Texas, Oklahoma, Kansas, Nebraska, the Dakotas, the eastern edge of Montana, Saskatchewan, and Alberta. Rising over a mile (1.6 km) high on thermals (rising columns of warm air) then gliding northward at up to 60 miles per hour (100 km/h), the cranes average about 30 miles (50 km) per hour and cover 200 to 400 miles (325-650 km) each day, depending on winds and weather. They may pause for several days along the way, to wait out storms or headwinds. Strong crosswinds or bad weather can sometimes blow them off course but the birds' migratory instincts usually lead them back to the migratory corridor. More often, it seems, the birds will stay on the ground to wait for good weather and favorable winds.

During migration, they do their flying during the day, usually resting at night, and sometimes using the same staging areas (rest stops and feeding areas) year after year. Not all the whoopers that leave Aransas each spring arrive safely at Wood Buffalo Park. On or near the ground, while feeding or resting, the migrating whoopers are vulnerable to predators, including bobcats, wolves, coyotes, foxes, raccoons, and golden eagles. Flying near the ground, especially at dawn or dusk, they sometimes collide with power lines, wind turbines, or the guy wires of radio or cell phone towers. Late winter storms can bury food sources along the way and expose the birds to bitter cold. Those who do reach Wood Buffalo usually arrive two to three weeks after leaving Aransas. Stopovers along the way tend to be short. Apparently, the urge to move north and begin nesting is very strong.

Most established pairs will return directly to the same nest or nesting territory each year. In new pairs, the male will often look for a new nesting territory near the nest where he was hatched and fledged. Non-breeding, subadult cranes behave very differently. Their first few days on the nesting grounds are spent in what graduate student and ICF intern Lara Fondow described as "the Spring Wander."

Not long after arriving at the nesting site, each whooping crane pair will stake out and defend a nesting territory. The size of each territory varies with the availability of food plants and nesting sites. On average, a pair of whoopers will defend a territory of about 1,000 acres or 1.5 square miles (3.9 km2). The pair gathers plant material, including bulrushes, cattails, and sedge, and builds a nest. Most whooper nests are built on the bottom of the pond but floating whooper nests are not uncommon. The finished nest is a mound of vegetation about three to six feet (0.9-1.8 m) across and up to a foot (30 cm) above the water level. It is surrounded by vegetation so a crane sitting on the nest is hidden from view. Nest building activity is punctuated by courtship dancing.

The female lays two four-inch (10 cm)-long eggs in the nest, a few days apart. If the eggs are broken or stolen during the first few days, females might lay more eggs to replace the lost ones.

Both parents share in guarding and incubating the eggs. While one sits on the nest, the other feeds or rests nearby, ready to drive off any predators. The chicks hatch after about 30 days. Hatching is a drawn-out, exhausting process that can last for 48 hours or more as the chick struggles to break free of its shell. Chicks—about the size of an adult robin—are born with cinnamon-colored down, gray eyes, and webbed feet. They are good swimmers—they have to be to keep up with their long-legged parents. (Adult cranes have long toes with no webbing, well adapted to walking on the soft muddy bottom of a marsh.)

Cranes are protective, indulgent parents, constantly feeding and guarding their young chicks for the first few weeks. Through the summer, the chicks learn from their parents how to find their own food. By the end of the summer, cinnamon and white feathers and black wingtips have replaced the chicks' fuzzy down. Though the chicks become increasingly self-sufficient, whooper parents continue to feed and guard their chicks through most of the chick's first year.

Most whooper pairs produce two eggs each spring, but in most whooper families, only one chick survives the summer. ICF's Mike Putnam said that there are theories, but no one knows for sure why so few siblings make it to the fall. Weather, disease, and predators are factors in chick survival. Between siblings, competition for food and outright aggression have been well documented. Parental attention might also play a part. Some crane biologists note that Wood Buffalo Park is located near the northern limit of the whoopers' natural, historic range. They suggest that the nesting territories there might not provide adequate nutrition to support two adults and two growing chicks.

Whatever the reasons, in most nests only one of the two chicks survives to fledge, though sometimes a pair of siblings does make it through the summer together. Being an only child confers no guarantee of survival, either. By late summer or early fall in an average year, fewer than half of the whooper pairs that nested in spring have even one surviving chick. Crane researchers have been plotting the recruitment rate of Wood Buffalo's whoopers for several decades. ("Recruitment rate" refers to the percentage of nesting pairs who successfully raise a chick.) Mike Putnam explains that the annual recruitment rate at Wood Buffalo National Park, as determined by Canadian Wildlife Service biologists, appears to follow a cycle of nine to ten years, varying from a high of 79 percent to a low of just 12 percent. This periodic fluctuation seems to parallel similar recruitment cycles in snowshoe hares, arctic snowy owls, and ruffed grouse. Biologists have yet to discover what drives any of these cycles. "Ecologies are very complicated," Putnam says. "There are many, many variables. We can tell you that a pattern exists [in whooper or snowshoe hare recruitment] but, so far, no one knows why it exists." Some answers might come from long-term study associated with the Kissimmee Prairie non-migratory flock of whooping cranes established in 1993 and the Wisconsin-Florida migratory flock established in 2001. At both Florida sites, studying the whoopers' nesting behavior is much easier than at the breeding grounds in the remote Canadian wilderness.

By the age of three months—around mid-September, on average—the chick can fly. Now it has a better chance of evading predators and it can range farther from the nest in search of food. Short practice flights strengthen its wings for the long migration ahead.

As the days grow shorter, the whoopers begin to feel the urge to move south. Starting in September, they migrate in small family groups or small flocks of unattached subadults. By mid-October, the last cranes have left the nesting grounds in Wood Buffalo National Park on the long 2,500-mile (4,000-km) migration to Aransas NWR.

After two or three days of flying, the birds are in southern Alberta or Saskatchewan where they pause for several days or even weeks. There they feed on waste grain in the harvested farm fields, a rich banquet compared to the sparse autumn diet farther north. Rested and loaded up on calories, the cranes continue south, the last of them departing Canada by the end of October.

The trip from the grain fields of southern Canada to the Texas Gulf Coast takes between 10 and 30 days—up to 40 days for the juvenile flocks. Along the way, they make brief stops for food and rest, and to wait for favorable winds. With good weather and tailwinds, a few whoopers have completed the journey from Canada to the Gulf of Mexico in just seven days.

The whoopers trickle into Aransas a few at time between mid-October and mid-December. During the winter, the cranes stay in small family groups, each defending its own feeding territory of at least 250 acres (about 1 km2)—roughly one fourth the size of a whooper pair's nesting territory. The chicks spend their first winter in the company of their parents, learning to eat blue crabs. Juveniles that are at least a year old but that have not yet mated spend the winter in small groups on the edges of adult wintering territories. They are frequently chased away by adult pairs defending their territories, so the unattached birds move around a lot. Subadult flocks typically number two to seven birds, though they may be larger around a plentiful food source. Individual juveniles come and go from the subadult flock. They may join for a few days or for an entire season. As they find mates, they leave the flock. Among the whoopers, the most common group is a mated pair, with or without one or two chicks.

The young birds may pair off with mates as early as age two, though they won't reach sexual maturity until they are four or five years old. Some pair off before the spring migration and head north with their new partners. Others migrate north with other unattached subadults or by themselves. Chicks approaching one year of age normally migrate north with their parents, but occasionally split off and join a subadult flock, or head north on their own.

The trip from Aransas to Wood Buffalo takes two to four weeks. New pairs claim a nesting territory and might or might not build a nest the first year. At the nesting grounds, chicks that migrated north with their parents move away from the parents' nesting territory, and fend for themselves, while the parents begin a new breeding season. In her first breeding attempt, a young female often lays no eggs or lays infertile eggs. By their second or third year together, a mated pair usually produces one or two viable eggs, and the whoopers' life cycle begins again.[12]

Photo, © International Crane Foundation, Baraboo, WI.

---

[12] An average, a whooper produces her first egg at age five and her first fertile egg at age five or six.

THE NESTING HABITAT OF THE WOOD BUFFALO/ARANSAS whoopers is in one of the more remote and inaccessible areas of the vast Canadian Interior. The cranes nest in wetlands fed by small creeks that form several large wetland complexes in the northeastern corner of the park. Scattered through the large marshes along the Klewi, Little Buffalo, Nyarling, and Sass Rivers, the nesting areas cover about 150 square miles (400 km2). Here, the principal threats to the whoopers' survival are natural ones: small population, lack of genetic diversity, disease, predators, and weather. Chicks do not easily tolerate cold weather during their first week or two of life. Unusually low water levels in the marsh, caused by drought, can leave the nests and chicks more exposed to predators. Average seasonal temperatures in the Canadian north are growing warmer; but no one knows for sure how that might affect the marshes and their suitability for the whoopers. Since the current nesting area is at the far northern edge of the whoopers' historic range, warmer temperatures and longer summers might create a habitat better suited to the whoopers' needs. Or warmer temperatures might increase evaporation, drying up the marshes, increasing predation, and reducing the cranes' food supply.

Along the whoopers' migration route, just east of the Rocky Mountains, human activity continues to disturb, degrade, and reduce habitats that the cranes rely on for stopovers during migration. Fence and power line collisions are common risks, as is illegal shooting of the cranes.

The cranes' wintering grounds at Aransas NWR are right along the Gulf Intracoastal Waterway, a busy coastal shipping corridor. The wakes of commercial ships and recreational ships and boats combine with wind, waves, and storms to erode the barrier islands and destroy the cranes' saltwater marshes. Aransas NWR has lost more than 1,000 acres (4+ km2) to erosion, construction, and maintenance of the waterway in the past half-century. Flexible cement mats now line the banks throughout the crane habitat. They have halted the erosion but they will to be maintained over the long term.

Pollutants in the Gulf Intracoastal Waterway may affect the health and survival of the birds, and biologists fear that a chemical spill in the waterway could be disastrous for the cranes and their winter food supply. Researchers are studying the Wood Buffalo/Aransas whoopers' biology, life cycle, diet, and habitat in the hopes of finding ways to protect this fragile flock from another long slide—or sudden drop—to the edge of extinction.

The Wood Buffalo/Aransas population of whoopers is growing, but slowly. According to the Canadian Wildlife Service, in an average year, only 45 percent of nesting pairs at Wood Buffalo raise a chick to fledge. In the winter of 2006-07, the Wood Buffalo/Aransas population numbered 237 whooping cranes, including 45 chicks; both numbers were record highs. That winter, there were 353 whoopers in the wild and 145 birds in captivity, for total world population of 498 whooping cranes.[13]

LACK OF GENETIC DIVERSITY IS A MAJOR CONCERN of the conservationists working to save the whooping crane. According to Tom Stehn, the species lost two thirds of its genetic material when it went through the population bottleneck—when only 15 birds were present at Aransas in 1941. Two or more separate populations might eventually diverge through "genetic drift," the small genetic mutations and recombinations that occur naturally in any species. A single population can be genetically sound but only if it contains at least 5,000 to 7,000 individuals. Fewer than that, geneticists say, and the population loses genetic material with each generation.

A single population is also vulnerable to natural and manmade disasters. With separate populations, physically and geographically isolated from each other, a disease or environmental disaster that ripped through one population wouldn't jeopardize the entire species.

At present, the Aransas-Wood Buffalo population is the only "truly wild" population of whoopers in the world. Yet, the Whooping Crane Eastern Partnership (WCEP)—a coalition of federal, state, and private conservation interests—has established a new non-migratory flock at Florida's Kissimmee Prairie, through releases of captive-raised chicks. And WCEP is building a new free-flying, migrating eastern population of whoopers that nests in Wisconsin—mainly in the Necedah National Wildlife Refuge—and winters in Florida and other southeastern states. Each year between 2001 and 2006, and 2006, the newest members of the eastern population of whoopers have been hatched and raised in controlled conditions, and led by ultralight aircraft on their first southward migration. Most of those first-generation whoopers have returned on their own to Wisconsin, and in succeeding years, have migrated on their own to

---

[13] 2006-07 population figures provided by USFWS Whooping Crane Coordinator Tom Stehn.

Florida and back.

The oldest birds in those two flocks are now producing new young whoopers; two wild chicks were hatched at Necedah NWR in the spring of 2006. At Kissimmee Prairie, eight wild chicks have hatched and fledged. This second generation has been hatched and raised entirely in the wild. They will learn the ins and outs of whooperhood from their wild whooper parents, relying in part on the wild instincts inherited from their western ancestors. Like the western population of whoopers, the new flocks will be observed, studied, managed, protected, and fretted over by humans for years to come. And though the eastern population owes its existence to humans, the eastern whoopers are within a historic whooping crane range, living in freedom and in wild ways.

Chapter 12
Shall We Dance?

"TEX" WAS NOT YOUR AVERAGE, garden variety whooping crane. She looked and sounded like a typical whooping crane, but she suffered from a serious and permanent identity crisis: she thought she was a human being. Or maybe it was that she thought human beings were whoopers. Either way, she was one befuddled bird.

Tex was hatched at the San Antonio (Texas) Zoo in 1967, the daughter of a pair of whoopers named Crip and Rosie. Crip was famous among crane aficionados. Hatched in the wild, and captured with an injured wing at Aransas in 1949, Crip was placed at New Orleans' Audubon Zoo. Over 30 years, at various captive sites, he sired 17 chicks in captivity.

Crip's first mate at the Audubon Zoo was "Josephine"—celebrity among cranes in her own right. She too was born wild, in the small non-migrating flock of whoopers that was discovered living in the Louisiana coastal marshes in the late 1930s. That flock was cut in half to just six cranes after a hurricane hit the coast in 1940. Josephine was captured a year later because of an injury, and brought to Audubon Park Zoo, where she and Crip enjoyed a fruitful 15-year romance that produced eight chicks. By 1951, Josephine was the only living bird from of the Louisiana flock. She died in 1965 after a helicopter flew too low over the whoopers' enclosure. Panicked by the noise and the sight of that whirling, roaring "beast," she was fatally injured while trying to escape from the commotion.

Crip was lent to the San Antonio Zoo after Josephine's death. There he mated with Rosie and sired more chicks, including Tex.

Rosie and Crip successfully incubated and hatched Tex, but the chick had health problems. She was whisked away from her parents to be raised in more protected surroundings. Thus Tex spent her first couple of months growing up in the living room of the zoo's superintendent, Fred Stark. By the time she was returned to the zoo's whooper enclosure at about two months of age, she was more than a little confused.

DOUGLAS ALEXANDER SPAULDING DISCOVERED the phenomenon that we now know as "imprinting." Born in London around 1840, he began his working life as a laborer but talked his way into the University of Aberdeen in Scotland, where he studied philosophy and literature. Through a circuitous chain of events, Spaulding was appointed as tutor to the young Bertrand Russell, who later made his fame as a philosopher. Between lessons, Spaulding carried out groundbreaking explorations into animal behavior. Historians of psychology consider Spaulding the true father of ethology—the study of animal behavior—for both his methods and his discoveries. He was the first to recognize that learning and instinct interacted to determine behavior, and the first to describe the concept of imprinting. (Imprinting was "rediscovered" and popularized in the 20th century by the Austrian ethologist and Nobel laureate Konrad Lorenz.)

Spaulding discovered that when goose hatchlings were denied any contact with other geese, they quickly and easily accepted other creatures, including humans, as their rightful parents.

But imprinting goes beyond answering the question, "Who's my mama?" A very young gosling, imprinted on a chicken, will think it is a chicken—but not exactly. It will think its chicken foster parent is a goose, but not exactly. It will bond with the chicken's flock and it will learn some distinctly chicken-like behaviors from its surrogate parent. Yet it will also retain its goose instincts. When it comes time to pair off and mate,

George and Tex.

Photo, © *International Crane Foundation, Baraboo, WI.*

168

our chicken-imprinted gosling will seek its mate among the chickens, showing no interest in other geese. Its courting behaviors remain distinctly goose-like, but the chicken-imprinted goose will aim its courtship in the wrong direction—toward chickens—and will not respond to courtship displays from other geese, even though those displays are identical to its own courtship behavior.

When whooping crane eggs were placed in wild sandhill crane nests in the 1970s, the experiment failed to create a new, productive wild population of whoopers. Imprinting was a key factor in that failure. Each of the young whoopers imprinted on its sandhill foster parents. When the foster-raised whoopers reached sexual maturity, a few of the males tried to pair off with young sandhill cranes, showing no interest in the other whoopers in the flock. As for the young sandhills, they knew who they were. And it was all well and good to share the playpen with those funny-looking foster-cousins, but pairing off and mating with them was, well—dear me!—out of the question.

TEX WAS A CLASSIC CASE OF MISDIRECTED IMPRINTING. She had spent her crucial "formative" weeks in Fred Stark's living room, interacting with humans. She had imprinted on humans and had no real interest in other cranes.

From the San Antonio Zoo, Tex moved to the Patuxent Wildlife Research Center. Crane researchers hoped that there, among Patuxent's captive flock of cranes, Tex might sort it all out and pair off with another crane. At Patuxent, Tex reached sexual maturity and began making typical whooping crane mating displays—to her human keepers. For ten years, Patuxent biologists tried to get Tex to mate with another whooper. She would have none of it. She mostly ignored the feathered suitors they paired her with, but she would begin a courtship display when a human came near her pen.

The biologists at Patuxent talked it over with Dr. George Archibald at the International Crane Foundation, in Baraboo, Wisconsin, and he offered to take Tex on as a personal project. He hoped that under more controlled conditions at ICF, Tex might be persuaded to pair off with another whooper. If that failed, the staff at Baraboo was prepared to pair her off with George, artificially inseminate her, and hope for an egg.

Breeding cranes in captivity has always been a challenge. Zoos have bred cranes but not very often. At Patuxent, Dr. George Gee developed successful techniques for artificial insemination of cranes in the early 1970s. George Archibald studied the crane management at Patuxent as a graduate student at Cornell University. He and fellow student Ron Sauey would later found the ICF and make captive breeding one of ICF's most important goals.

For ICF, successful captive breeding and hatching sometimes required simulating the climate of a crane's wild nesting range at Baraboo. For Brolgas, a crane species nesting in northern Australia during the monsoon season, that meant watering the birds twice a day with "rain" from garden hoses. For hooded and Siberian cranes, that nest in the far north of Siberia, it meant artificial lights to simulate the long arctic days.

Crane eggs do best if they spend at least half their incubation period under live birds. Sandhill cranes proved to be excellent foster parents for that purpose. About halfway through the 30-day incubation period, the eggs are moved to the artificial incubator, where ICF staff simulate as closely as possible the care and conditions in the nest, from turning the eggs every few hours to cooling the eggs twice a day—to mimic the handoff when one parent leaves the nest to feed and the other parent settles onto the nest.

Through careful study and observation, creativity, and much trial and error, ICF successfully bred 13 of the world's 15 species of crane during its first ten years of operation (1973-83).

Tex arrived in Baraboo from Patuxent in the spring of 1976, the first whooping crane to reside at ICF's headquarters and research facility. Two weeks later, she was joined at Baraboo by Tony,[14] a whooping crane on loan from Audubon Park Zoo. At the time, Tony and Tex were two of only three surviving whoopers who were produced from captive parents, and two of only 84 whooping cranes in existence. They shared the same illustrious father—Crip. Tony's mother was Josephine, the last member of the extinct Louisiana flock of whoopers. An article in the Spring 1976 issue of ICF's newsletter, the Brolga Bugle, described Tony as a living relic, "[l]ike Martha, the last passenger pigeon, who lingered on at the Cincinnati Zoo long after the rest of her kind had disappeared for ever." But through his

---

[14] As already noted, cranes are famously difficult to sex. When Tony hatched, the staff at Audubon Park named the chick "Georgette," after former zoo director George Douglass. Georgette soon had a brother named "George." When it was discovered that Georgette was a male, he was rechristened "George II," alias, "Tony." Perhaps his androgynous nickname was a hedge by the zoo staff against future surprises.

father, Crip, Tony also carried the genes of the Wood Buffalo/Aransas flock—the world's last remaining wild whoopers. Said the Brolga Bugle:

> "Tony embodies, therefore, not only the final over-whelming tragedy of extinction, but also a continu-ing hope that the tall majestic whooper will not fol-low Martha and her kind to oblivion."

The mood at ICF that spring was definitely hopeful. Although Tony had so far been a bachelor, he appeared to be in excellent health. He and Tex were placed in adjacent pens that allowed them to get acquainted without any risk of fights or feather pulling. (Though not as fierce as Siberian cranes, whoopers are jealously ter-ritorial and can be extremely aggressive toward each other.) ICF staff reported that both birds were responding well to their new surround-ings and that they were occasionally dancing and calling together. These were not full blown mating behaviors—being more on the order of "flirting"—and there was little chance that Tex would actu-ally accept Tony as her mate, given her history. But the dancing and unison calling were positive signs. They should have triggered hor-monal changes in both the birds that are necessary for production of eggs and semen.

But it soon became obvious that Tex wasn't really interested in Tony. She was far more interested in her human keepers. In the early summer of 1976, ICF Director and "Head of Propa-gation" George Archibald moved into Tex's pen. Behind a chicken wire divider, George set up his office in the enclosure, with a desk and an old manual type-writer. "During those first eventful weeks together," George wrote in the ICF Bugle,[15] "I learned to wake to an unusual alarm clock—Tex blasting 110-decibel calls beside my bed at dawn's first light." When Tex wanted to dance, George danced, waving his arms, jumping up and down, and throwing sticks in the air. George spent most of the spring and summer of 1976 in the pen with Tex, and the two became solidly bonded.

In the spring of 1977, George returned to Tex's pen for several weeks, spending every day with her, from dawn until dark, seven days a week. They danced and when the time was right, Tex was arti-ficially inseminated with semen from one of Patuxent's whoopers. At

---

[15] Vol. 8, No. 3: July 1982

age ten, Tex laid her first egg. It was infertile.

The next spring, 1978, George moved in with Tex again. Again they danced and again she was artificially inseminated. This time the egg was fertile, but the embryo died just before it was due to hatch. In 1979, she laid a third egg, but it was soft-shelled and it cracked. Hopes of continuing Tex's genetic line were crumbling. Her parents, Rosie and Crip, were both dead and she had no living siblings.

If Tex produced no offspring, an important genetic line and a source of genetic diversity would be lost to the world's remaining whoopers.

Mike Putnam, ICF's Curator of Birds picked up the story. In the spring of 1980, George was working in China. Yoshimitsu Shigata, a Japanese ornithologist, had asked to fill in for him, bonding and dancing with Tex. But Tex didn't fancy Shigata and she laid no eggs that spring.

"She was a peculiar bird," Putnam said. "It turned out that she hated women and oriental or red-haired men. If you were sort of medium height to tall and had darkish hair, that was okay; that was what she liked in men." After Tex rejected her Japanese suitor, another ornithologist tried to take up with her. "He was about my height and had a beard like me," Putnam explained, "but he had red hair and Tex didn't want anything to do with him. George and I looked enough alike in height and build and hair color that she liked us both."

Putnam began dancing with Tex in the spring of 1981. His full-time duties at ICF didn't allow him to spend as much time with Tex as George had:

> "About three times a day I'd go down to her pen and dance with her and try to be a mate to her, and I did that seven days a week for two months, then scaled back to six days a week because I was kind of burning out. When I showed up at her pen, Tex would dance right away and make pre-copulatory calls, and she seemed like she was ready. But she never really got all the way there. I just didn't have enough time in the day to spend with her."

Tex laid no eggs in 1981. It was not a good year for whooper production. The captive flock at Patuxent yielded only one chick that spring; there were no chicks hatched by the sandhill crane foster parents in Idaho; and only two wild whooper chicks arrived at Aransas with the fall migration. With the loss of several adult and sub-adult birds over the summer,[16] the total number of whoopers counted in December 1981 was 109—eleven fewer than a year before.

George returned from China, and in the spring of 1982 he and the biologists at Patuxent agreed that it was time for an all-out effort to get Tex to reproduce. George thought that getting Tex out of her pen into a wider nesting territory might help, so the two of them moved to a 10-acre hayfield not far from the ICF crane compound. The staff built George a little

George Archibald and Tex "at home" in their hayfield.
Photo, © International Crane Foundation, Baraboo, WI.

shack on the hill, just big enough for a bed and a desk. The hayfield was their "nesting" territory and Tex defended it fiercely—in her own mixed-up way. When wild sandhill cranes landed in the field, she ignored them. If a human other than George entered the territory, she would do her best to drive the intruder away. George danced with her every morning and evening, and spent a lot of time just being with her, doing the things that a male crane would do—hunting for earthworms, gathering material for a nest, and helping her defend their hayfield.

In mid-April, after nearly a month of George's constant companionship, Tex seemed ready for artificial insemination. Frozen semen from male whoopers at Patuxent was stored at ICF but it was found that half the semen cells were dead. Fresh semen was collected at Patuxent and put on a commercial flight from Baltimore, MD to Madison, WI. An ICF aviculturist picked up the sample at the airport, brought it the last 45 miles to Baraboo, put it in a syringe and used it to inseminate Tex. This cross-country relay race was repeated

---

[16] Coyotes claimed several birds in Idaho; others died in collisions with power lines and barbed wire fences. In Wood Buffalo National Park, fires and drought made nesting difficult in 1980 and 1981.

every two to three days for two weeks, through the end of April. On May 1, Tex showed signs that she was producing an egg; she was lethargic and showed little interest in food. George stayed close to her, as a male crane would have done.

On May 3, 1982, she laid a fertile egg. It was whisked away and replaced with a fake sandhill egg. Her real egg was given to an experienced sandhill crane foster parent and tended with the utmost care.

At ICF, incubating eggs are weighed as part of a daily check on growth and health. Mike Putnam explained that a normal crane egg will lose about 15 percent of its weight (mostly in water) during its roughly 30 days of incubation. Tex's egg was losing water at twice that rate. After two and a half weeks, concerned ICF biologists took the egg from its sandhill foster parents and placed it in a high-humidity incubator. That didn't help.

"So we called Bernie Wentworth, a professor of poultry science at the University of Wisconsin, Madison," Putnam said, "and we asked him 'what should we do?' And he said, 'I'm coming up.'" Putnam continued:

> "He showed up with this vat of cold liquid. It's a technique the poultry industry uses to introduce antibiotics into eggs to prevent infection. You take an egg—a hot egg from an incubator—and you plunge it into cold water. The contents of the egg contract and since the shell is porous, the contraction draws water into the egg. So every day we'd take the egg out of the incubator and dunk it in cold [50° F./10° C.], sterile water, and the egg would jiggle around a little bit as the embryo moved around. Then we'd put it back into the incubator. In that way, we were able to stabilize the egg's weight loss and, in fact, it actually gained a little bit of weight before it hatched."

Tex's egg hatched on June 1, 1982. The healthy, robust chick was named "Gee Whiz" in honor of Dr. George Gee of the Patuxent Research Center.

The story of Gee Whiz and of Tex and George's seven-year "romance" captured worldwide attention. Photos of George dancing with Tex were published and broadcast all over the world. "The man who dances with cranes" even showed up in a political cartoon in a prominent US newspaper.

After Gee Whiz was hatched, George was invited to appear on Johnny Carson's "The Tonight Show." He was concerned about that appearance, scheduled for late June, fearing that Carson might focus on the humorous side of the story and might try to make George look foolish. But George knew that the show offered a tremendous opportunity to spread the word about ICF and its work to a nationwide audience.

On the day of the broadcast, George was in his Los Angeles hotel room, thinking about the show, reading his Bible, and marshalling his mental and emotional strength, when the phone rang. It was ICF calling with the news that a tragedy had struck the crane compound. Deeply saddened, George prepared for the show.

That evening, his concerns about being made to play the fool went unrealized. Carson appeared to be fascinated by the story of Tex. "Doc Severson, Johnny Carson, and Ed McMahon, could not have been kinder," George recalled. "I had a wonderful time with them." Near the end of the interview, Carson asked gently, "George, shall we tell the audience the sad news?" Solemnly, George revealed that Tex was dead—killed by a raccoon raiding the crane enclosures the night before.

ON THE MORNING OF APRIL 22, 1982—just hours before George Archibald appeared on The Tonight Show, ICF aviculturist Lisa Hartman went to Tex's pen to check on the bird. Hartman found a large female raccoon guarding Tex's partially eaten remains. The raccoon had torn a hole in the nylon netting over the crane's pen, and killed Tex sometime during the night. It was the first killing of a crane by a raccoon in the ten years of ICF's existence. A county sheriff's deputy destroyed the raccoon and the staff assumed that the attack was an isolated incident. Sauk County Sheriff Alan Shanks thought otherwise. He told the ICF staff, "They'll be back tonight."

As a precaution, five ICF staff members camped near the main crane pens, spending a quiet, uneventful night. But the next morning, another crane was found killed and partially eaten, in a pen not far from Tex's pen. ICF was swamped with telephone calls from members expressing condolences, and from news reporters looking for details, while the staff desperately sought measures to protect the remaining cranes.

At the suggestion of the Wisconsin DNR, electric wire was strung around the main breeding pens at the east end of ICF's property, where the attacks had occurred. Live-catch traps were set around the breeding center and along the property's eastern border. Cranes that had indoor shelters were locked inside at sunset. That night, a militia of staff members and volunteers patrolled the breeding unit in shifts.

George Archibald arrived back from Los Angeles around midnight and joined the "guards" near the breeding unit. They were chatting about George's appearance on national television when they heard the chilling and unmistakable sound of crane alarm calls coming from the far end of the ICF property. They raced toward the sound—George scaled a nine-foot chain link fence along the way—to find another crane dying, its throat torn open.

Three cranes killed by raccoons in three nights—the situation was devastating and desperate. The pens could be raccoon-proofed but it would take time—days or weeks—to complete the job. In the meantime, there weren't enough staff and volunteers to keep all the cranes safe at night. Dennis Jameson, the local DNR warden, suggested that ICF go on the offensive against the raccoons. He knew a local raccoon hunter who could help. Jameson helped push through the necessary hunting permits that same day. That night three hunters and two Red-Boned Hounds went raccoon hunting at ICF. Over the next few weeks, they would destroy several raccoons. The cranes remained safe while ICF staff and volunteers worked on making all the pens on the property predator-proof.

After George's Tonight Show appearance, the press picked up the story of Tex's death and followed it with high interest. Archibald and Sauey were forthright in discussing the raccoon hunts, and not everyone was pleased at the news. ICF was criticized—in angry letters and in the media—for facilitating the hunting of one wild species while championing the preservation of another. Sauey called the decision to hunt the raccoons, "inescapable." In the July 1982 issue of the ICF Bugle, he wrote:

> "Our responsibility to the rare and endangered birds in our custody was our primary consideration. . . To further jeopardize the lives of our cranes, some so rare that the entire world's population would fit into one of our 60' x 60' pens, in an attempt to avoid killing a few members of a widespread and abun-

dant species seemed illogical and an abrogation of
the stated purposes of ICF. Moreover, raccoon hunting is a temporary expedient, and we are confident
that we can have raccoons and captive cranes living
in harmony again once we complete our plans to
predator-proof the enclosures."

The raccoon hunts ended in mid-summer of 1982, as work was
completed on the pens. Once all the electrified fences were up and
running, the hunts were no longer necessary. The new fencing extended several inches below ground level, to prevent unwanted guests
from burrowing in. Electric and non-electric barriers were carefully
engineered to thwart a variety of predators native to the area.

Gee Whiz fledged in early September 1982. Tex's celebrated offspring lives on at ICF in Baraboo. Now almost 25 years old, Gee
Whiz has sired at least 14 whooping crane chicks and has at least one
grandchild. Several of his progeny have been released into the wild.
Others have gone to breeding programs at Calgary and New Orleans.

In 1981, it had seemed as though the growth of the world's
whooper population was stalled, even sliding backwards. Perhaps the
arrival of Gee Whiz in 1982 signaled good luck. In the following year,
1983, the whooper population rebounded. In Idaho, 28 whooper
eggs were placed in wild sandhill crane nests; 26 hatched and a
record 19 chicks fledged. At Patuxent, five breeding pairs of whoopers produced 31 fertile eggs (about half were sent to Idaho) and the
center increased its captive flock from 25 to 35 birds. In Canada,
biologists counted a record 24 nesting pairs at Wood Buffalo
National Park; the previous record was 19. That fall, 12 chicks were
banded at Wood Buffalo and seven of them completed the migration
to Aransas NWR in Texas. In November 1983, ICF estimated the
world population of whoopers at 149, up from 109 two years earlier.
It certainly looked like a "Gee Whiz!" year.

Chapter 13
New Flocks, New Hopes

BY 1989, THERE WAS GROWING OPTIMISM for the future of wild whooping cranes. Since the winter of 1982-83, the Wood Buffalo/Aransas flock had doubled in size to 146 cranes, after six good breeding years in a row. Crane specialists at ICF in Baraboo, Wisconsin and the USFWS Patuxent Wildlife Research Center in Maryland had learned much about captive breeding, hatching, and rearing of cranes, in part through experimental work with sandhill cranes. Since 1964, the Canadian Wildlife Service (CWS) and the US Fish & Wildlife Service (USFWS) had been working closely together to create a captive breeding program for whooping cranes at Patuxent. Most of the eggs for that program came from wild whooper nests in Canada's Wood Buffalo National Park.

Crane biologists at Patuxent established the first long-term captive breeding program for cranes in North America, and they were the first to work toward reintroduction of captive-bred cranes into the wild. They pioneered successful techniques for caring for captive cranes and encouraging captive cranes to breed. By modifying poultry diets, they created several varieties of pelletized "crane chow" to provide good nutrition for the birds from hatching to old age. To protect the cranes from diseases, they determined safe dosages of drugs and developed new vaccines.

Patuxent's staff learned new ways of managing the birds' behavior, to encourage pair bonding and breeding. Dr. Gee pioneered artificial insemination of cranes and cryogenic storage of crane semen. By 1989, Patuxent researchers had begun developing the techniques that would allow captive-raised whoopers to be released into the wild, to bolster existing wild flocks and create new ones.

With 44 whooping cranes in 1989, Patuxent was the headquarters for captive breeding of whoopers. ICF had one whooper—Gee Whiz—in Wisconsin, and a few zoos had single male whoopers, whose semen could be used for artificial insemination. Officials at the USFWS and CWS were more than pleased with the success of their captive breeding program, but they began to worry that they might have too many of their eggs—and whooping cranes—in one basket at Patuxent.

There was good reason to worry. An outbreak of equine encephalitis had hit the center just a few years earlier. Carried by mosquitoes, that virus took the lives of seven of Patuxent's whooping cranes. At Baraboo in the late 1970s, ICF suddenly lost 22 of its captive cranes to a previously unknown strain of the herpes virus. In the wild and in captivity, cranes are susceptible to a whole menu of bacterial and viral diseases. They can also be threatened by severe weather and other natural and manmade disasters. With nearly all of its captive whoopers in one location, the joint US-Canadian effort faced the possibility that a disease or other disaster could devastate the breeding program and the species. US and Canadian officials decided to split the flock. In August 1989, they announced that half of Patuxent's captive flock—22 whoopers—would be transferred to the ICF in Baraboo, Wisconsin.

Patuxent biologists and staff met with their ICF counterparts at Baraboo to lay the groundwork for the transfer. The main topic of discussion was deciding which birds would move to Wisconsin and which would stay in Maryland.

Each bird was carefully profiled. One of the principal goals of the transfer was to ensure that whatever genetic diversity currently remained in the species would be preserved at both sites. Genetic diversity is already low among whoopers. All of the world's whooping cranes are descended from fewer than 20 individuals that survived in the wild and in captivity in the 1940s. The biologists wanted all of those genetic lines to be represented at each breeding center.

Other goals were to ensure that each center had roughly an equal number of successful and promising breeding pairs, that each center would have a roughly equal number of birds of the same ages, and that birds with behavioral problems would be divided equally between the centers.

Before 1989, ICF's focus had been on the captive management and breeding of endangered Asian and African crane species. Its new

Baraboo headquarters, opened in 1983, included two public areas—the Johnson Exhibit Pod and the Crowned Crane Exhibit—and a 12-acre complex of pens called "Crane City." There, 17 pens (12 of them newly constructed) were reserved for the whoopers coming from Patuxent. To manage the incoming flock, ICF also added a half-time veterinarian, a full-time veterinary assistant, and a full-time aviculturist to its staff. The National Fish & Wildlife Foundation and the USFWS provided some of the funding for the new facilities and employees. In a 1989 issue of the ICF "Bugle" newsletter, George Archibald wrote: "It was decided that, for the whoopers, ICF's focus would be on breeding, while Patuxent's focus would be on research and captive propagation for future releases." That division of labor has blurred somewhat since then. Patuxent remains the primary center for research into the management, biology, breeding, and reintroduction of whooping cranes. ICF also sponsors research and educational activities focused on the whoopers. Both centers continue to produce captive-bred cranes for release into new wild flocks.

A public ceremony at ICF on September 16, 1989 honored the whooping cranes and celebrated the completion of their new "residential street" in Crane City, where the thoroughfares bear such names as "Sibe Street" and "Brolga Boulevard." The festivities ended with the raising of a new street sign for "Whooper Way."

The whooping cranes were flown from Patuxent to Baraboo aboard a US Marine Corps Reserve C-130 cargo plane. The first group of 8 birds arrived on November 8, 1989. A month later, the third and last shipment was greeted at the Baraboo airport on December 7 by more than 400 middle-schoolers from Baraboo. An article in the ICF Bugle described the scene:[17]

> "The eager kids worked hard to control their energy, because they didn't want to disturb the cranes. Filing out into the frigid air, after a presentation in the hangar, the children lined up on either side of an aisle leading from the tail of the airplane. They held banners and signs with messages like, 'Back from the Brink,' and, 'Whoopee! The Whoopers Are Here!' When all was ready and the kids were quiet, a [Marine Reserve] color guard marched forward, fol-

---

[17] ICF Bugle, Vol. 16:1, Feb 1990, p 8

lowed by the first crate. As the color guard stood at attention, the children came up to greet the crane chicks and bestow gifts of fish and cranberries."

THE FOLLOWING SPRING, ICF STAFF PLAYED MATCHMAKER to several new pairs of cranes. ICF's own Gee Whiz was paired with "Faith," a five-year-old female from Patuxent. Another Patuxent female, "Ginger," was paired with "Napoleon," who had been raised by sandhill crane foster parents at Grays Lake, Idaho, before being captured and brought back to ICF. In all, there were seven pairs of whoopers at Baraboo that spring. Gee Whiz and Faith seemed most likely to bond and produce eggs that season.

Earlier that year, while crane biologists were working out the details of splitting Patuxent's flock, the Canadian Wildlife Service (CWS) put out a call to Canadian zoos and other facilities that might be capable of managing a captive whooper breeding program. Canada is the summer home for the Wood Buffalo/Aransas whoopers, and there was strong support for establishing a captive breeding program somewhere in Canada. The Calgary Zoo, in Calgary, Alberta, was chosen as the site, and it remains the only captive breeding facility for whoopers in Canada.

Calgary's whooping crane breeding program is located at the Devonian Wildlife Conservation Centre, a 320-acre complex five miles outside the city and away from the zoo's public exhibits. In addition to whooping cranes, the centre also breeds rare Mongolian wild horses and Canada's most endangered mammal, the Vancouver Island marmot. Biologists at the center also conduct conservation research on burrowing owls, leopard frogs, and other animals.

The Calgary Zoo received its first two whooping cranes from Baraboo in 1992 and began building a small captive flock over the next few years. Zookeeper and Whooping Crane Flock Manager Dwight Knapik explained that, in the beginning, "We were hoping and trying to get as many pairs as we could breeding naturally. Unfortunately, we really only had one successful pair that has produced most of our chicks over a number of years.'

In 2003, a crane biologist from the Audubon Zoo in New Orleans, Louisiana visited the Calgary Zoo to instruct the zoo staff in artificial insemination techniques. Knapik and a colleague also spent some time at Patuxent, learning the techniques from the crane experts there.

"With the training, with the birds getting used to the technique, and with us getting used to the technique," Knapik said, "we had our first success in the spring of 2005, with a couple of chicks from eggs fertilized through artificial insemination, and then four more birds in 2006."

"It's been a long, slow process and we're still working on some birds who haven't responded to the techniques." But, he added, artificial insemination has been helpful. Knapik said whooping cranes are the most difficult species of crane to breed, though no one knows exactly why. "One of the reasons might be loss of genetic diversity," he said. "When the whoopers went through a population bottleneck in the middle of the last century, and they were down to 21 birds, they lost a lot of genetic diversity."

For the past 40 years, the captive breeding facilities have been trying to retain as much genetic diversity as possible. And so far, the most effective way to do that is through artificial insemination, using genetic contributions from as many individual whoopers and as many genetic lines as possible, Knapik said. Across the whole population of whoopers, he added: "We believe that we have right now, more and better genetic diversity in the captive flock than there is in the wild flock."

IN MAY 1989, TERRY KOHLER received a call from George Archibald. The Kohlers' Windway Foundation, which Mary Kohler managed, had been contributing to ICF for several years. In April 1989, Terry had agreed to fly Sumner Matteson of the Wisconsin DNR to Alaska in the Kohlers' Cessna Citation jet, to collect trumpeter swan eggs. That flight, the first of eight annual trips, was scheduled for early June 1989.

George and Sumner were friends and colleagues, and Sumner had told George about his upcoming trip with the Kohlers. George was calling Terry to ask a favor: Would it be possible for the Kohlers to fly up to Fort Smith, Northwest Territories (the nearest airport to Wood Buffalo National Park) in early 1990, to help the ICF and the USFWS retrieve whooping crane eggs for the captive breeding programs at Baraboo and Patuxent? Once again, Terry's characteristic reply was, "When do we leave?"

Early on May 28—Memorial Day—1990, the Kohlers' Citation jet departed Chetek, Wisconsin, bound for Fort Smith. Tom Mahan, an ICF aviculturist was onboard, with special suitcases for transporting the eggs. Terry and Mary Kohler were pilot and copilot. They cleared customs and refueled in Brandon, Manitoba, before arriving at Fort Smith at noon, local time. Terry later wrote:

> "It is worth noting that although Whoopers are really quite dumb, and they certainly have lousy migration habits, such as waiting too late in the season and traveling in groups of two to perhaps five, instead of huge flocks as the Sandhills do, they sure are beautiful, and they sure pick beautiful places to breed. The Fort Smith area, and Wood Buffalo Park in particular, are incredibly wild, attractive, and haunting in their appearance."[18]

Ernie Kuyt, a Canadian Wildlife Service (CWS) biologist, and Jim Lewis, USFWS Whooping Crane Coordinator, were waiting at the Fort Smith airport. With them were a dozen whooping crane eggs, collected the day before from wild nests in Wood Buffalo National Park. Traveling by CWS helicopter, Kuyt, Lewis, and two other crane experts—Rod Drewien, University of Idaho, and CWS biologist, Brian Johns—had visited 12 nests and collected the eggs, leaving at least one viable egg in each nest. The gathered eggs had been flown back to Fort Smith and placed in an incubator to await the Kohlers' arrival.

At the airport, Kuyt and Drewien carefully moved the eggs from the incubator to the suitcases Mahan had brought from Baraboo. Each suitcase contained foam cradles for the eggs, a thermometer, and an all-important hot water bottle. (The Vollrath egg carrier was designed and built after the 1990 trumpeter swan egg trip. It was first used for trumpeter and whooper eggs in 1991.)

During the trip back to Wisconsin, the eggs had be kept between 99.0° and 99.5° F. (37.2° to 37.5° C.). A drop to a few degrees below 99.0° for a short period of time would not harm the eggs. But a rise of just one degree could be fatal to the embryos. Jim Lewis joined the flight back to Wisconsin and he and Mahan had their work cut out for them, monitoring temperatures and tending the eggs. The airplane's onboard coffee dispenser provided hot water to replenish the water bottles, about once an hour. Adding water was a delicate task because the temperatures inside the suitcases could spike rapidly.

---

[18] Terry Kohler's personal notes, unpublished.

Mahan and Lewis spent most of the five-hour flight staring at the thermometers—replenishing the hot water bottles when temperatures dropped, and cracking the lids of the egg cases when temperatures rose too high. With a half-hour stop for fuel and customs in Minot, North Dakota, the Citation touched down at Baraboo just after seven p.m. The 12 eggs were quickly transferred to incubators at ICF.

The next day, during a routine egg check, Mahan placed the eggs on a table and made crane-like "purring" sounds to them. Five of the eggs moved around as the embryos inside responded to Mahan's purring. Peeping sounds came from two of them. Those two were moved to the hatchery and hatched the following day, May 30, 1990. They were the first whooping cranes to hatch at ICF since Gee Whiz made his entrance eight years earlier.

One of the 12 whooper eggs was infertile. The others hatched successfully. That fall, eight of the chicks fledged at ICF. The Kohlers would make eight more annual trips to Fort Smith at their own expense, retrieving whooper eggs for the captive breeding programs at Baraboo and Patuxent.

As a species, the whoopers retained very limited genetic diversity, but new eggs from the Wood Buffalo flock helped to maintain that diversity within the world's most endangered species of crane.

No whooper eggs were collected from Wood Buffalo after 1996. Since then, Dwight Knapik explained, the captive breeding programs at Patuxent, Baraboo, and Calgary have been producing enough eggs to meet everyone's needs. In the future, more eggs might be collected from Canada's wild nests, to help ensure the greatest possible genetic diversity in the captive flocks. Biologists might gather eggs from specific wild pairs whose genetic legacy is not well represented in the captive population.

As the Whooping Crane Recovery Team held its more-or-less-annual meeting in July 1990, there was good and bad news for the whoopers. The 22 birds transferred to ICF from Patuxent the previous winter had not produced any eggs, and only three new chicks had fledged from the flock remaining at Patuxent. Of the 11 fertile eggs brought to ICF from Wood Buffalo, eight fledged. At Aransas, the flock that arrived in the fall of 1989 included 20 new chicks, and 141 cranes had migrated north in the spring of 1990. The total number of whooping cranes in the wild and captivity had increased to 235.

There were 32 nests at Wood Buffalo in 1990, where the cranes were expanding their nesting range southward into new, unoccupied territories. But Canadian biologists reported that the nesting wetlands were drying out, possibly entering a period of drought. In the past when water levels had declined at the nesting grounds, the birds' reproductive success also had declined.

In Wyoming, power lines were being marked with bright yellow balls, reducing the number of collisions between cranes and power lines. In Idaho, the Grays Lake whoopers had produced no eggs and no nesting pairs.

In Florida, biologists were evaluating possible sites for creating a new non-migratory wild flock of whooping cranes. The USFWS and the Florida Game & Freshwater Fish Commission hoped to begin releasing captive-raised birds in 1992.

In Texas in the spring of 1990, there were three oil spills in the Intracoastal Waterway, which runs through Aransas National Wildlife Refuge. Though they did not harm the refuge, those spills were a pointed reminder that the world's last surviving flock of wild whooping cranes was all too vulnerable. The members of the Whooping Crane Recovery Team left their 1990 meeting with a heightened sense of urgency to establish more wild flocks as a hedge against disaster.

PLANNING FOR A NEW EASTERN FLOCK OF WHOOPERS was underway as early as 1980. The idea was to recreate a non-migratory flock like the one that existed in Louisiana until the late 1940s. Migration multiplies the hazards, especially for the younger cranes. Migratory flocks also tend to winter over larger ranges; for birds in a small, reintroduced flock, that would make it harder to find mates. For the next attempt at creating a new flock, non-migratory made the most sense.

Was migration instinctive or learned behavior for cranes? By 1980 all of the world's existing whoopers were either captive or living in wild migratory flocks. No one knew whether or not a non-migratory flock could be created with chicks from migratory parents. To try to find the answer, biologists from the Florida Game & Freshwater Fish Commission placed 34 sandhill crane eggs into the nests of wild non-migratory Florida sandhill cranes. Half of the eggs in the study came from captive sandhills at Patuxent; the other half came from the nests of wild migratory sandhill cranes in Wisconsin and Idaho. The cross-fostered chicks were caught and fitted with radio collars at about two months of age, just before they fledged.

Then they were tracked for at least two migration seasons.

Chicks raised in captivity also were introduced into the non-migratory flock using a technique called "soft-release." In captivity, those chicks were raised in isolation from humans, taught to find food by crane-suited keepers wielding crane puppets. They too wore radio collars for tracking. At the release site, these birds were held in a large fenced-in area and allowed to acclimate to their new surroundings. After three to four weeks they were allowed to come and go from the pen. Food and water were provided in the pen as long the birds kept coming back. Gradually, they spent more and more time away from the pen, and eventually they stopped returning altogether.

In the Florida experiments, sandhill chicks hatched by non-migratory foster parents and chicks introduced into the non-migratory flock did not migrate. They stayed in the release area and within the local range of the non-migratory Florida sandhill cranes. Biologists concluded that whooping cranes, raised in captivity and soft-released into the wild, would also remain non-migratory—despite their migratory forebears.

Finding the right release site was critical if a new flock of whoopers was to succeed. While one group of biologists was studying the migratory/non-migratory issue, another was evaluating sites for the new flock. Leading candidates included Michigan's Upper Peninsula (for a migratory flock), Georgia's Okefenokee Swamp, and several sites in Florida. Early in the 20th Century, there was a migratory population of whoopers that nested around the Great Lakes and wintered on the Atlantic coast in the southeastern U.S. The last of that population was shot in Florida in the late 1920s.

Louisiana was also on the list of possible sites; it was home to a small flock of non-migratory whoopers until 1950. But a large population of snow geese winters in Louisiana, and biologists feared that whooping cranes could be mistaken for snow geese and shot during the state's goose hunting season. In contrast, Florida had no snow geese and allowed no goose hunting. In 1990, the US Fish & Wildlife Service chose the Kissimmee Prairie in central Florida as the most promising site for establishing a new non-migratory flock of whooping cranes.

The Florida Audubon Society's Ordway-Whittell Kissimmee Prairie Sanctuary and adjacent Kissimmee Prairie Preserve State Park protect the largest remaining parcel—50,000 acres (202 km²)—of

Florida's "dry prairie" habitat, an ecosystem that once covered 2.8 million acres (11,330 km2) in the state.

A "dry prairie" isn't really very dry during most of the year. A typical dry prairie ecosystem, the Kissimmee Prairie is a mix of freshwater wetlands and open grasslands. It is very flat with a very shallow water table that keeps the soil very wet for three seasons of the year. In the spring dry season, the soil turns sandy and fires are common. Most of the prairie is covered by saw grass and other grasses, along with saw palmetto, low shrubs, and forbs (non-grass, broadleafed herbs). Near the prairie's wetlands, you will find cabbage palms, live oaks, and southern slash pines. Though the soil is shallow and nutrient-poor, and it alternates between extremes of very dry and very wet, the dry prairie supports an abundance of plant and animal life. With 100 to 200 plant species per acre, this is one of the most diverse plant ecosystems in North America. And it supports a long list of water birds, wading birds, and prairie birds, some of which are found nowhere else in Florida. The Audubon Society's list of local birds includes: the Florida Sandhill Crane, Audubon's Crested Caracara, Burrowing Owl, Florida's Mottled Duck, Florida Grasshopper Sparrow, most of Florida's herons and egrets, White and Glossy Ibis, Wood Storks, Limpkins, Least and American Bitterns, King Rails, Anhingas, and various ducks. While much of Kissimmee Prairie is public lands, it also encompasses several large cattle ranches and farms. Some of the ranches have been in the same families for generations, and many of the landowners have worked to restore native grasses and to rid their lands of invasive species. The Kissimmee Prairie is an excellent habitat for cranes and other birds, in part because so much of it has been kept in, or restored to, a natural condition.

Of special interest to the Whooping Crane Recovery Team, Kissimmee Prairie was (and is) home to a large and successful non-migratory flock of sandhill cranes. Two other flocks of non-migratory sandhill cranes—in Mississippi and in Cuba—were struggling for survival. If the Florida sandhill cranes could thrive at Kissimmee Prairie, the Whooping Crane Recovery Team reasoned, whooping cranes should have a fighting chance there, as well.

THE FIRST GROUP OF 14 WHOOPING CRANE CHICKS was released at Kissimmee Prairie in January 1993. They came from Patuxent and Baraboo, where they had been hatched and raised in isolation from humans. Isolation techniques developed at Baraboo kept the birds from becoming accustomed to humans. The chicks were taught to feed and forage by aviculturists dressed in white "crane suits," with hand/arm puppets shaped like whooping crane heads. Any contact between the chicks and un-costumed humans was accompanied by recorded crane alarm calls.

The chicks were brought to Florida and released at about eight months of age. Terry Kohler and his company pilots flew the birds from Maryland and Wisconsin to Florida. Each bird made the five-hour flight in a specially designed crate that kept it visually isolated from the pilots and crew. Talking was also kept to a minimum during the flights.

From the airport, the chicks' crates were transferred to a pickup truck for the trip to the release site. That leg of the journey took about an hour and a half. The birds were put in the soft-release pen after dark, when they were less likely to be stressed and could be more easily handled. Each bird was fitted with a radio transmitter on a leg band, and each bird's wings were "brailed" (bound) to keep it from flying out of the open-top pen. The wing brail is a simple strap that limits the range of movement of a bird's wing, making flight impossible. The brails used during soft release are made of clear plastic and fastened with rivets. They cause no harm to the bird. During the trip from Maryland or Wisconsin to Florida, the brails help prevent injury while the whoopers are in their crates.

One night in mid-February 1993, after the chicks had spent four and half weeks in the pen, their wing brails were removed, allowing them to fly out of the pen. They seemed reluctant to leave (or unaware that they could leave), and 24 hours later, 12 of the 14 whoopers were still in the pen. It was early March before all 14 had ventured outside the enclosure. For a few weeks after that, some of the birds returned to the pen occasionally for food and water.

Young cranes' movements during the "spring wander" probably set the boundaries of their lifetime ranges. Wandering around during their first two years, they discover where to find food and resting/nesting sites. The newly released whoopers stayed close to the release site until May 1993, when they began wandering farther afield. Biologists who tracked them by radio concluded that the birds' wanderings were not migratory behavior but the normal movements of young non-migratory cranes. So far, everything was going pretty much according to plan and the team began planning for more releases in late 1993 and early 1994.

The Kohlers' company pilots flew the second group of five whoopers to Kissimmee Prairie in November 1993. Based on lessons learned from the first release, things were handled somewhat differently this time. The whoopers were brought to the release pen in small groups of four or five birds. The smaller groups were easier for the biologists to manage, and assimilated more easily into the existing flock of now-wild whoopers. (Still, the new birds were greeted with "mixed enthusiasm,"[19] as they sorted out their places in the flock's pecking order.) Evidence from sandhill crane studies also suggested that cranes tended not to seek mates among the group they were released with; so several smaller groups might produce more mating pairs than one large group. The small groups were released one after the other with intervals of several weeks between groups. That assured a higher number of "experienced" birds to help guide each set of newly released birds in learning the ropes. Between January and March of 1994, Windway pilots flew 14 more whoopers to Kissimmee Prairie. All of those birds were successfully soft-released.

Based on sandhill crane studies, biologists had predicted that 40 to 60 percent of the Kissimmee whoopers would survive their first year after release. Predation was a major threat. Potential predators (known to prey on sandhill cranes) included dogs, alligators, eagles, and raccoons.

Bobcats, especially, presented a serious risk to the cranes and, as one whooper after another began to fall victim to these nocturnal feline hunters, the team cleared brush around the release pen to give the bobcats less cover for stalking, and worked on ways of conditioning the cranes to spend more time in the water, where they would be safer from predators.

The goal of the Florida whooping crane project was to create a stable flock of 100 to 125 birds, with 25 successful nesting pairs, by the year 2020. To meet its goal, the whooping crane recovery plan called for the release of 200 to 250 cranes. The long-term survival rate for the released whoopers was expected to be around 50 percent.

The local bobcats had other expectations.

---

[19] Steve Nesbit, a biologist with the Florida Game & Freshwater Fish Commission, was a member of the Whooping Crane Recovery Team and wrote about the 1993-94 releases in the August 1994 issue "The ICF Bugle."

FELIS RUFUS FLORIDANUS IS ONE OF TWO WILD FELINES native to Florida—the other is the Florida panther (Puma concolor coryi). The male bobcat is about the size of a Border collie, averaging 39 inches (1 m) in length and weighing about 25 pounds (11 kg). Females are smaller, averaging 36 inches (92 cm) long and 15 pounds (7 kg). The cats' short, dense, silky fir is dark brown with black spots. Their legs are striped and their belly fur is usually white. Their large, tufted ears are white with a black outline. Their tails are short, a bit over 5 inches (14 cm).

Florida bobcats live in every county in Florida and nearly every state in the U.S. In Florida, their population is high enough that they are not listed as endangered or threatened, though hunting and trapping of bobcats are controlled. Florida panthers and wolves used to control bobcat numbers, but those predators have all but disappeared from the state. Coyotes occasionally prey on bobcat kittens, but are no match for the adults. Today, the bobcat's most important predator is man—hunters and trappers

As predators themselves, bobcats kill and consume a wide variety of small animals and birds. On average, rabbits and rats make up about 70 percent of a bobcat's diet, which makes the cat a welcome pest controller in many parts of Florida. Only rarely will a bobcat kill prey as large as a deer.

The bobcat's favorite habitats are shrubby swamps and the open, grassy boundary areas between woods and swamps. These areas offer lots of small animals for food, good cover for hunting, and good sites for dens.

Recent estimates put the population of Florida bobcats at about 80 bobcats and kittens for every 100 square miles (260 km2). Of course, local densities vary, depending on local habitat and the availability of prey. Bobcats are solitary and territorial; home territories average 2,900 to 4,900 acres (10 to 20 km2). A male and female might share the same territory, but adults rarely spend time together except to mate.

Florida bobcats are declining in number as their habitats are lost or fragmented by human development. Biologists estimate that a self-sustaining population of bobcats means 200 individuals occupying 159,000 acres (645 km2) of forested habitat with adequate prey animals. Wild habitats over 100,000 acres (400 km2) are becoming increasingly scarce in Florida.

As local bobcat populations shrink and disappear, the pests they control—rabbits, rats, and mice—will grow in number. And as Florida continues to lose its wild lands to development, its bobcats may yet end up on the endangered species list.[20]

THE WHOOPING CRANE RECOVERY TEAM had predicted that the first whoopers released at Kissimmee Prairie would have a first-year mortality rate of 40 to 60 percent from all causes. But by August 1994, 33 whoopers had been released and 18 of them had been killed by bobcats. Four months later, only 11 of the 33 whoopers remained; bobcats had taken the rest. Terry Kohler wrote to the team expressing his concern over the predation rate and his reluctance to "fly any more bobcat food" to Florida.

To be sustainable, the flock needed more than a 33 percent survival rate. The bobcats' appetite for whooping cranes was putting the entire project in jeopardy. Ruefully, the team concluded that the large, permanent soft-release pen was set up in the wrong place, in an area that was more suitable to bobcats than to cranes.

That winter, biologists from the Florida Game & Freshwater Fish Commission and the USFWS put their heads together and came up with a new approach, involving two major changes beginning with the 1995 releases. In place of the large, permanent release pen, they began using smaller temporary pens that could be easily and quickly put up and taken down. The lightweight plastic pens could be moved around as water levels and other conditions changed, so the birds would be released into habitats that provided the best food supplies and better protection from predators.

In central Florida, most of the best habitats for cranes are outside the reserve's public holdings, on private land. The state and USFWS enlisted private landowners in the area around Kissimmee Prairie and from 1995 through 2001, released 186 whooping cranes in six privately owned marsh habitats.

The birds' mortality rate was cut in half. From 1995 through 1997, 70 percent of the whoopers survived their first year in the wild. After 1997, first year survival rates dropped to about 50 percent,

---

[20] Ecosystems are never simple. The Florida panther used to range through most of the state. Today, Florida's largest wild predator is found almost exclusively in the southern part of the state. As a result, raccoon populations have grown dramatically in the rest of Florida. That puts stress on the raccoons' food supplies, which include Atlantic sea turtle eggs. The decline of the Florida panther may be one of the factors that have put the Atlantic sea turtle on the endangered list.

probably due to the drought that affected water levels and crane food supplies statewide.

THE KOHLERS WERE STILL MAKING ANNUAL FLIGHTS to Canada's Wood Buffalo National Park to help ICF collect whooper eggs for Baraboo and Patuxent, and to Alaska to collect trumpeter swan eggs for the Wisconsin DNR. Their Windway corporate pilots were transporting whooper eggs from Baraboo to Maryland and Idaho. Terry was piloting his Bell 407 "JetRanger" helicopter to help with wildlife surveys for the Riveredge Nature Center, Trout Unlimited, the Wisconsin DNR, ICF, and the U.S. Fish & Wildlife Service. The Kohlers and Windway donated the costs of all these flights.

Each year from 1993 to 2004 Terry and Windway pilots made several flights from Baraboo or Maryland to Kissimmee Prairie to deliver a new batch of crane chicks to the soft-release pens and the non-migratory flock. Most were made in Windway's Cessna 208 Caravan. In November 1997, Windway made the trip in the company's highly modified Grumman "Aleutian Goose" amphibian—a unique aircraft with an interesting history.

Windway's Goose was built in July 1944 for the U.S. Navy and operated at various Naval Air Stations on the east and west coasts. In 1952, the Navy sold the airplane to the U.S. Fish & Wildlife Service. It sat in storage in Anchorage, Alaska until 1968, when USFWS had it converted to an "Aleutian Goose" by Volpar, Inc. Volpar replaced the two radial piston engines with Garrett turboprops, lengthened the nose 40 inches (about 1m), reinforced the hull so the airplane could land on glaciers, added retractable wingtip floats, and upgraded many other aircraft systems. Its gross weight increased from 12,500 to 15,000 lbs. (5,770 to 6,800 kg). USFWS routinely operated it at 17,000 lbs. (7,700 kg). The new engines extended its range to over 2,000 miles (3,200 km) between fuel stops. With the addition of an auxiliary fuel tank, the Goose once flew for 17 hours nonstop.

The USFWS and the US Department of the Interior[21] flew the airplane all over Alaska for wildlife surveys, fish surveys, bay and land surveys, and pipeline surveys. It carried sensors, cameras, data recorders, and tracking and locator systems, including a sonar system for tracking whales and other marine life. A variety of radios and

---

[21] FWS became part of the Dept. of Interior in 1973.

antennas allowed its crew to communicate with everything from satellites to submarines.

Windway bought the aircraft in December 1992 for its Rio Puelo Lodge, a fly-fishing lodge near Puerto Montt, Chile. Mechanics stripped 200 lbs. (90 kg) of antennas and electrical wire from the aircraft, upgraded its avionics, stripped and repainted it, and made changes to improve safety and passenger comfort. Under Chilean registry, the Goose carried clients (who came mainly from North America and Europe) to and from the otherwise inaccessible Rio Puelo Lodge and to and from fishing spots in the area. Notable passengers included an ESPN video team filming a segment for the program, "Fly Fishing the World," and singer-songwriter John Denver, who caught the Lodge's largest brown trout (32"/ and 16 lbs) during the film project.

The Lodge closed in 1995, and the Kohlers returned the Goose to the U.S. and obtained U.S. aircraft registry.

All of its modifications gave the airplane greater power, payload, and durability, and made the Goose an ideal platform for research and recreation. As flown for the Lodge, it could carry up to nine passengers and plenty of luggage. Though it was a "demanding" airplane to fly, according to its Windway pilots, the Goose took to the water like its feathered namesake with smooth, stable water landings and takeoffs.

Terry decided, since the Goose was back in the States, that it might be the perfect airplane for delivering whooping crane chicks to Florida. It had the room, the payload, and the range to do the job, and it could land on water, near the release pens. That could reduce the amount of time the chicks had to spend in their crates.

On November 1997, the Goose landed at Baraboo. ICF staff members put aboard ten six-month-old crane chicks raised at Baraboo, each riding in its own wooden crate. Also on the passenger list for that trip were Trey Finney, a wildlife artist and illustrator for Walt Disney Studios, and Chicago Tribune reporter Luann Grosscup. The pilots were Paul Jumes, Windway's chief pilot, and Jeff Kohler, Terry's nephew.

Flying to Florida in the Aleutian Goose took about five hours. The Cessna Caravan that was used on most of Windway's "crane lifts" always landed at the Kissimmee airport. In the Goose, the pilots intended to land on Lake Kissimmee, nearer the soft-release pens. That would cut an hour or so off the birds' normal journey from

The Kohlers' "Aleutian Goose." At right, ICF and Windway staff members load crane chicks bound from Wisconsin to Florida.

Photos, © International Crane Foundation, Baraboo, WI.

Baraboo to Kissimmee. But by the time the flight reached Florida, rising winds were kicking up waves on the lake. The Goose could easily handle the chop, but transferring the whoopers' crates from plane to boat on the rough lake would be too risky for the birds and their handlers, so Jumes landed the Goose at the Kissimmee airport instead.

An article about the Goose and the cranes appeared in the *Chicago Tribune* a few months later.

The Aleutian Goose flew one more whooping crane mission in February 1998, carrying chicks from Patuxent, Maryland to Kissimmee. In June of that year, it was sold to a new owner who could make use of its unique capabilities.

IN THE SPRING OF 2000, TWO ENORMOUS WHITE BIRDS appeared on a dairy farm near Sandusky, in Michigan's "thumb," landing on a flooded forty-acre field near owner Mark Batkie's home. Mark didn't recognize the birds, but with help from the Internet, he soon identified them as whooping cranes. He assumed they were stopping off on their return migration from Canada, and he made an effort not to disturb them.

The birds disappeared in early June, but not to Canada. They moved just a few miles to a wetland on the property of the Michigan Peat Company. Eastern Michigan's bogs have been a source of commercial peat for many years. Harvesting the peat leaves large, shallow depressions in the bog that fill with water and provide good habitat for cranes and other waterfowl. Vito Palazzolo supervised the peat harvest for the company, and he discovered the birds on the bog. After he, too, searched the Internet to identify them, his wife Sheila contacted the Whooping Crane Conservation Association. When USFWS employees showed up, they found that both birds were tagged, and their origins could be traced. That solved one mystery and created another. The two birds were members of non-migratory flock at Florida's Kissimmee Prairie. What were they doing in eastern Michigan?

Hatched five years earlier, in 1995, and raised in isolation from humans at Patuxent Wildlife Research Center, the two wandering whoopers were released on the Kissimmee Prairie in early 1996. They made eyes at each other and in 1999 eloped to a wetland located near Inverness in northwest Florida. But the Inverness wetland was shrinking, a victim of two years of hard drought in Florida. When the wetland dried up in April of 2000, the two whoopers vanished. Crane watchers assumed they had relocated to another Florida wetland. Unobserved, the birds headed north. Maybe some dormant migratory instinct kicked in. Or maybe they were just looking for a wetter place to live. It's impossible to know what they were thinking. ("Probably not much," said one crane biologist. "Cranes are beautiful but really pretty stupid.")

In early May, they were spotted near Sandoval, in south central Illinois, 750 miles northwest of Inverness, Florida. They remained there on a flooded field until May 14. The next day, they appeared on Mark Batkie's dairy farm, 600 miles to the northeast of Sandoval. Three weeks later, they moved to the peat bogs.

The cranes remained on the peat company's marsh for six weeks, possibly attempting to nest and breed. For more than a month, the company kept its feathered guests secret from the public, wanting them to be left undisturbed. In mid-July, the company finally put out a news release about the birds. That sparked public interest and 70 people attended a special program on whooping cranes at the Sandusky Public Library on August 17.

A week later, Terry Kohler flew ICF's George Archibald to Sandusky to see the cranes and to look for signs of nesting. Archibald and Palazzo found two large nest platforms in the marsh but no eggshell fragments in either nest. Like many young pairs, these cranes were establishing a territory by building nests but had not yet bred successfully—a typical pattern for bonded pairs in their first year together.

A single young sandhill crane was often seen in the company of the two whoopers on the peat company's marsh. Though they had tried to drive the sandhill crane away in June, the whoopers seemed to accept it during the rest of the summer. A pair of sandhill cranes nested elsewhere on the same marsh and Archibald thought the young sandhill might be a year-old chick, driven away from its parents' nesting territory as they began a new breeding season. The sandhill cranes that breed in Michigan winter in Florida. Archibald hoped that the two wandering Kissimmee whoopers would follow sandhill cranes back to Florida in the fall, or find their own way as winter settled in. Though there were lots of guesses, no one really knew what the cranes might do or where they might go.

ICF biologists Kristin Lucas and Anne Lacy arrived at the Batkie farm on November 8, in a radio tracking van donated by Alliant Energy Corporation. (The two birds were already wearing radio transmitters for tracking.) At dawn the next morning, the cranes could be seen near the Batkies' barn. For two weeks, Lucas and Lacy stayed with the Batkies, checking the cranes' nesting area each day and waiting for the birds to move. Finally on November 21, the roost was empty and the cranes' radio signals were coming from overhead and heading south.

The birds had been foraging all summer in fields south of the Batkies' farm, but on this morning, they didn't stop to eat. Their radio signals kept moving south and it looked as though they might be heading for Florida. Several more ICF staff members joined the tracking team and the van headed south in pursuit of the birds. Lucas contacted Windway pilot Mike Frakes, who flew Windway's Cessna 182 Skylane from Sheboygan, Wisconsin to join the chase.

For four hours, the ground team in the van tracked the birds south toward Canada and Lake Erie. (The southwestern corner of Ontario is south of Michigan's thumb.) Frakes rendezvoused with the van at Marine City, Michigan, about 50 miles (85 km) north of Detroit, and tracked the birds south into Canada, while the van drove ahead to Sandusky, Ohio, on the south shore of Lake Erie.

In the plane, Frakes and Koji Suzuki, an ICF field ecology intern, followed the cranes' radio signals but could not spot the birds in the November snow squalls. With daylight fading, Suzuki picked up the day's last signal from Ontario's Point Pelee National Park, on the tip of a peninsula jutting southward into Lake Erie. Then Frakes called off the search, to land the plane for the night.

That evening the ground crew backtracked through Detroit to

Point Pelee. Arriving at the park at 10:30 p.m., they searched unsuccessfully for the birds' radio signals. Early the next morning, they searched the area again, but the tracking receiver was silent.

Frakes and Suzuki were airborne early, searching fruitlessly over western Ontario, and then turning south across Lake Erie. In northern Ohio at mid-morning, they finally acquired a tracking signal from one of the cranes—the female. While the van yo-yoed back through Detroit, Frakes and Suzuki followed the signal. The snow squalls had moved east and the day was clear and perfect for flying. Just before 1 p.m., Suzuki spotted the female crane—"a tiny white speck just above a deep green forest." But though they circled and searched and listened, they found only one crane. The male's radio signal had gone silent.

Afraid of losing the female's signal again, Frakes and Suzuki followed her southward. That evening, near a southern Ohio coal mine, in a large pond in the midst of a desolate "moonscape" with no trees or vegetation, the female crane rested alone. Her companion was never heard or seen again. Most likely, he was lost to the bad weather and cold waters of Lake Erie.

The next morning, Day 3 of the crane's southward odyssey, the ground crew moved in carefully to observe the female. To the team, the blasted landscape seemed an odd setting for a whooping crane. At 10 a.m. on a freshening breeze, she rose into the air, circled the pond once, and headed south.

She spent two and a half days resting at a pond near Chucky, Tennessee, and then flew over the Appalachian Mountains to South Carolina. Three days later, she arrived at the wetland near Inverness, Florida, the last place she and her mate had been seen before heading north the previous fall. She wasn't quite finished. A day later, on December 1, 2000, 11 days after leaving the Batkie dairy farm, she settled at Kissimmee Prairie, the same place where she had been released as a chick four and a half years earlier. She remained in Florida until her death a few years later.

The two errant cranes were more than just a footnote in the story of Kissimmee's whoopers. They had demonstrated that a whooper raised in captivity and released at a wintering site retained some instinct to migrate north in the spring and to return in the fall, uncoaxed and unaided, to the place where she was released.

ALSO IN THE SPRING OF 2000, WHILE THE TWO ERRANT

whoopers were heading north, two wild whooper chicks hatched at Kissimmee Prairie. The parents were costumed-raised whoopers, the female from Baraboo and the male from Patuxent. The female laid two eggs and both hatched—the first wild whooping cranes to hatch in the United States since the 1940s, when Louisiana's non-migratory flock disappeared. One of the two Kissimmee chicks died a few weeks after birth. It was a sad event but not unexpected. In the wild, it is common for only one whooper chick to survive out of a clutch of two.

The severe drought in Florida that year did nothing to improve the chicks' chances. Cranes sleep in the water and build nest mounds in the water, to protect themselves and their chicks from predators. Water levels were low throughout Florida in 2000, and although the parents found water, the marshes and lakes were shallow and offered less protection than in wetter years. But the second chick thrived, replaced its down with cinnamon-colored feathers, and began its early attempts at flying.

There are two especially dangerous times in a whooper chick's life: In the first few days and weeks after hatching, the chick is entirely dependent on its parents for food and protection. And when the chick prepares to fledge, its practice hops and early flights take it farther from the safety of its parents. Most chick mortality occurs during one or the other of these two periods. Once the chick has fledged, it is able to evade most predators and it can find its own food, though it will stay with its parents for most of its first year, gradually becoming more and more independent.

Hopes were high for the surviving chick. In late summer, it began exercising its wings and making short wing-flapping hops—a prelude to its first real flights. But just a few days before it would have fledged, the chick was caught and killed by a bobcat.

The following year, 2001, was a good year for the captive breeding programs at Patuxent and Baraboo, which were producing chicks for release at Kissimmee Prairie and for an experiment, begun in 2000, to create a new migratory flock east of the Mississippi River. In the Florida non-migratory flock, several pairs made nesting attempts in 2001, but there were no new eggs and no new chicks.

In the spring of 2002, a pair of Patuxent-raised whoopers produced the second clutch of eggs to come from Florida's non-migratory flock. The pair nested on private land owned by Gene and Tina Tindell, and from their home, the Tindells watched the chicks' development and reported regularly to the staff of the Florida Fish & Wildlife Conservation Commission. The Tindells' property provided an excellent location for Commission biologists to observe and film the whooping crane family, and the Tindells allowed the commission staff to use their yard day and night, to record the chicks' progress.

The whooper pair had begun nest building on the Tindells' property around Christmastime 2001, the earliest documented example of whooper nest-building behavior. Two eggs appeared in early February and the first chick hatched on March 13, 2002, followed by the second chick two days later.

Just two days after that, a surveillance video camera placed near the nest captured the death of the younger chick. While the parents were away from the nest feeding the older chick, a bald eagle carried off the younger sibling. Observers named the surviving chick, "Lucky."[22]

Whooping cranes acquire some of their parenting skills through trial and error. After the eagle's attack, Lucky's parents guarded him much more closely and moved him away from the exposed nest to a bushy area where he would be better protected from eagles. When the eagle attacked again three weeks later, the female whooper protected Lucky while the male aggressively drove the predator away.

Six weeks after Lucky's hatching, the marsh began to dry up. The water level continued to fall through the spring, making the marsh and the whoopers' nest more accessible to bobcats and other predators. As the water levels fell, Lucky's parents several times abandoned one nest platform and built another in deeper water. It was another new discovery for the biologists; no one had ever seen whoopers building new nest platforms this late in the chick-rearing cycle.[23]

Early in the summer, when Lucky was nearly the same size as his parents and very close to fledging, a pair of bald eagles landed near the nest. The response from the whooper parents was immediate and furious. One of the eagles was scared off by the whoopers' attack; the other was slower and not so fortunate. Caught on the ground by the whoopers, the eagle was pinned and battered seriously enough to require rescue and treatment by local wildlife rescuers.[24]

---

[22] Lucky's story is chronicled in detail in Patuxent Research Center's "Whooping Crane Reports," at http://whoopers.usgs.gov/.

[23] Young chicks sometimes use the nest platform to stay dry, especially at night.

Lucky's wings grew stronger and his "test hops" grew longer until in early June he was officially fledged—able to make sustained flights of several hundred yards. Not since the 1940s had a wild whooping crane hatched and fledged in the United States. Lucky offered proof that a new flock of non-migratory whooping cranes could reproduce in the wild.

As of October 2006, the Kissimmee Prairie whoopers have hatched and fledged eight whooper chicks—four of them in 2006. All of the chicks have survived so far, save one. In 2004, at age 2, Lucky fell victim to a bobcat.

BETWEEN 1993 AND 2004, A TOTAL OF 221 WHOOPERS were released into the wild at Kissimmee Prairie. The most recent release, of five birds, was in December 2004. In late 2006, the population of the non-migratory flock was counted at 50 whoopers, including 12 nesting pairs. The actual population was probably a bit higher, since not all of the non-migratory whoopers can be located at any given time.

The lion's share of the Kissimmee whoopers came from Baraboo or Patuxent. The Calgary Zoo provided just 16 of the 221 birds released at Kissimmee Prairie between 1993 and 2004. "Moving live birds, fertile eggs, bird semen, or even blood samples across the border into the U.S. is a real headache in terms of all the permitting and regulations," Calgary Zookeeper Dwight Knapik explained. "As much as we can keep birds here and pair them, without having to move them around [to other facilities], we will do that." But it's not always possible, he added. The release projects are in the United States, so Knapik and his staff will continue wrestling the red tape, to send fertile eggs and live birds across the border.

Future releases to the non-migratory flock are on hold, according to Marty Folk, crane biologist with the Florida Fish & Wildlife Conservation Commission. "We have concerns about the low productivity and high mortality of the flock," Folk said. "And we want to direct the chicks from the breeding centers toward the migratory flock" that is being established in Florida and Wisconsin. The non-migratory flock continues to serve as a laboratory for studying the whoopers in the wild.

---

[24] Patuxent's "Whooper Report" noted with irony that several of the staff at Patuxent had worked for years on efforts to reintroduce the once-endangered bald eagle. Those staff members watched in frustration as two species they had fought to save were engaged in a take-no-prisoners competition for survival.

"We're playing detective," Folk said. "We're trying to figure out why the birds have these huge ups and downs in their breeding seasons." There seems to be a correlation between the birds' productivity and the winter rains just preceding the breeding season. Folk added, however, that the rainfall in 2006 was the lowest ever recorded in Florida, and the birds still fledged a record number of chicks.

"We're also studying the birds' behavior to see if they're doing something wrong," he said. The non-migratory flock has been producing lots of eggs but few chicks. He added:

> "Sometimes it's a fertility issue and sometimes it's not. When the birds incubate past the normal period, we go out and collect the eggs and analyze them for signs of fertility and we look at how developed the embryos were. There are eight or ten different things that could be factors influencing productivity. That's where we come in with our detective work, trying to determine why the birds aren't hatching a lot of their eggs."

It might be something physiological in the birds, he said, it might be related to weather or water levels, or it might be something else. "It's all very preliminary," he said, "but at least we feel like we're beginning to get at some of the reasons why we've had several poor years for productivity."

Part IV
Follow Me!

Photo: © *www.operationmigration.org*

"We shall never achieve harmony with land, any more than we shall achieve absolute justice or liberty for people.

In these higher aspirations, the important thing is not to achieve but to strive."

—Aldo Leopold

Chapter 14
A Bird-Brained Idea

WEDNESDAY, OCTOBER 17, 2001, Necedah National Wildlife Refuge, in Central Wisconsin, about 7:15 a.m.—The weather is clear and cold (25° F. / -4°C.) with light winds from the Northwest. Most of the leaves have fallen from the trees and the refuge is clothed in autumn tans and browns. Heavy frost sparkles in the early morning sun.

On a short makeshift grass runway in a remote corner of the 43,656-acre (176 km2) refuge, three pilots, Joe Duff, Bill Lishman, and Deke Clark, advance the throttles on three Cosmos® ultralight aircraft.[1] The whine of two-stroke engines assaults the ears. The pilots are dressed in shapeless white "crane suits." Partway down the runway, they pass a large camouflaged holding pen at the edge of the marsh. A member of the ground crew, also dressed in a crane suit, opens the door to the pen and eight young whooping cranes rush out, hopping, flapping their wings, and calling in obvious excitement. A speaker mounted on Joe Duff's ultralight broadcasts recorded crane calls and after a few running leaps down the runway, the cranes take flight in pursuit of Duff's aircraft. As they catch up to him, they form a staggered line spread out from his wing. The young cranes "surf" the wave of air—the vortex—that rolls off the airplane's wingtip, only rarely flapping their wings. Clark flies second lead, ready to pick up any birds that drop out of formation, and try to get them to fol-

---

[1] "Ultralights," also called "microlights" (in England and New Zealand) and "ULMs" (in Italy and France) are simple, lightweight single-seat aircraft designed for economical sport flying. In the United States, an ultralight is defined by strict limits on weight, maximum speed, stall speed, and fuel capacity. Regulations prohibit night flying and flights over populated areas. No license or training is required for ultralight pilots, though no one should try to fly an ultralight without some instruction.

As pilot Joe Duff lifts off, the whoopers form up on his ultralight's wing.

Photo: © www.operationmigration.org

low his ultralight. Lishman flies as chase pilot and scout.

Leveling off just a few hundred feet above the ground, Duff heads south from the Refuge where the cranes have spent the summer and fall paradoxically learning to follow the ultralights and learning to act like wild cranes.

Over the next 48 days, the birds and aircraft together will migrate in short hops, 1,250 miles (2,011 km) to a new winter home in Florida's Chassahowitzka National Wildlife Refuge. It will be the first time in nearly 100 years that migrating whooping cranes have been seen in the Eastern United States. If all goes as planned, the cranes will migrate back to Necedah NWR on their own in the spring. And each year after that, they will make the journey south and return north as wild whooping cranes.

On this day, they will fly just 29.3 miles (47.1 km) on the first leg of their migration. Since they fledged in August, the young cranes have been gaining strength and confidence in the air, but today's 45-minute flight is the longest they have made in both distance and duration. They will need more practice and better tailwinds before they can fly longer and farther at a stretch.

They arrive at their first stop just before 8:00 a.m. There, more costumed handlers set up a temporary holding pen where the birds will spend the night protected from predators. They will also be protected from any contact with humans. Their handlers are forbidden to speak, cough, sneeze, or make any other human sounds near the birds. With recorded crane calls and crane puppet heads, the handlers lead the cranes to the pen or to a foraging area nearby.

Each day, weather permitting, the cranes will follow the ultralight for an hour or so, taking advantage of the smooth, cold air of early morning. They will spend the rest of the day on the ground, doing what wild cranes do: feeding, bathing, preening, and socializing.

Their journey will require a small army of staff and volunteers, the hospitality of dozens of private landowners, and the cooperation of two nations, two provinces, and 22 states. Supporters will provide more than $300,000 to cover the cost of the migration. And the cranes' progress will be followed closely by news media and well-wishers around the world.

Planning for this project has been intense, and hopes for success are high. But the outcome is by no means certain. One bird died during the training period. Another was removed from the group because its wing feathers did not form properly. One of the cranes flying with the group today may not be strong enough to keep up with the ultralight and the other seven birds in the flock. Already the trip has been delayed by two days of gusty headwinds at Necedah. A million things could go wrong.

But on this day, the wind cooperated. Seen from above, Wisconsin's autumn landscape presented an almost unnatural beauty in the morning sun. And the young whoopers, their white plumage still mottled with juvenile tan, were majestic in flight. They seemed truly excited to get off the ground, and made their longest flight yet with little sign of fatigue. With a small step of 29 miles, their journey has begun.

ESTABLISHING NEW FLOCKS OF WILD whooping cranes is considered essential for preserving the species in the wild. If the world's most endangered crane continues to exist in a single wild flock—the Wood Buffalo/Aransas population—the species will be too vulnerable to natural or man-made disasters. Aransas NWR lies along the Gulf Intracoastal Waterway, the third busiest waterway in the United States,[2] and that causes special concern for the cranes. A major oil spill or chemical spill in the shipping lane could threaten the survival of the Aransas/Wood Buffalo whoopers.

---

[2] Completed in 1949, the 1,300-mile Gulf Intracoastal Waterway is a manmade shipping canal that runs from Brownsville, Texas to St. Marks, Florida. It provides access to all the inland waterways of the Gulf Coast. With a minimum width of 125 feet and depth of 12 feet, it is designed primarily for barge traffic. The Texas section of the

In 1989, half of the captive breeding flock of whoopers at the Patuxent Wildlife Research Center was transplanted to Baraboo, to ICF. At the time, Patuxent had the only major breeding program for whoopers. Creating a second breeding center at ICF helped ensure that a single catastrophe wouldn't wipe out the entire captive population and its irreplaceable genetic lines. Launching a third captive breeding program at the Calgary Zoo in 1992 added another measure of security for the captive population.

Creating new wild flocks, geographically isolated from each other, would provide similar safeguards for the wild members of the species. The USFWS' Whooping Crane Recovery Plan calls for the creation of two new self-sustaining wild flocks, one migratory and one non-migratory. The non-migratory flock was established at Florida's Kissimmee Prairie, beginning in 1993. For that flock, one of the principal challenges facing avian biologists was how to teach captive-raised cranes to survive as wild birds. To keep the young birds isolated from human contact biologists employed strict and elaborate protocols. That approach worked, and it proved that captive-raised cranes can learn to live in the wild.

Establishing a new migratory flock separate from the Aransas/Wood Buffalo flock offered new and imposing challenges: How does one teach young cranes to migrate? Can isolation-rearing techniques, so successful with the non-migratory flock, be sustained over a migration route of a thousand miles or more? Would young captive birds taught to migrate to their wintering grounds be able to find their way back on their own to viable nesting grounds?

Sparrows, robins, warblers, thrushes and other songbirds seem to have migration routes "hardwired" into their brains. Young songbirds migrate alone over thousands of miles, some to Central or South America, mostly flying at night and often with no parents or older birds to lead the way.[3]

Not so for cranes and swans. While these birds appear to possess an instinct to migrate, they depend on their parents to teach them where to migrate and where to winter. In the cross-fostering experiment at Grays Lake, Idaho, the whooper chicks hatched by sandhill cranes did follow wild sandhills south to their winter range in New

---

canal is 423 miles long and carries 60% of the canal's total annual tonnage—about 65 million tons of cargo.

[3] Avian biologists know very little about songbird migrations, especially about how the birds navigate.

Mexico, and back to Grays Lake in the spring. But the cross-fostered whoopers were sexually imprinted on sandhills and failed to produce any new whoopers. Without new whooper chicks, there could be no self-sustaining new flock.

All of the whoopers in existence today carry the genes of the last wild migratory flock. The two Kissimmee whoopers who migrated on their own to Michigan added to the evidence that whoopers possess an instinct to migrate.[4] The challenge, one of many, was to find a way to teach young cranes how and where to migrate.

KENT CLEGG GREW UP ON A RANCH NEAR GRACE, IDAHO, 35 miles (55 km) from Grays Lake National Wildlife Refuge. When he was a teenager, his family spent summers on a second ranch near Grays Lake. It was a small ranch and a big family—there wasn't room for all the boys at the summer ranch, so in 1977, the summer before his senior year in high school, Kent took a summer job on the maintenance crew at the refuge. The whooper/sandhill cross-fostering project was underway at the time and Rod Drewien, a biologist from the University of Idaho, asked Kent to help with the project. "I'd work on the maintenance crew during the day," Clegg said, "and then I'd help at night to band and mark sandhill cranes that they could use as foster parents" for whooper eggs.

Drewien was apparently impressed with Clegg's work; a year later, he invited the young man to spend the winter in New Mexico, tracking the birds they had banded and marked the summer before. Clegg searched for the birds in New Mexico and Old Mexico that winter, and his interest and involvement in the project grew as he spent the next ten years working with Drewien, tracking Grays Lake's cross-fostered whoopers.

"We kept running into the same problem" at Grays Lake, Clegg said.

---

[4] A pair of captive-raised whoopers released at Kissimmee Prairie might have been driven in part by their migratory instincts when they headed north in the spring of 2000, and summered in Michigan. Biologists believe the two cranes were looking for suitable nesting habitat, and that they left Florida because the state's wetlands had been greatly reduced by a prolonged drought. After six months in Michigan, the birds began a return migration to the south on their own. The male disappeared over Lake Erie but the female returned on her own to Kissimmee Prairie, where she had been released in early 1996. She never migrated again.

"We were imprinting the whoopers on sandhills and they were flying around as individual birds, not associating with each other. I spent a lot of time out tracking them and watching them and I kept thinking, there's got to be a way to raise a group of them so they will imprint to each other, and then to somehow figure out how to show them a migration route."

In the late 1980s, Clegg attended a trumpeter swan conservation conference in Salt Lake City, Utah. At the conference he met Bill Carrick, a prominent Canadian filmmaker and naturalist. Carrick had trained a group of Canada geese to follow his airboat so he could film them. To get the geese up in the air and make his films more realistic, Carrick purchased an ultralight aircraft and tried to train the geese to follow that, but his ultralight flew too fast for the geese to keep up.

Carrick's project caught the interest of Canadian wildlife sculptor Bill Lishman. Working with Carrick and flying a slower ultralight, Lishman raised several Canada geese and trained them to fly in formation with the aircraft.

At the meeting in Salt Lake City, Clegg recalled, he told Carrick, "If I could raise a bunch of whooping cranes and get them to follow an airplane, I could get them to imprint on each other and lead them together on a migration." Clegg had already been teaching tame sandhill cranes to follow ground vehicles—pickup trucks and all-terrain vehicles (ATVs)—around his Idaho ranch. An ultralight, Clegg told Carrick, might offer a way to get past the major problems that had plagued the cross-fostering project for 15 years.

About the same time that Clegg and Carrick were comparing notes in Salt Lake City, Bill Lishman was releasing a 28-minute video documentary called "C'mon Geese." It told the story of teaching Canada geese to follow his ultralight. The film won six international awards and was broadcast in many countries.

That July 1989, at the Experimental Aircraft Association's (EAA's) annual fly-in convention[5] at Oshkosh, Wisconsin, Terry Kohler saw the video and bought a copy. Returning home, he called George Archibald at ICF to tell George about the film. Did George

---

[5] EAA's "AirVenture Oshkosh," is held each summer in late July. The weeklong gathering typically draws 12,000 aircraft and 750,000 people to Oshkosh, Wisconsin's municipal airport. It is the largest aviation gathering in the world.

think it was even possible, Terry asked, that whoopers could be taught to follow and migrate behind an ultralight piloted by a human?

"I ignored George's horrific laughter," Terry wrote,[6] "and sent him the video." A week later, Terry called again. He had taken the liberty, he told George, of calling Bill Lishman to ask whether Lishman might be interested in working with George Archibald, a fellow Canadian, and ICF to, "explore this migratory thing with whoopers." Bill Lishman said "YES!," Terry recalls. George Archibald said, "Maybe."

A few months later, George brought up the idea at a meeting of the International Whooping Crane Recovery Team. He expected something akin to the incredulous response he'd given Terry when the idea was first proposed to him. Instead, team members were intrigued by the idea. FWS Whooping Crane Coordinator Jim Lewis thought it was a good idea. Tom Stehn, a USFWS biologist at Aransas who later became the USFWS Whooping Crane Coordinator, recalls:

> "My reaction was, the ultralight project wasn't going to work. And it was because cranes don't fly and flap their wings the way geese do. They don't fly in a straight line; they use thermal currents and they soar and that's the way they make their migrations. I thought, you were fighting the basic biology of the species, hoping that it would follow the ultralight."
>
> . . . [But] here was this group basically offering to fund themselves, and all they needed from the Whooping Crane Recovery Team was whooping cranes to do it with. We had nothing to lose by trying. We came out of that meeting saying, 'By all means, we endorse the basic research,' to see if the technique would work. I personally did not think it would.
>
> The miscalculation I made was the vortices coming off the wing that would kind of act like a thermal current. Once we realized that that would be a way that the cranes would save energy and not have to flap so much, then it became feasible. And that just took basic research, doing it once with sandhill cranes."

---

[6] Kohler, Terry, unpublished article.

That year, 1990, Lishman ran afoul of officials from the Canadian Wildlife Service (CWS). He was raising another flock of Canada geese to follow his ultralight and he was working with Dr. William Sladen, director of the Airlie Center in Virginia,[7] to raise a group of hybrid trumpeter/tundra swans and teach them to follow his ultralight. Their ultimate aim was to help reintroduce trumpeter swans to the eastern United States. A number of avian biologists were criticizing Lishman's work as "unscientific." CWS officials said he didn't have the requisite permits to be messing about with wild birds. For the moment, both projects were grounded.

Meanwhile, Kent Clegg was still leading tame sandhills around the valley with his pickup truck and thinking about an ultralight-led crane migration. In 1992, he was ready to approach Jim Lewis, USFWS Whooping Crane Coordinator. Lewis was supportive but the Whooping Crane Recovery Team was moving slowly on the idea. Clegg persisted, bringing it up several times over the next two years.

In 1994, on one of those trips around the valley, Clegg's sandhill cranes flew 38 miles (61 km) behind his pickup. That same year, Clegg took the ultralight idea to Lewis once more and, Clegg recalls, "Lewis told me, 'if you prove that you can get [cranes] to follow an airplane, we'll consider it.'"

Out east, Bill Lishman had sorted out his wildlife permit situation and had been raising and training Canada geese to follow his ultralight. In the fall of 1993, he led a group of 18 "honkers" on a 375-mile (600-km) migration from Ontario to Virginia. The next spring, 13 of those geese returned on their own to Ontario.

That same spring—1994—Clegg raised a group of sandhill cranes, got them to follow an ultralight around the valley where his ranch is located, and filmed it. Like Carrick and Lishman, Clegg raised the birds to imprint on him and his ultralight. He wasn't planning to release these sandhills into the wild, so he didn't worry about how tame they were. The object of this first step, he said, was simply to prove that cranes could and would follow an aircraft. "We did everything we could to get them to follow us," he said, including sleeping with the birds.

Then, Clegg recalls, "I went back to Jim Lewis and said, 'I can do that. Now can I raise some whooping cranes?' And [Lewis] said,

---

[7] The Airlie Center (www.airlie.org) is a conference center located on several hundred acres of wildlife habitat. The Center and the Airlie Foundation is active in environmental education, research, and policy-making.

'No, it doesn't go quite that fast.'"

EACH AUTUMN, THE WILD SANDHILL CRANES (Grus Canadensis) that summer in Idaho and the surrounding states migrate south for 800 miles (1,300 km) along the spine of the Rocky Mountains, over some of the most rugged mountains and canyon lands in the United States, to winter along the Rio Grande River in central New Mexico. Some 15,000 to 20,000 sandhill cranes congregate each winter in and around Bosque del Apache National Wildlife Refuge, near Socorro, New Mexico, at the northern edge of the Chihuahuan desert. The refuge ranges from 4,500 feet to 6,300 feet (1,375 to 1,925 m) above sea level and offers a wide variety of habitats, from wetlands and floodplains to desert foothills and mesas. Much of the 57,000-acre (230-km2) refuge is maintained as wilderness. In the moist bottomlands, the refuge staff cultivates corn, winter wheat, clover, and native plants to provide food for cranes, ducks, geese, mule deer, elk, and other wildlife. Local farmers plant corn and alfalfa on the refuge, harvesting the alfalfa for their cattle and leaving the corn for the wildlife. With the ample food supply, the woods and marshes along the Rio Grande River make the refuge an excellent habitat for the cranes and more than 350 other species of birds that winter there or live there year-round.

For 1995, the International Whooping Crane Recovery Team gave Clegg the go-ahead to raise a group of sandhills at his ranch and lead them on a migration to Bosque del Apache NWR in New Mexico—the wintering ground for the Grays Lake cranes. This group of birds would be released into the wild flock in New Mexico. Clegg would have to raise them to be wild.

With funding from public and private donors,[8] and working with USFWS staff and volunteers, Clegg began hunting for sandhill crane eggs at Grays Lake in April and May of 1995. The eggs they found were given a "float test" at each nest site to estimate when they would hatch, and then returned to their nests. Twenty eggs were removed from the nests about four days before their estimated hatching dates and taken to an incubator at the Clegg ranch. When the eggs pipped (when the chick broke the first tiny hole through the shell), they were moved to a hatching container furnished with natu-

[8] Financial support for the project came from Canadian Wildlife Service, International Crane Foundation, National Biological Service, US Fish & Wildlife Service, Windway Capital Corporation, and World Wildlife Fund-Canada.

ral nesting materials and an infrared heat lamp.

Clegg made a recording of his imitation of a sandhill crane brood call—the call a parent crane would make to summon and comfort its chicks. As the chicks began to pip, this recorded call was played for them. On the tape, the call lasted about 5 seconds and occurred about twice a minute. It was played off and on, for up to half an hour at a time, during the roughly 30 hours that it took each chick to struggle out of its egg. All 20 eggs hatched successfully.

Typically, the older chicks in a brood pick on the younger. Clegg grouped the hatchlings by age—six to eight chicks in each group—to reduce aggression. Nonetheless, two of the youngest chicks were killed by others in their groups.

After they hatched, the sandhill chicks were moved outdoors to small holding pens, then, at five to ten days of age, to a larger (50x100 feet, 15x30 m) pen, and finally to an island in a creek located within the larger pen. There were bowls of crane food on the island, and a full-sized crane decoy kept the chicks company there. A heat lamp suspended over the island and a transparent windbreak kept the chicks warm at night. The pen protected the chicks from the local riffraff, which included coyotes, raccoons, golden eagles, and red-tailed hawks. The creek flowing through the pen meant the chicks always had fresh water, which meant a much lower risk of disease.

A few weeks after the cranes hatched, Clegg and his helpers took them out into a natural environment—streams and fields near the ranch. Within two days, the chicks were eating bugs off the ground, playing in the water, and bathing. Each morning, Clegg led the young cranes out of the pen, across an open field, to a ditch bank where they could forage in the water and in the field. There, too, the crane decoy kept the chicks company, while Clegg disappeared from their sight. During the day, the cranes fed on grain, seeds, insects, and earthworms—their natural foods. Every 15 to 30 minutes, observers who remained hidden at a distance checked up on the cranes' progress and well-being. Each evening, Clegg appeared at the ditch bank and called the birds to him by imitating the sandhill crane brood call. Then he led them back across the field to their pen. At night, a video camera kept watch over the chicks.

Wild cranes roost in water as protection against predators. It's a survival tactic that Clegg's chicks had to learn. Over a period of about seven weeks, the water level in the pen was gradually raised, eventually flooding the island. By the time they fledged, the chicks were comfortably roosting in the water each night.

While aviculturists at Patuxent and ICF were using costumes and puppets to raise cranes in isolation near total isolation from humans, Clegg took a different approach. He believed that if he raised the birds as a group that they would imprint on each other, not just on him. He explained:

> "[T]hey'll imprint to you, but only until they've developed enough that you no longer fit in their scheme of things. And once they are old enough, they sort of ostracize you from the group, because you're the odd duck out."

The young chicks would follow Clegg when he called but when he walked away, they didn't seem to care. "They would just go off and do their own thing," he said.

> "They got very used to me not being around. And also they imprinted very strongly on each other and relied on each other for warnings and everything else. We would see an eagle fly over and the chicks' instincts would kick in, and they'd start calling and warning each other."

Clegg said he spent just enough time with the birds to keep them following him, but not enough time that they cared when he left. And each day when he took the birds out to the field and then disappeared, "they would just interact with each other." The goal, he said was to create an environment for the chicks that was as close as possible to their natural environment. "We wanted everything that's innate to them to kick in and everything that comes to them naturally would take over. We were very successful in raising birds that way."

"To me," he added, "it just isn't critical, the emphasis on costumes and all that stuff. That's one approach but there's another way of doing it." It was more important, he concluded, to give the chicks a natural environment and give them the chance to be cranes. "We gave them every opportunity to be wild."

When the chicks were about three weeks old, they were introduced to the sounds and sights of the ATV and the ultralight. Every couple of days, the ultralight was flown over their pen, and then left idling nearby for a short time. That gave the birds a chance to grow accustomed to its noise and appearance, and the wind from its propeller. Using his brood calls, Clegg taught the birds to run after his ATV and his taxiing ultralight.

Three of the chicks died of unknown causes over the summer. The remaining 15 chicks all fledged successfully in August. Clegg encouraged them with brood calls to follow the ultralight into the air. They were reluctant at first and, initially, only one or two birds would follow Clegg aloft. But within five days, all 15 birds could be seen trailing after the ultralight in low-level flights around the ranch. At first, they flapped along in an unorganized gaggle behind the aircraft. Gradually, one by one, they learned to conserve their energy by "surfing" on the ultralight's wingtip vortices.

Flight brought new hazards for the birds to learn and avoid. A collision with a power line near the ranch took the life of one young crane, soon after it fledged. Another crane became entangled in a wing strut during a practice flight. That chick survived, but lost a foot. One crane was killed when it flew into the ultralight's rear-mounted propeller during a flight around the ranch. Flights were suspended while the team quickly designed and installed a metal guard to protect both the cranes and the propeller from any more such mishaps.

During one flight around the ranch, two golden eagles attacked the cranes, diving on the flock from above and behind. All but one of the cranes managed to out-maneuver the eagles. That one survived the attack but with an injured wing.

As the young cranes gained strength and experience, the flights became longer, stretching in wider circles around the valley. When the cranes began to pant or to fly with their mouths gaping, the pilot knew it was time to rest. By early October, the sandhill cranes were following the ultralight for up to 25 miles (40 km) at a time.

KENT CLEGG'S FIRST AIRPLANE WAS A WRECKED ULTRALIGHT he bought from a neighbor. His father was a licensed Private Pilot and owned a small airplane, and Kent learned the basics of flying while riding with his dad. He also spent many hours in the air with USFWS pilots during wildlife surveys.

In the mid-1980s, he recalled, one of his neighbors up the valley had an ultralight and crashed it. The man's wife wouldn't let him repair it. "I knew it was wrecked," Clegg recalled, "and I knew where it was, and I kept asking him if he'd sell it to me, and he wouldn't." After about the third offer, Clegg realized he was talking to the wrong person. "I called his wife one day when he was at work, and she sold me the airplane."

Clegg rebuilt it, took it out to a field on his ranch and started practicing, taxiing back and forth. "And finally the thing was off the ground, and the next I knew I was up there so high I didn't know how I was going to get back down. But the law of gravity seems to take care of that." After three or four years of flying the ultralight, Clegg went to a local flight school and earned his Private Pilot's License.

The aircraft he used for the migrations was a Dragonfly, manufactured in Australia. Clegg and his team had worked hard to find the right ultralight—one that he could feel comfortable flying in the mountains and over the rugged terrain that lay along the migration route. The Dragonfly was ideal. Designed for towing hang gliders aloft, it had a big main wing for plenty of lift, big "flaperons"—combined ailerons and flaps—for good control, and a lower-than-average cruising speed. While many commercially designed ultralights cruise at 60 to 80 mph (100-135 kmh), the Dragonfly cruises at just 45 mph (75 kmh), and its stall speed[9] is less than 20 mph (33kmh). Widely used for stock management on Australian cattle and sheep stations, the Dragonfly is strong and maneuverable. It can take off at 26 mph, (22 knots) in 195 feet (60 m), and land in less than 400 feet (120 m). It has a single seat and 3-axis flight controls,[10] and weighs about 370 lbs (170 kg) with a pilot and full fuel load. Clegg's Dragonfly was assembled for him in Florida. He went there for test flights and then shipped it to Idaho. "We were actually training birds while I was learning to fly it," he recalled. "I wasn't super-comfortable with it at first, but by the time we were done, it's probably the best airplane I've ever flown."

Planning was intense for the first ultralight-led crane migration in 1995. Clegg flew the entire route ahead of time with a neighbor—an airline pilot—in the neighbor's Cherokee 140, a four-seat, single-engine airplane. "We sort of mapped out the whole route," Clegg recalled. "We were going to land here, and then we were going land there. Are there any ponds down there? We want the birds to experience a pond."

During the actual migration, the preplanned route gave way to nature. "We didn't fly where we wanted to go," said Clegg. "We went

---

[9] In simple terms, "stall speed" is the speed at which an airplane is no longer moving fast enough to produce enough lift to stay aloft.
[10] Control stick for ailerons (roll) and elevator (pitch), and rudder pedals (yaw).

wherever the birds could go, however long they could stay up, however long fuel lasted, and where winds blew us." Nothing turned out to be pre-determined, he said, except the fact that once they left the ground, they were going to come back down "at some point. That was the only thing you could count on."

Clegg's first migration flight would offer other lessons, as well.

AS KENT CLEGG PREPARED TO LEAD HIS SANDHILLS south by ultralight in 1995, a group of USFWS biologists led by David Ellis at Patuxent, was teaching greater sandhill cranes to follow a truck on migration.[11] Ellis and his assistants dressed in blue and white jackets and wore red caps to mimic the sandhill crane's red crown. To teach the cranes to follow the "cranemobile" (a converted Army ambulance), the trainers ran behind the slow-moving truck, flapping their arms. In August, four of the sandhill cranes were driven from Maryland to Garland Prairie in northern Arizona in the cranemobile. The four-day trip was very stressful for the birds and the remaining six birds in the study were flown to Arizona in the Windway jet. The sandhill chicks were already conditioned to follow the trainers and the truck. They were soon flying after the cranemobile, for up to 9 miles (15 km) at a time. As the truck led them through a variety of settings—through prairies, forests, and developed areas, and past fences, power lines, and other features—lead trainer Brian Clauss rode in the open rear door of the truck calling to the cranes and encouraging them. A crane decoy fastened to the rear of the truck and flags flapping from the roof provided additional cues to the birds. All six birds carried leg-mounted transmitters. The team would come to regret the choice of solar-powered transmitters when the birds wandered off after dark.

In early October, the cranemobile led ten sandhill cranes from Garland Prairie, 385 miles south (620 km) to the Buenos Aires National Wildlife Refuge in southern Arizona. There were three vehicles and six

---

[11] Ellis, et al (1997): "Results of an Experiment to Lead Cranes on Migration Behind Ground Vehicles," Proceedings of the Seventh North American Crane Workshop, pp 114-122. This was not the first time Ellis taught cranes to follow a truck. From 1990 to 1992, he and other staff at Patuxent taught small groups of sandhill cranes to follow a car or truck so the biologists could see at close range how wearing various backpack harnesses with tracking transmitters affected the birds' flight performance. In 1994, in preparation for a truck-led migration, they taught several sandhill chicks at Patuxent to walk up a ramp into the back of a pickup truck and to ride in the pickup bed. The only problem encountered was the flightless chicks' tendency to walk off the sides of the ramp.

people in the convoy. The lead car scouted traffic conditions and hazards; the cranemobile was in the middle; and the tail car kept a running audio log and searched for straggling cranes.

The 13-day migration trip from Garland Prairie to Buenos Aires NWR included plenty of difficulties. In its report, the team noted, "Our southward passage included many unique and bizarre interactions between trainers, cranes, railroad trains, police, a jogger, eagles, bystanders, and oncoming vehicles."[12]

Power lines presented the greatest hazard to the birds; there were three collisions (1 fatal) and many near misses. Golden eagles attacked the cranes several times; no cranes were injured but each attack scattered the birds and disrupted the trip's progress. Some of the birds flew on their own back to Garland Prairie after the eagle attacks, and had to be retrieved.

Part of the route wound through a dense forest that made it impossible for the trainers to keep the cranes in sight when the birds flew above the trees. But the most serious problem was the heat. Early October should have brought the first hard frost to the high desert. Instead, midday temperatures topped 85° F. (30° C.) during the last two thirds of the trip. The cranes easily overheated and dropped out. Only six of the nine surviving cranes arrived at the refuge behind the cranemobile.

At the refuge the birds were penned over the winter to protect them from predators and to encourage them to imprint on their new surroundings. In the spring, the cranes were released from their pen in the hopes that they would migrate back to Garland Prairie. Most of them left the refuge. Then the project went awry. Some of the birds spotted "civilians" wearing red caps, landed, and began following those people around. Others landed in fenced-in schoolyards, apparently because the school fences resembled their winter pens. That spring of 1996, none of the cranes migrated north along the route they had followed behind the truck the previous fall. They were rounded up and trucked back to Mormon Lake, near Garland Prairie, to spend the summer.

---

[12] Ibid., p118. The Proceedings are available on ICF's Web site: www.savingcranes.org.

Chapter 15
It Works!

OUT EAST, BILL LISHMAN WAS STILL TEACHING Canada geese to migrate behind his ultralight. In October 1995, he led a flock of 38 geese 400 miles (640 km) from the north shore of Lake Erie to the Airlie Center, in Virginia. Six weeks later, 36 of those geese were led another 415 miles (670 km) south to a wildlife refuge on South Carolina's Atlantic coast.

As Kent Clegg was rearing sandhill cranes for migration to Bosque del Apache NWR, Lishman and his team began working with sandhill cranes at a rearing area near Blackstock, Ontario that they had previously built for rearing Canada geese. Lishman's team collected sandhill eggs from wild nests along the north shore of Lake Huron. The young cranes were raised in isolation by caretakers dressed in crane costumes that disguised their human forms, especially faces and hands. The handlers used crane puppets and recorded crane calls to interact with the chicks. The birds were also exposed to recorded ultralight engine noise, and then gradually to the ultralight itself. To encourage the cranes to follow the ultralight, costumed "parents" would run alongside the taxiing aircraft. The pilots were also costumed. The cranes followed the costumed parent and, later, the ultralight alone.

Lishman began with eight sandhill crane chicks hatched in late May 1995, but mortality was high for the young sandhills. Two of the chicks died less than a week after hatching. The six remaining chicks responded well to training with the ultralight, but two of them developed severe leg deformities. Those two were euthanized about five weeks after they hatched. During one of the training sessions behind the taxiing ultralight, one of the chicks broke its leg. The pilot was alone with no other handlers and didn't see the accident, so no one knew whether the chick had collided with the airplane or just stumbled. It survived but it was out of the program.

In mid-September, as the experiment moved into its final phase, the team prepared to move the three remaining chicks from their rearing pen to a new pen and runway. A costumed handler approached the chicks' pen carrying one of the large cardboard boxes used to transport the chicks. Inside the pen, the chicks were excited, possibly due to the break in their routines that day. Startled by the cardboard box, one of the chicks jumped, collided with part of the pen, and broke its neck. That left just two sandhill cranes for the project.

By the fall, when they began following the ultralight into the air, the birds had clearly imprinted on the airplane. If it was rolled out of sight into its hangar before the birds were back in their pen, they would get very agitated, often circling over the hangar and calling. The handlers learned to leave the airplane on the runway until the cranes were back in their pen.

Lishman led the cranes on short cross-country flights over preplanned routes. The birds were at first reluctant to leave the pen area, but after a few flights they were happy to follow the aircraft. Lishman and his co-authors later wrote that they had made some significant discoveries while flying with the sandhill cranes.[13] The cranes were willing and able to follow the ultralight to altitudes as high as 4,000 feet (1,200 m) and over distances up to 40 miles (64 km) from their starting point. When the birds encountered thermals—rising columns of warm air—they would make good use of them, just as wild cranes do. The captive-reared cranes soon showed themselves to be experts at riding thermals upward. Observing them at close range in flight, the pilots noted that the cranes were very efficient at climbing (in thermals) and at descending—much more efficient than the ultralight or the Canada geese, probably due to the cranes' comparatively light wing loading.[14] In thermals, the cranes could ascend much faster than the ultralight, though they seemed reluctant to climb more than about 90 feet (150 m) above it. The cranes also descended relatively quickly. Canada geese have fairly high wing loading, and they descend and land very much like airplanes, with a shallow glide, a

---

[13] Lishman, et. al., "A Reintroduction Technique for Migratory Birds: Leading Canada Geese and Isolation-Reared Sandhill Cranes with Ultralight Aircraft," *Proceedings of the North American Crane Workshop 7*, 96-104.

[14] An aircraft's (or bird's) "wing loading" is the ratio between its total weight and its wing area.

flare of the wings to generate a stall, and a running landing. Cranes have a much lower wing loading and can safely descend much faster and more steeply, to an almost vertical final approach.

When Lishman's crane flights ended in early October, the sandhill cranes were returned to captivity.

OUT IN IDAHO, KENT CLEGG'S CLASS OF sandhill cranes hatched in early May 1995 and was introduced to his ultralight about three weeks later. Every few days, Clegg flew the airplane in a low pass over the pen, then landed and briefly left it idling near the birds' pen. Over the summer, the birds learned to follow an ATV, then the taxiing ultralight, and finally the flying ultralight, encouraged by Clegg's brood calls.

Shortly before they left on migration, the cranes were fitted with bright yellow leg bands with black numbers for easy identification, and with solar-powered transmitters (with battery backup) for radio tracking.

On the morning of October 16, Clegg led the 11 sandhill cranes south away from the ranch on the world's first ultralight-led crane migration. Two birds that were injured earlier in the summer during flight training were left behind. Clegg was worried that they might not be able to keep up with the Dragonfly.

A second ultralight joined the flight, a Challenger flown by Errol Spaulding of Ririe, Idaho. Spaulding is a heavy-duty mechanic who loves to fly and has flown a wide range of ultralight and experimental aircraft.

With its much faster cruise speed (100 mph, 160 km/h, max.), Spaulding's Challenger could scout ahead for landing sites and wind conditions, and fly "high cover" to protect the cranes from eagle attacks, which typically came from above and behind the flock.

A four-person ground crew rode in three vehicles. A pickup truck and a lightweight four-wheel-drive truck were the chase vehicles. A heavier pickup towed the ultralight's trailer; it carried the portable pen that was used along the route, and would carry the Dragonfly back to Idaho at the end of the trip.

The 11 birds settled in quickly. Flying in formation and riding on the ultralight's wingtip vortices required more wing flapping than a simple glide, but was much more efficient for the birds than flapping along on their own.

On most days, the morning flight would begin about 9 a.m. and last for an hour or two. When the birds or the pilots decided it was time to land, the portable pen was set up and the birds were rested during the day. If the winds died down enough in late afternoon, the team would make a second flight just before sunset, then pen the birds for the night, to protect them from predators. In a single day, the flights covered anywhere from 25 to 120 miles (43 to 217 km). The birds averaged about 30 mph (50 km/h) in flight with sprints up to 42 mph (70 km/h).

During the afternoon flight on Day One, about 75 miles south of the Clegg Ranch, one of the cranes disappeared. It showed up back at the ranch three days later.

On the second day of the migration, two of the birds quickly showed signs of tiring during morning flight, and were unable to keep up with the rest of the flock. When one bird dropped out of formation to land, the other birds tried to join it. To keep the flock in the air, the two stragglers were carried in the trailer for much of the trip. One of the stragglers was later diagnosed with coccidiosis, a common ailment among cranes that can cause respiratory problems.

Kent Clegg's ultralight parked next to the cranes' traveling pen.

Photo, © *Kent & Peter Clegg.*

The second morning's flight also saw the first of five eagle attacks during the migration. As the flock crossed a high pass in the Bear River Mountain Range, two of the cranes lagged below and behind. In a diving attack from behind, a pair of golden eagles struck the two cranes. One crane was hit and driven to the ground 1,500 feet (460 m) below. The other crane dodged the initial strike and took off with the eagle in hot pursuit. The two were last seen disappearing over a ridge. The ground crew recovered the remains of the first crane; the second was never found.

The rest of the flock scattered. The ultralights landed and the birds followed them to the ground, panting and wild-eyed. It took several hours in the portable pen to calm them down. Still, the team made two more flights that day, covering a total of 83 miles (134 km).

Eagles typically attack in high-speed dives from above and behind. The momentum of the attack can drive their razor-sharp talons deep into the victim's lungs or other organs and carry both predator and prey to the ground. During the 1995 migration experiment, the cranes often gave the first warning of an attack when they crowded in under the wings of the Dragonfly. As the migration went on, the pilots learned to head off attacking eagles. In the Challenger, Spaulding carried a shotgun loaded with "cracker shells." The shells fired a small charge that exploded about 50 yards (45 m) out of the barrel. That was usually enough to discourage the eagles. There were four more attacks, and eagles were seen on two other occasions, but none of the other cranes was injured by eagles during the 1995 migration.

From the Clegg Ranch near Grace, Idaho to Bosque del Apache NWR near Socorro, New Mexico, the migration covered 748 miles (1,204 km). It took 11 days and a total of 23 hours in the air. Only one day passed without any flights. On October 2 in southeastern Utah, snow and high winds kept the ultralights on the ground.

Around mid-day on October 26, the aircraft and seven cranes landed at the refuge, not far from a large gathering of wild sandhill cranes. A group of refuge staff and reporters greeted the birds, and then moved away from the landing area. As Clegg walked the seven birds toward the wild cranes, several wild birds came near, calling to Clegg's birds. Clegg slipped away, and early that evening, as the wild birds began flying back to the marshes where they would spend the night, Clegg's birds followed. But as they flew with the wild birds, they got high enough to spot the Dragonfly parked some distance away. All seven birds turned, flew to the ultralight, and landed. With the wild birds out of sight, Clegg led his birds into their pen for the night.

The next morning, the wild cranes were back in the adjacent field and Clegg's birds joined them to feed. During the day, the pen and aircraft were moved away. At dusk, the wild birds flew off to their night roosting sites, but the seven Clegg birds stayed behind. When the humans chased them to encourage them to follow the wild birds, the cranes flew off, but there was no way of knowing where they spent the night. Their solar-powered transmitters, even with battery backups, had proven inadequate to the task all through the trip; after dark, their signals couldn't be tracked.

On October 28, the third day on the refuge, only five of the seven Clegg birds were spotted feeding with the wild cranes. Late that morning, the remains of the two missing cranes were found in high grass, apparently killed by coyotes. That evening, when the wild cranes flew off to their nighttime roosts in the marsh, the five Clegg birds went along.

The next morning, October 28, the team could find only two of their birds. Searchers found one of the missing birds hiding in tall grass. It had a minor wound in one wing, from a shotgun pellet. That bird was treated and released, and it rejoined the wild cranes.

On October 28 and 29, some 60 hunters gathered for a crane hunt on private land near the refuge. Clegg and his team assumed that the hunt would not be a problem; there was plenty of crane food on the refuge and no apparent reason for the cranes to wander outside the refuge and into the hunt area. But on October 29, a hunter brought the remains of two of Clegg's cranes to a hunter checking station. They had been flying with wild cranes when he shot them, he said, and he saw their orange leg bands before he fired, but didn't know that they were significant.

Two more hunts were scheduled for December. The refuge staff wrote and distributed flyers to educate the hunters about the research project and ask them not to shoot any more cranes wearing bright orange leg bands.

In November, the Clegg crane diagnosed with coccidiosis was released on the refuge after treatment, and immediately joined the wild cranes. The "homesick" crane that returned to the ranch on the first day of the migration was also released into the wild flock. Two days later, he disappeared and was never found.

The four surviving Clegg cranes spent the winter on the refuge, living with the wild cranes. As they had on the Clegg ranch, the birds fed in the fields each day and spent each night roosting in water, in the nearby marshes. When humans approached them, they flew away, just like the wild birds. In the spring, all four migrated north with the wild sandhills cranes, along a different route than the one Clegg had led them on the previous fall. In March, they were seen in southern Colorado's San Luis Valley, an important staging area for the region's wild cranes. A month later, two of the Clegg cranes were spotted with wild sandhill cranes about 30 miles (50 km) from the Clegg Ranch. The two others were not seen again.

In spite of the eagles, the hunters, and all the other obstacles and pitfalls, Kent Clegg and his team had proven that it is possible to raise a group of cranes, lead them on a long migration, and at the end of it, integrate them successfully into a population of wild cranes. "We flew those cranes to New Mexico," Clegg said, "and in 1996 I was ready for whooping cranes but [the International Whooping Crane Recovery Team] said, 'no, you need to do it again.' So we did it again."

DAVID ELLIS AND HIS TEAM REPEATED the truck-following experiment in the fall of 1996.[15] Fourteen captive-reared sandhill cranes were raised at the Patuxent Wildlife Research Center and then flown to Camp Navajo, on a remote corner of the Navajo U.S. Army Depot near Belmont, in northern Arizona. The blue and white jackets and red caps were gone in 1996, replaced by gray ponchos and a gray hood. The team also used two gray plastic crane decoys to encourage the birds to follow the cranemobile.

The 360-mile (600-km) migration began on October 12 and took eight days, compared to 13 days the year before. It followed nearly the same route as before. In 1995, hot weather in the Sonoran Desert exhausted the cranes and made long flights difficult. In 1996, cooler weather allowed for longer flights. And aggressive measures by the trainers reduced the number of golden eagle attacks to zero. The cranes' only brush with an eagle in 1996 occurred when they flushed one from the top of a power pole, and on that occasion it was the eagle that (in Huck Finn's words) "lit out for the Territories."

When they reached Buenos Aires NWR, the cranes were rather socialized to humans and certainly had the potential to become "nuisance birds," like the 1995 class. The trainers trucked the 1996 class north to a wetland near Gila Bend, Arizona (SW of Phoenix), about a third of the way back to Navajo Camp. There, they released the cranes one or two at a time into a flock of wild sandhill cranes. Once they settled into the wild flock, the cranemobile birds seemed to have no more interest in humans.

---

[15] Ellis, David, et al., "Results of the Second (1996) Experiment to Lead Cranes on Migration Behind a Motorized Ground Vehicle," Proceedings of the North American Crane Workshop 8; pp 122-126.

Meanwhile, the class of 1995 still hadn't made much progress at migrating on their own. Five of the eight were lost during the summer, probably to coyotes or bobcats. In the fall of 1996, they headed south after some prodding, but not along the 1995 route. They continued to look for human company, and, once again, they were gathered up and penned over the winter of 1996-97 at Buenos Aires NWR.

IN IDAHO, ON OCTOBER 16, 1996, KENT CLEGG'S Dragonfly ultralight (painted white with black wingtips, to look like a whooping crane) led seven captive-reared sandhill cranes southward from the Clegg Ranch at the start of the second ultralight-led migration to Bosque del Apache NWR. High winds caused more problems for the birds and the ultralight, than in 1995. On the best of days, the thermals rising off the spine of the Rocky Mountains are too violent for an ultralight. Unable to use the thermals, the birds had to work extra hard to climb over the high passes and ridges along the route. In 1996, strong headwinds and crosswinds added to the strain on the cranes and the pilots. When the birds struggled to climb, Clegg had to slow the Dragonfly to near stall speed to avoid outrunning the cranes. At near stall speed, the plane has little lift and maneuvering is tricky. On Day Two, Clegg nearly crashed into the treetops while crossing a ridge. A few days later, trying to stay with the birds on a long climb, he made a forced landing on a highway when his lift ran out. That day, the cranes were loaded into the trailer and given an elevator ride to the top of the pass. With no cranes to worry about, Clegg could maintain plenty of speed in the aircraft to clear the ridge safely.

On good flying days, some of the cranes almost seemed to be playing with the airplane. In his journal of the flight, Kent's brother Peter Clegg described some of the birds' antics:

> "[One bird] will fly out ahead of Kent and then gradually float back until his feet are touching the controls. Then he'll drop down and fly right between the tires. One of the birds will float right out and try to lay [sic] prone on the wing during flight. It's their version of body surfing."[16]

During one flight, Peter wrote, "one of the birds drifted back

---

[16] Peter Clegg, 1996 Migration Project, published online; www.clegg.org.

close enough for Kent to tickle its feet." But toying with the airplane could be risky for the cranes.

> "Just before landing, [crane #]102, Kent's favorite, most loyal flyer, almost bought the farm. Somehow she had gotten over the wing and near the tail section of the plane. The Dragonfly uses cables for stability and has a cable running from the top of the rudder to the outside of the elevator. As Kent looked back 102 had tangled herself in the cable. He immediately thought, 'She's history!' Last year a bird had caught itself in the wing strut and immediately snapped its leg. #102 went over backwards with wings flapping and did a couple of somersaults in the air. Kent waited for her to spiral down but instead she recovered from the stall, regained controlled flight, and was soon back on the wing with the rest. A closer inspection on landing showed no lingering aftereffects."[17]

The 1996 migration took 15 days, including a total of five days grounded due to bad weather or high winds. (Clegg's 1995 ultralight

"One of the birds drifted back close enough for Kent to tickle its feet."   Photo, © Kent & Peter Clegg.

---

[17] Ibid. "102" was the number on the crane's yellow leg band.

migration took 11 days.) There were four golden eagle attacks but none were successful. All seven birds completed the trip, though two of them rode part of the way in the ground vehicles. Crane #105, one of the two males in the flock, had trouble keeping up during most of the trip. (Peter Clegg wrote that #105's problems might have come from a too-hearty appetite.) Crane #107 had developed a nerve problem in her left leg over the summer. In flight, it would hang down a bit, "like a rudder in the water," and slow her down.

On October 30, the cranes arrived at Bosque del Apache NWR, after the end of the two-day crane hunt on adjacent land.

> "High over head, the Dragonfly with its white fuselage and black tipped wings started its descent. Kent and the cranes started a long slow spiral directly above the refuge hay field where they were to land. The birds tucked their wings in the parachute position and followed in lazy descending circles. 102 stayed right on Kent's wing the entire time. At about 100 feet, Kent straightened the plane, lined it up between the irrigation ditches and set it down in a perfect landing. The cranes spread their wings wide and flapped them a couple of times as they stepped out of the sky and onto the ground. The journey was over."[18]

In an adjacent field, hundreds of wild sandhill cranes were feeding on the corn. The ultralight birds followed Kent to the cornfield. As they began mingling with the wild cranes, Kent slipped into the high corn and disappeared from their sight.

The next day, two of the ultralight cranes apparently joined a group of wild cranes flying south into Mexico, where many sandhills spend the winter. The rest of the ultralight birds spent the winter on the refuge with the wild cranes and with three surviving ultralight cranes from the class of 1995. In the spring of 1997, all of the ultralight cranes migrated north with the wild cranes, staging in Colorado's San Luis Valley before heading north and scattering across Utah, Idaho, and Wyoming. The ultralight cranes did not stay together and none of them returned to the Clegg Ranch. Instead they each followed the wild sandhills to nesting grounds in the region.

---

[18] Ibid.

Meanwhile, four cranemobile cranes, survivors of the class of '95, had spent the winter penned at Buenos Aires NWR, to keep them out of mischief. They were released in the spring of '96 and headed north in April along the route back to Mormon Lake, near where their truck-led migration had begun in the fall of 1995. It was a promising start but 85 miles (140 km) north of the refuge, they landed on a golf course. They were captured and moved a short distance to a more isolated location, in the hopes that they would continue their migration. There, the team later reported, a coyote or bobcat injured one of the birds.

> "The three remaining cranes apparently became disoriented after we moved them; they flew 125 km [75 mi] east (not north) and landed in a state penitentiary. When they were released from jail, they flew west and were never seen again."[19]

The cranemobile had been a limited success. Clegg and his team had proven that captive-raised sandhill cranes could be led by an ultralight on a long migration route, could be integrated into a flock of wild cranes at the wintering site, could learn survival techniques from the wild cranes, and could make a return migration on their own.[20] It was time to try it with whoopers.

---

[19] Ellis, et al., "Fate of the Survivors . . ." Proc. of the North Am. Crane Workshop, 8:2001; p 129.

[20] The 1996 migration team included: Kent Clegg, pilot & "lead crane;" Mignon Clegg, ground crew; Jim Lewis (USFWS), project collaborator; Errol Spaulding, Challenger pilot; Sharon Spaulding, ground crew; Peter Clegg, ground crew & author; and Ron Hill, camera lead.

Support for the 1996 ultralight migration project came from Newton Heuberger, Friends of the Bosque del Apache NWR, Portneuf Valley Audubon Society, Whooping Crane Conservation Association, Windway Capitol Corp., and World Wildlife Fund of Canada.

Chapter 16
Whooping Cranes, at Last!

KENT CLEGG'S 1997 ULTRALIGHT-LED MIGRATION to Bosque del Apache actually began in Maryland, at the Patuxent Wildlife Research Center where five whooping crane eggs hatched in late May. As they pipped, they were introduced to Clegg's own brood call—a respectable imitation of a crane's brood call. Three more whooper chicks of similar age were transferred from Patuxent's costume-rearing program. (They were originally slated for release into the non-migratory flock at Kissimmee Prairie.) When the youngest of the chicks was about two weeks old, they were flown to the Clegg Ranch in Idaho, in Windway's Cessna Citation. One died of infection shortly after arriving in Idaho. The other seven fledged.

At the ranch, volunteers had been raising a dozen sandhill chicks, hatched from eggs collected at nearby Grays Lake. Three of the sandhill chicks died; nine fledged.

The rearing techniques were the same used for the classes of 1995 and 1996. For most of the summer the sandhills and whoopers were penned separately but exercised together. Clegg explained:

> "When we raised the whooping cranes, we integrated them with a group of sandhills because we knew that when we got to New Mexico the whoopers were going to have to associate with about 10,000 sandhills on the Rio Grande River. So we raised a group of sandhills and . . . we integrated the two groups and got the whoopers to associate with the sandhills. And yet the whoopers were old enough that they didn't imprint to the sandhills. The whoopers were larger birds and, to them, the sandhills were just something to associate with and beat on but not

imprint to. . . [T]he whoopers tended to hang together as a group within the integrated flock."

Over the summer of 1997, the whooper and sandhill chicks learned to follow Kent's brood call, then his Polaris® ATV, and finally the ultralight making short flights away from the ranch. In the early fall, another whooper died of a respiratory infection. Two whoopers died after flying into their pen wall one night. One of the sandhills, a dominant male, was kicked out of the program for insubordination.

Young whoopers at the Clegg Ranch.

Photo, © Kent & Peter Clegg.

On Sunday, October 12, the migration pilots and ground crew gathered at the Clegg Ranch: Tom Stehn, Whooping Crane Coordinator for the US Fish & Wildlife Service, on the ground crew; Jim Lewis, Tom Stehn's predecessor as whooper coordinator, now retired from FWS, on the ground crew; Peter Clegg and Scot Mcbutch, writer and photographer, respectively, on the ground crew; and Errol Spaulding, chase pilot, this year flying a RANS S-7 homebuilt airplane.

The next morning, October 13:

> "The clear sky from late last night was covered with scattered morning clouds. Light filtered through to highlight the reds of autumn against the new snow. The valley was checkered with fields of bright green from new hay, and the contrast of the three seasons' colors was beautiful."[21]

It looked like an auspicious day to start a new adventure. At mid-morning, the Dragonfly was parked near the birds' pen. Kent started the engine and taxied away slowly. He had rigged a system that allowed him to open the door of the pen as he taxied. The pen door swung open and cranes came trotting out, excited and ready to fly. The Dragonfly lifted off the runway with a dozen cranes—eight grey sandhills and four whooping cranes in their juvenile plumage, white mottled with tan. All 12 birds carried brightly colored ID tags and leg-mounted radio transmitters.

Soon after takeoff, one of the sandhill cranes had second thoughts and circled back to the pen. Kent circled back and retrieved the bird "on the fly" but soon one of the whoopers peeled off and headed home. Several attempts to reassemble the flock only left more of them back at the pen. Finally, Kent landed about a mile from the pen to keep the birds he still had with him from jumping ship.

Kent conferred with Jim Lewis and Tom Stehn and they agreed that the birds would be more likely to stick with the ultralight if the migration started in unfamiliar surroundings. They gathered up the birds, herded them into the trailer, and took them about 15 miles (25 km) south along the intended flight path. The winds had picked up and there would be no more flying until late afternoon. The ground crew set up the portable pens—one for sandhills and one for whoopers—and waited for the winds to calm down late in the day.

That evening, the winds did not abate. It was too windy to fly and the crew headed back to the ranch for the night, leaving Scott to spend the night with the birds. On the first day of the world's first ultralight-led whooping crane migration, the cranes had covered just 15 miles—on the ground.

So much for good omens.

---

[21] Peter Clegg, "The 1997 Whooping Crane Migration," at www.clegg.org.

The next morning was cold and clear—perfect flying weather. Kent circled the pen and the cranes lifted off and fell in behind him. Almost immediately, a whooper—the lone male whooper in the group—dropped out of formation and headed north, taking one of the female whoopers with him. Kent wheeled around picked him up, but the bird dropped out again. Kent was about to land and exile the troublemaker to the trailer for the day, when all four whoopers tucked into formation on a southerly heading. They were off.

South of Logan, Utah, they approached the difficult mountain pass between Paradise and Eden, Utah. Two years earlier, golden eagles had killed two ultralight-led sandhill cranes as they climbed toward this pass. One year earlier, with the birds exhausted from the climb and Kent slowing to near stall speed to keep them together, the Dragonfly had almost tangled with a tree at the summit. This year, the birds were flying high and strong, and sailed right over the heights.

The cranes flew 62 (103 km) miles that morning. About a mile before touchdown, one of the sandhill cranes dropped out and landed. At the landing site, the ground crew was about to go look for it when it appeared high overhead. Kent's brood call brought the bird drifting downward to land, and it was penned with the others.

Around 4:30 that afternoon, the Dragonfly took off again, leading the birds another 30 miles (50 km) before sunset. As Kent landed and shut down, one of the sandhills ventured too close and was struck by the propeller. Though the bird was not killed outright, its injuries were severe, and it was euthanized.

On Wednesday, Day Three, the birds put another 90 miles behind them. They were flying well and keeping up an amazing pace for so early in the trip. The pass south of Daniel's Canyon, near Morgan, Utah, was another major hurdle and the team planned to land the birds in the canyon and trailer them to the pass, to avoid exhausting them. But this year the birds were flying well; they pushed for the top and sailed over it without trouble.

Errol Spaulding flew "top cover" in his RANS S-7. Like a fighter pilot guarding a formation of bombers, he intercepted and discouraged several golden eagles that morning. One especially persistent eagle tried repeatedly to join the cranes' formation. Finally, a cracker shell fired from Spaulding's shotgun sent the "bogie" packing.

Wednesday afternoon's flight began just below another imposing mountain pass near Soldier Summit. As Kent circled to gain altitude, the birds struggled along behind him, beating their wings and panting heavily. They cleared the pass by just 40 or 50 feet, with the birds scattered but still following the Dragonfly. Once over the pass, they fell back into formation on the long, gentle descent. Wednesdays' distance was another 90 miles (150 km).

The four whoopers got along amiably enough with their smaller sandhill companions, but they tended to do their own thing, a little apart from the sandhills. In the air, the four whoopers generally formed up on one of the ultralight's wings, while the eight sandhills trailed after the other. On Thursday, Day Four, Peter Clegg wrote, "[T]he whoopers seemed to be holding their own party."[22] First, the whooping cranes dropped into formation behind Spaulding's RANS. Kent circled past with the sandhills, and the whoopers followed, but "the gang of four" was hanging back and flying just a few feet off the ground. The ultralight was heading low down a small valley, with the whoopers trailing behind when a golden eagle stooped and struck a straggling female whooper. The honking horn from a ground vehicle scared the eagle away, and Jim Lewis hopped a fence and ran to the crane. She was standing in the field with blood on one leg, but at least she was standing. The rest of the birds formed up tightly on the ultralight and followed it out of the valley toward Green River, Utah. Kent ran into headwinds on the way and landed at the Green River airport after two hours and forty minutes of flight, with almost no fuel left in the Dragonfly's tanks. They had come 90 miles in one stretch.

Spaulding, who had been close behind Kent's ultralight a few minutes before, was nowhere to be seen and couldn't be raised on the radio. Nearly frantic with worry, the crew quickly pumped 15 minutes worth of fuel into the Dragonfly and Kent took off to search for the missing pilot. All twelve birds dutifully followed along. Clegg circled back and landed, while the ground crew rushed to set up the pens and get the birds inside. As the last bird was being herded into the enclosure and Kent was firing up the Dragonfly, Spaulding's red and white RANS came over the ridge.

Spaulding landed at the airport and climbed out looking a bit shaken. He had been intercepting eagles that were diving on the Dragonfly's tail, he told the crew. He was turning hard, in a steep bank about 200 feet off the ground, when his engine quit. He quickly leveled off, hit the starter once (without success), and landed in

---

[22] Ibid.

short brush, rolling to a stop just short of a deep ravine. The culprit was a slightly bent fuel tank vent. With the plane (and its tanks) level, the engine fired right up, and Spaulding took off and flew to the airport to repair the vent.

Throughout the migration project, "there were risks," Kent said,

> "but you didn't think about it too much. We were trying to do something worthwhile, we were out on the cutting edge trying to figure out how to work with the cranes. We were careful. Errol is probably one of the most experienced pilots I know and that's why he was there."

With all the excitement and another 90 miles (150 km) behind them, the team decided to call it a day. The injured crane was taken to a local veterinarian for treatment. A diving eagle aims for its victim's lungs or vital organs. This crane was lucky; she escaped with two lacerations to her upper leg.

Friday October 17, Day Five, was another perfect weather day. The pilots spotted several eagles during the morning flight but with Spaulding discouraging them, the raptors kept their distance. The cranes spent more than two hours in the air that morning, covering 82 miles (132 km).

That evening, Clegg took off about 5 p.m. with seven birds in tow, but they were disorganized and seemed nervous, flying low to the ground. Spaulding spotted an eagle high above them. Diving from about 10,000 feet of altitude, the eagle rocketed down toward the cranes, its wings tucked tightly against its sides. Peter Clegg described the mayhem that followed:[23]

> "Peeling off one of the sandhills [the eagle] missed a direct hit and circled back for another attack. Kent locked on and flew directly at it sending the eagle right over the upper wing at the center of his plane. One sandhill was still hanging with him and as he looked back, the determined eagle had made a 180[-degree turn] and was bearing down on the crane. Errol peeled off the eagle in a three-G turn just in

---

[23] Ibid.

the nick of time. The eagle still wouldn't give up and as it pumped its way back to the flock, Errol cut it off again. He said he tried to plant it right on his skylight. . . That was enough for the eagle and it retreated into the cedars below.

"The birds were wildly out of formation. When they sense danger, they all flock in a mad scramble to get near the [Dragonfly]. Wings and feathers are everywhere as they crowd the front of the plane and the cockpit. In the scramble for position, one whooper maneuvered too close and hung itself up on the plane's ballistic chute canister. Kent cut the throttle and nosed downward to keep the crane from going through the prop. Fortunately there was no injury.

"Another eagle appeared. This time Errol was ready with the shotgun and scared the eagle off before it got too near the birds. By now the cranes were very upset and continued to crowd the plane. Kent had to set down to keep them from getting tangled in [the ultralight's rigging] or caught in the propeller. [Both pilots] landed on a hill near the highway and waited to see if the cranes would settle down. [The cranes'] eyes were wild and they were panting as they walked around the planes."

The cranes were safe and the pilots were safe. They counted their blessings and called it a day with a total of 92 miles (148 km) traveled. Saturday, October 19, Day Seven, was uneventful by comparison. The weather was perfect, there were no eagle attacks, and the route took the planes and cranes over some spectacular landscapes. They traversed the Four Corners region (where four states come together) and flew into New Mexico. They were over Navajo land now, and passed Shiprock, a magnificent "volcanic

Wild-eyed after the eagle attack.
Photo, © Kent & Peter Clegg.

neck" formation towering nearly 2,000 feet (600 m) above the table-flat desert. They landed at sunset after two flights totaling almost 100 miles (160 km).

From here on, there were more and more spectators and well-wishers along the route. The news media were following the flight and Peter Clegg was posting a daily log on the Internet.

On Saturday, the whooper that was injured by the eagle two days earlier returned to the flock. A vet had treated two lacerations on her upper leg, and she was limping a bit but flying around the pens. She rode in the trailer the rest of the way to Bosque del Apache. With all the people around, the team was concerned for the injured whooper's safety, in case she dropped out of formation along the way.

One of the sandhill cranes also rode most of the way in the trailer. Weaker than her mates, she had respiratory problems and could not keep up with the flock. Both trailered cranes were released into the wild at Bosque del Apache NWR.

Sunday morning's flight was a good one, covering 64 miles. Penned during the day on the Grants-Milan Airport, the cranes and planes attracted a large gathering of spectators and reporters—large enough to cause concern over the cranes. The afternoon's flight took them to a more isolated landing site, after covering 84 miles for the day.

Monday, October 20, Day Eight was another perfect weather day and the cranes were flying well, roughly paralleling Interstate 25. As Peter Clegg followed along on the ground,

> ". . . [A] couple of the birds started to drop and Kent radioed that something was bothering them. Suddenly I caught sight of a military jet heading right over the top of them. It wasn't just one but six of what appeared to be F-16 fighters in low altitude, high-speed flight. It was just like shooting a grenade launcher into the flock. Several birds shot up and out and the rest dived for the deck. Kent was wildly banking the plane trying to see what was happening and where the birds were going. One after another, the F-16s streaked over head—probably completely oblivious to what was happening below them."[24]

---

[24] Ibid.

Together, Kent Clegg and Spaulding managed to round up the scattered birds and get them back into formation on the Dragonfly. With the morning's takeoff 60 miles (100 km) behind them and Bosque del Apache NWR just 40 miles (66 km) ahead, Kent found an isolated spot and set the flock down for the day.

Kent Clegg and some friends check the day's distance on the GPS receiver.
Photo, © Kent & Peter Clegg.

On Tuesday, October 21, Day Nine, the ultralight lifted off into a clear, calm sky, with the cranes following in good order. Peter wrote: "It was a smooth, leisurely flight down the center of the valley and took a little less than an hour. No eagles, no jets, and only a little tail wind to speed things up."[25]

Their landing site on the refuge, scouted the day before, was an open hay field near a huge gathering of wild sandhills. Not far away was another large gathering—of people who had come to see the ultralight-led cranes arrive at the reserve. Kent circled the crowd in the Dragonfly, the white ultralight with its black wing tips looking like a huge whooping crane. Behind it three whoopers and seven sandhills soared gracefully toward the landing site. The RANS followed high and behind.

Kent chopped power and the ultralight touched down in the cut hay field and rolled to a stop. The cranes "parachuted" down around him. The ultralight-led migration was over.

The pilots and ground crew penned the cranes to keep them away from the crowd of people. Then they flew the airplanes away and out of sight. The next day the ultralight birds were released as a group into the wild flock of sandhill cranes. "We opened the gate on the little pen they were in," Clegg said, "and I walked out slowly toward the cornfields" where the wild cranes were feeding.

> "And this was nothing the birds hadn't done a hundred times back in Idaho. They went out and started feeding on the natural foods. And of course down there,

---

[25] Ibid.

there are thousands of sandhills all around. It was more sandhills than they were used to seeing but they went out and started integrating. And while they were feeding and doing what comes naturally, I just went into the cornfields and disappeared and they just never saw me again."

Clegg placed a whooping crane decoy in the Rio Grande River where the wild sandhills roosted at night. He parked his ATV in the feeding area as another "security blanket" for the ultralight cranes. Within a few days, all of Clegg's cranes were feeding and roosting with the wild flock. The whooper that had been attacked by an eagle on the way south recovered quickly; after a few days, she had no trouble flying with the rest of the flock.

In among the wild sandhills was one old whooping crane, one of the cross-fostered whoopers from Grays Lake, Idaho. More than once, the young whoopers who had just arrived at the reserve sought out the older whooper and kept company with him.

In November, a one-day sandhill crane hunt was held on land near the reserve. Every hunter was given a pamphlet describing the migration project and how to identify the ultralight birds. But on the day of the hunt, one of the ultralight sandhills disappeared, apparently wandering off the reserve. And at one of the hunter check-in stations, a sportsman turned in a bright yellow ID leg band and a radio transmitter.

Kent stayed at the reserve for about ten days while the birds integrated into the wild flock. He explained:

"I had a white whooping crane decoy that we had got them sort of imprinted to, and I would just put that decoy wherever I wanted them that night or that morning, like out in the Rio Grande River on a sandbar, and then I would go out there and call them. And they would get up in the air and fly over and see that decoy and land by the decoy. And I would be hiding somewhere, so they would associate the voice with the decoy.

"And that took a couple of days of conditioning to get them flying to the river and to the fields. And they'd pick up on the wild birds quickly, as well. So at a certain time of day, everything gets up and goes over to the river to roost and then goes back to the fields to feed, and [the ultralight birds] just sort of fell into that pattern and learned that routine."

While the decoy helped the ultralight cranes learn to be wild, it was also indirectly responsible for the loss of two of the ultralight whoopers. "What I hadn't realized," Clegg said, is that

". . . the Rio Grand River changes almost daily. I would put the decoy out there and leave it for two or three days. And a sandbar connected to the bank and a coyote ran right out that sandbar . . . and one of the cranes was killed. Within a couple of weeks we lost two whooping cranes. But the others learned from it and had we had a bigger group or been able to do it again, we could have corrected a lot of those things."

The following spring, in March of 1998, the two surviving young whooping cranes flew north from Bosque del Apache NRW, apparently had second thoughts, and returned to the reserve. The next day, they headed north again and this time kept going. One of them was the whooper that had been injured in an eagle attack while following the ultralight. Tracked by satellite, the two cranes settled for a time in Colorado's San Luis Valley, apparently following wild sandhills to that well-used staging area. In March, it is late spring at Bosque del Apache but the snows have not yet melted in the north where the birds spend their summers. The cranes wait in the San Luis Valley, while the warm weather works its way up the latitudes.

Six young sandhill cranes also left the Bosque del Apache that spring. Companions of the two ultralight-led whoopers, the sandhills also staged in the San Luis Valley. Later that spring, all eight birds flew north and spent the summer scattered around Idaho, Utah, and Wyoming. Though none of Clegg's birds ever returned to the ranch on their own, those who survived migrated north on their own and found suitable summering areas, usually in the company of wild sandhill cranes. Most of the ultralight-led cranes returned to Basque del Apache in subsequent winters. The last of Clegg's whoopers was seen there in February of 2000.

OUT EAST, BILL LISHMAN AND JOE DUFF HAD FOUNDED
Operation Migration in Canada in 1994, to continue their groundbreaking work and carry out further migration studies.[26] They
embarked on another migration test with sandhill cranes in the fall of
1997. Clegg's birds were always led to areas where they could integrate into a large flock of wild cranes. But what would happen if
cranes were led on migration to a wintering ground where there were
no other cranes? Would those captive-reared cranes survive and would
they migrate north on their own in the spring? Those were the questions Operation Migration set out to answer in the fall of 1997.[27]

The study began with 18 greater sandhill cranes hatched from
captive breeding cranes at Patuxent. They were raised by costumed
handlers who wore gray ponchos and red baseball caps with a face
veil attached.[28] The chicks were raised in two groups, separated by
ages (up to 20 days apart). At Patuxent, the cranes were introduced to
a portable replica of an ultralight, complete with engine sounds. They
were taught to follow their handlers to the replica and then follow the
replica as it taxied. On July 31, 1997, when the youngest of the birds
was 40 days old, all 18 birds were flown by Canadian Armed Forces
Air Command to a training and fledging area at the southern tip of
Lake Scugog, near Perry, Ontario, about 160 miles (260 km) north of
Toronto. None of the cranes had fledged at that time.

In Ontario, the birds were placed in a pen divided in two. The
cranes were penned separately in a younger group and an older
group, to try to minimize aggression. Still, on the day they arrived at
their new home, one of the younger cranes was injured by its pen
mates and had to be euthanized. Three days later, one of the younger
chicks died of septicemia.

Until the chicks fledged, the costumed trainers would lead them

---

[26] Operation Migration is a registered Canadian charitable organization based in Port
Perry, Ontario, about 50 miles (80 km) northeast of Toronto. While has worked closely ICF in recent years, OM is not and never has been a branch, section, or department
of the International Crane Foundation. There seems to be a fair bit of confusion about
this in the public's mind. OM and ICF are separate entities working together toward a
common goal.

[27] Duff, et al., "Results of the First Ultralight-Led Sandhill Crane Migration in Eastern
North America," Proc. North Amer. Crane Workshop, 8:2001; pp 109-114.

[28] Earlier experiments had shown that the most effective costume for crane handlers—
to minimize the birds' socialization to humans—was a shapeless poncho-like garment
that extended at least to the wearer's knees, with coverings that disguised the wearer's
face and hands.

each day to the runway nearby and encourage them with brood calls to follow the taxiing ultralight. Duff wrote that there were problems in the training, caused by several factors: the delay in bringing the birds to Ontario while they waited for the youngest to reach 40 days of age, the difference in the ages of the two groups (about 20 days), and the large number of birds in each group. The birds were reluctant to follow the aircraft. And there was another unexpected complication. While the airplane was taxiing,

> "Caretakers would . . . run beside the aircraft in an effort to protect the chicks from the wheels and propeller. By this means, we inadvertently conditioned the birds to follow the handlers and not the aircraft."[29]

Unusually bad weather, reluctant and uncooperative cranes, dominance issues in the flock, and a minor airplane crash all conspired to slow the training. It wasn't until early October that the older group of birds would follow the ultralight well enough to give the pilot control over the direction and duration of the flight. The younger group never did graduate from the class. They would only follow the airplane for a short distance before peeling off and heading back to the runway.

On October 24, Duff took off and headed south, with the older group of 8 birds following along. The migration route took them east up the shore of Lake Ontario and around the eastern end of the lake, then south to the Airlie Center, near Warrenton, VA, a distance of 536 miles (863 km). They had originally planned to go straight south across Lake Ontario, but training delays caused a late start for the migration, and Duff and his team deemed it too risky to cross the open lake so late in the season.

The younger group of birds followed along in a trailer. The team made 14 stops along the way. At half of those stops, the young birds were brought out of the trailer and allowed to mix with the older birds, and the pilots tried to coax all 14 birds to follow the ultralight. The younger birds never did catch on. Sadly, at one stop, as Duff was trying to lead all 14 birds, one of the older birds was struck by the ultralight's rear-mounted propeller and was killed instantly.

High winds, rain, and snow plagued the project and it took 21 days to reach the Airlie Center. When the weather allowed them to

---

[29] Ibid., p 111.

fly, the birds flew well, surfing on the ultralight's vortices and show-ing no signs of fatigue.[30] At one point, the cranes dropped out of for-mation to climb on a rising thermal, but most of the time they stayed close to the aircraft, the lead bird soaring a foot or two behind the ultralight's wing.

The flight arrived at the Airlie Center on November 13. There the cranes were penned at night and released to forage during the day. The ultralight led them on "familiarization flights" around the area. Costumed handlers provided food daily at the pen and a costumed mannequin was left in the pen to encourage the birds to stay nearby. In February, the pen was dismantled. The birds spent their days for-aging and continued to spend their nights close to the pen site. The old and younger birds now seemed to be living and flying together as a single flock.

On March 13, four months after arriving at their wintering grounds, all 15 cranes flew away. A NASA satellite tracked the seven older cranes to the shore of the Chesapeake Bay. A few days later, they returned to the Airlie Center on their own. The six younger birds were reported wandering around a suburb of Baltimore, Maryland about 80 miles (135 km) from the Airlie Center. These cranes had all been trailered south in the fall and they were proving too tame for the study, or for their own good. They were captured and "retired" to a zoo in Omaha, Nebraska.

Two weeks later, on March 28, the seven older cranes (all ultra-light-led in the fall) left Airlie for good. They migrated around the west end of Lake Ontario, and a few days later, six of them were seen about 20 miles (30 km) west of the runway where they had fledged and trained in the fall. The seventh bird wandered off to Ohio and was captured.

For a few days the flock wandered east and west, never north. They seemed to know the latitude of their fledging ground but not the longitude. Like their younger counterparts, they were proving too tame to be left on their own, and on April 5, the team gathered them up and led them by ultralight back to the fledging grounds. The team hoped the birds would stay there, where fields and marshland offered excellent habitat for summering cranes. But within a few days the birds were wandering off and getting into mischief. By midsummer,

---

[30] The cranes' average speed was about 30 mph (51 km/h); their highest cruise speed was nearly 40 mph (65 km/h). Their longest sustained flight during the southward migration was 75 miles (124 km) in 2 hours and 20 minutes.

all six were back in captivity.

The project had achieved its primary goal. Cranes had been led by ultralight to a wintering ground where there were no other cranes. And they had made the return migration on their own in the spring. The rearing and training techniques used in the project could be refined to reduce the birds' tendencies to seek out human company.

In 1998, Operation Migration (OM) set out to promote more wildness in the captive-raised cranes by reducing the time the birds spent in contact with human trainers, and by improving the training procedures for ultralight-led migrations. OM planned to train a group of captive-raised sandhill cranes to follow an ultralight, trailer the cranes most of the way south, and then fly them behind an ultralight to a wintering ground. The hope was that trailering the birds would minimize the birds' contact with humans and flying them the last few miles would give them a sense of what direction to go when it came time to migrate north.

At Patuxent and at Scugog Lake, costume-rearing protocols for these birds were much tighter than the year before, with a strict "no talking" rule in force. In 1997, the cranes had learned to follow the trainers who ran alongside the ultralight, not the ultralight itself. To correct that in 1998, the chicks were placed inside a circular fence 30 feet (9.15 m) in diameter and 2 feet (61 cm) high. The ultralight, with its wing removed and its pilot in full crane costume, taxied around the outside of the fence. The chicks learned to follow the ultralight around the inside of the fence, and never associated it with walking handlers. Birds that were slow to catch on were placed in a small round "jealousy pen" in the center of the round training pen. From there, they could watch their pen-mates following the ultralight. In later training at Scugog Lake, chicks that had been trained in the round pen would ignore human handlers to follow the ultralight.

At Scugog Lake, the chicks' pen was modified to give it a much more natural look and to remove or disguise any evidence of humans. Instead of being led around each day by human handlers, the birds were released to forage and interact on their own, outside the pen and under the watchful but unseen eye of their human keepers. These and other refinements cut by nearly 80 percent the amount of training time it took to get the birds to follow the aircraft in flight—to about 60 hours. The real test of these improved methods would come in the spring, after the birds had been taken south. At their wintering ground uncostumed humans would approach them away from their release pens. If the cranes flew away at the humans' approach the experiment to increase the birds' wildness would be a success.

The 15 cranes left Scugog Lake by trailer on October 15, 1998 and arrived at a private airport in Green Sea, South Carolina on the 19th. En route, one of the cranes was attacked and injured by another, and was euthanized.

At the airstrip owned by Earl and Shirley Shaw, the crew penned the birds for two days to wait for better flying weather and to give the birds a rest. On October 21, OM Pilots Joe Duff and DeWitt "Deke" Clark, each flying a Cosmos® weight-shift controlled ultralight, led 14 cranes 61 miles (108 km) to the Tom Yawkey Wildlife Center on South Carolina's Atlantic coast. The Center's 31 square miles (80 km2) offer a variety of habitats from salt marshes to upland forests. OM chose it for its isolation, suitable crane habitat, and the absence of any wild cranes.

During the 75-minute flight to the Yawkey Center, two of the cranes dropped out of formation and disappeared.[31] The other 12 arrived safely. They were penned for a few nights, led on a few local flights around the wildlife center, and then released. The birds were monitored and periodically visited by costumed handlers through the winter. In the spring, when uncostumed humans approached the flock, the birds flew away.

Though they did not migrate back to Ontario, they did wander north into parts of North Carolina, staying in isolated areas. There were no reports of any of the cranes approaching humans or populated areas. OM had succeeded in promoting a greater degree of wildness in the birds and its methods would be used with refinements in the ultralight-led whooper migrations that followed.

OUT IN ARIZONA, DAVID ELLIS AND HIS CREW were still trying to find a safer alternative to leading crane migrations by aircraft or by truck. Their idea was to trailer a group of young sandhill cranes along a migration route from the Fish Springs NWR in west central Utah to the Gila River basin in southwestern Arizona. Along the way, the birds were released at intervals ("stages") along the route, encouraged to fly at those stops, then recaptured and trailered to the next stop. The team hoped that the birds would learn the migration

---

[31] One of the missing birds was never found. The remains of the other were discovered in Central Florida a year later, in November 1999.

route while avoiding the major risks to the birds (golden eagles, power lines), to the humans (rough terrain, engine failures), or both (crane-vehicle collisions). The group made two stage-by-stage migrations, in 1998 and in 1999. In both, the main difficulty was recapturing the cranes at each stop. Several birds in each study either couldn't be caught or were removed from the studies because they were too difficult to catch.

After wintering on the Gila River, none of the stage-by-stage cranes migrated back to Fish Springs. Some of them headed north into Utah but turned around and flew back to Gila River. In the end, the team concluded that the method showed some promise, but wasn't yet practical.[32]

The members of the Whooping Crane Recovery Team weighed the results. With Kent Clegg's successes in the west and Operation Migration's successes in the east, it appeared that the way was open to establish a new wild flock of whooping cranes in the United States.

---

[32] David Ellis, et al., "Results of the Utah-Arizona Stage-by-Stage Migrations," Proc. North Amer. Crane Workshop, 8; pp 132-138.

Chapter 17
Dress Rehearsal

THE BIG QUESTION AT THE SEPTEMBER 1999 MEETING of the Whooping Crane Recovery Team (WCRT) was, Where should the new migratory flock be established? USFWS Whooping Crane Coordinator Tom Stehn recalls:

> "A small team of crane experts led by Dr. John Cannon spent a year looking for possible sites for the migratory flock. They looked for suitable habitat, abundant foods, size (because Aransas is huge), isolation from humans, lack of hunting, and lack of power lines."

Over the spring and summer of 1999, Terry Kohler piloted Windway's Bell 407 helicopter in an aerial survey and filming of all of the well-known sandhill crane nesting areas in Wisconsin, looking for the best place to anchor the northern end of a new whooping crane migration route. "We covered a heck of a lot of Wisconsin," Terry recalls, flying at 20 to 25 knots, at 50 to 150 feet (15 to 45 m) off the ground. The survey located and filmed over 300 sandhill crane nests. A preliminary analysis narrowed the choice to three sites in Wisconsin: Crex Meadows, Necedah NWR, and Horicon Marsh."

Michigan's Seney NWR was also considered as a possible rearing site for the reintroduction of migratory whoopers. One of the FWS's most experienced and knowledgeable crane experts, Dr. Richard Urbanek, lived and worked at Seney, and had studied the sandhill cranes there for decades.

The fact that Seney also supports a large and growing population of reintroduced trumpeter swans might have worked both for and against it as a whooper-rearing site. In the end, the WCRT favored Wisconsin sites in part because of their proximity to the ICF headquarters at Baraboo.

ICF hosted the WCRT meeting at Baraboo that fall. Terry Kohler brought two Windway aircraft to the meeting, including the Citation, and flew the team members on an aerial tour of the three sites.

Crex Meadows is a 30,000-acre (121 km2) state wildlife refuge in northwestern Wisconsin. About half the refuge is wetlands, mostly sedge marshes. It has been one of the key sites for the reintroduction of the trumpeter swans to the region. The 43,000-acre (174 km2) Necedah NWR in central Wisconsin includes wetlands and hardwood savannah, and was already home to several threatened or endangered species, including bald eagles, Karner blue butterflies, Blanding's turtles, and timber wolves. The Horicon Marsh wetland, at 17,000 acres (68 km2), is the largest freshwater cattail marsh in the United States. It is a critical habitat for more than 200 species of ducks, cranes, egrets, herons, marshbirds, and shorebirds.

The WCRT's nod for a whooping crane rearing site went to Necedah. Crex Meadows is too close to Minnesota and to the whoopers that migrate between Canada and Texas, Stehn said, and it was full of trumpeter swans. Horicon Marsh is a very popular hunting spot and much of the marsh is too deep for cranes.

For wintering sites, the team narrowed the choice to two: Chassahowitzka National Wildlife Refuge in Florida and Marsh Island State Wildlife Refuge in Louisiana. In 1998, Terry and Mary had flown crane biologists around Louisiana to survey possible wintering sites there. The most promising site was Marsh Island, located between Vermilion Bay and the Gulf of Mexico, about 45 miles (75 km) south of Lafayette, Louisiana. Its 70,000 acres are mostly treeless salt marsh and a major wintering ground for snow geese and other waterfowl. Recent counts have found roughly 30,000 geese and 50,000 ducks there.

Chassahowitzka NWR, 65 miles north of St. Petersburg, Florida on the Gulf of Mexico, has more than 31,000 acres of salt marshes, estuaries, and saltwater bays. It was created in 1941, mainly to preserve the waterfowl habitat at the mouth of the Chassahowitzka River. Home to over 250 species of birds, the refuge also harbors two dozen species of mammals and 50 species of reptiles and amphibians. Among its denizens is the endangered West Indian Manatee.

"We decided Marsh Island was too close to Aransas," Stehn

recalls; "the [whooping crane] flocks might intermingle. Chassahowitzka seemed to have what we needed, including an abundance of blue crabs."

Necedah has proven to be a good choice, providing good sites for rearing and training captive-raised whoopers and suitable nesting habitat for wild cranes. Chassahowitzka proved to be less than ideal, according to Tom Stehn:

> "In fact, we did a terrible job selecting Chassahowitzka because it's really not suitable for whoopers. On the uplands, the vegetation is much too dense for the cranes; the only ways to make it suitable are to burn it off or mash it down. And you can't do that over acres and acres. There are salinity problems because the marsh is actually open to the Gulf. And there are the tides."

The extreme tides at Chassahowitzka cause roosting problems for the cranes. One day the marshes will be too deep for the cranes, Stehn explained, and the next day, the same marshes are too shallow for roosting in safety from predators. To solve the problem, refuge managers have constructed an "oyster bar"—a sloping artificial sandbar built up with tons of oyster shells brought in, load after load, by helicopter and dumped into the marsh. The oyster bar provides a wide range of water depths. And as the tides move in and out, the cranes move around to find the right depth for roosting.

"The abundance of blue crabs fooled us," Stehn said.

> "But we've adapted the project to make Chassahowitzka a very suitable location for the cranes' first year in Florida. The first-year cranes are penned every night and we provide food for them all winter. In the spring, they migrate back to Wisconsin. Their second year in Florida, they'll come to Chassahowitzka for a few days, out of habit, then disperse to find better habitat on their own. So it has really worked out very well, though not the way we originally planned it. The proof is in the very high survival rate of whooping cranes that come to Chassahowitzka—much higher than at Kissimmee Prairie."

Chassahowitzka's shortcomings were unrecognized in the fall of 1999. They were just a few of the many unknowns confronting the Whooping Crane Recovery Team as they approved plans for an ultralight-led sandhill crane migration from Wisconsin to Florida—the next step toward establishing a new migratory flock of whooping cranes in the eastern United States.

IN EARLY MAY 2000, TERRY AGAIN FLEW HIS BELL 407 around to wild sandhill nests in the Necedah area, to collect eggs for the first ultralight-led Wisconsin-Florida migration. Richard Urbanek and George Archibald did the actual egg collecting from the helicopter. At each nest, the eggs were "float tested" by floating them in a bucket of water and imitating the cranes' brood call—a kind of "purring" sound. If the embryos were close to hatching, the eggs would move around as the embryo responded to the brood call. The biologists collected 38 eggs over two days. A few eggs, found to be too young, were returned to wild nests; 23 eggs were flown to Patuxent on a Windway aircraft, and the rest were incubated at ICF. By late June there were three cohorts of seven sandhill chicks each, two at Patuxent and one at Necedah. On June 30, Windway Chief Pilot Mike Mauer flew 14 prefledged sandhills from Patuxent to Necedah to begin flight training.

While the Operation Migration (OM) team had three groups of chicks available to them, they only had two training sites at Necedah. Each had a predator-proof pen at the water's edge, close to a short grass runway. The two pens were separated by a lake, to keep the two groups of birds from mingling. At a third training site, the runway proved too soft and wet for safe use. The team focused its efforts on the two groups of Patuxent chicks.

Over the summer, the birds learned to run behind the taxiing ultralight, then to fly behind it. One of the most difficult and complicated aspects of the training was the isolation protocol. Everything possible was done to avoid exposing the birds to human voices, figures, and artifacts. The pens had view blocks on their landward sides to control what the birds could see, and to allow handlers to complete some tasks without costumes. The gray poncho-like costumes were meant to disguise the human form. Crane puppet heads and recorded crane calls added to the disguise.

The birds were kept overnight in their pens to protect them from predators. At night in the pens, the birds could eat all they wanted of

A handler in a whooping crane costume uses a crane puppet to teach a chick to forage.

Photo, © *www.operationmigration.org*

a specially formulated, pelletized "crane chow." Each day, after an hour or so of early morning flight training, the cranes were allowed to fly free, to forage and to socialize. Though free flight caused some worries for the protective handlers, it helped the birds learn to be wild. In early August, one of the groups returned to their pen in the afternoon, in the company of 15 wild sandhill cranes. That was a good sign; the OM sandhills were willing to socialize with wild birds. But if the OM birds decided to join the wild Necedah flock, the ultralights could be left flying all by themselves. The biologists considered penning the birds during the day, but decided instead to monitor the cranes more closely during free flight, use brood calls to keep them closer to the pens, and hope for the best.

By mid-August 2000, each group of seven birds was flying behind the ultralight, and the two groups were merged into one. The dominant bird from each group now sought to dominate the combined group. The two faced off immediately, and the bird from group #2 came out on top. To the team's surprise, all of the birds in group #1 immediately became submissive to all of the birds in group #2. It took a few more weeks for the overall pecking order to sort itself out, but the group #2 birds remained dominant. Gradually, the pecking order was established and the flock became more cohesive. There were fewer and fewer challenges and each bird needed less and less "personal space."

It took a while, Joe Duff explained, for humans to learn what motivated the cranes and how to adapt training methods and facilities to meet the cranes' needs. Next to each of the crane pens at

Necedah is a makeshift runway. The side of the pen that faces the runway is made of camouflage-painted plywood panels that provide a view block. At the beginning of each training session, handlers opened double doors in the plywood section of the pen and the birds came out onto the runway.

At first, said Duff, they came out in a string, single-file. The first few would take off behind the ultralight, he said, "and the rest are left in the pen, or you'd take off in the middle and leave half the birds on the ground. . . And you don't get this nice formation."

> "So you have to get them all out of the pen at once [but] that's crowding their space. Over the years, we'd get birds that just wouldn't come out of the pen, and we'd think, they're afraid of the aircraft, but it turns out they're gate-shy. . . They won't go through that damn door because when they do, something bad happens. They get crowded into their friend and their friend beats the hell out of them. So we've done things like make the doors wider. We sometimes leave the doors wide open and put a net across there so the birds can see there's nothing bad out there."

Duff said they also park the aircraft outside the pen and wait to start the engine until the birds are all out of the pen, "so they're not running out to this screaming airplane."

> "There's a whole bunch of little things that we've learned, but prior to learning those things, you'd have a bird that wouldn't come out of the pen and you couldn't figure out why. So you'd coax him out and then finally end up pushing him out, and that made him even worse. Now he hated the gate and then he wouldn't come anywhere near the handlers, and then he wouldn't follow the aircraft. And, first thing you know, he's left behind in the training, he's left behind socially, and you've got a bird that drops out."

Some of the birds had trouble learning to surf the aircraft's wake. Ultralight training begins with the birds running up and down the runway behind the airplane, and then progresses to the birds flying in "ground effect"[33] behind the ultralight. At that stage, the birds can get a few feet off the ground but are not yet strong enough to climb. As the birds get stronger, the ultralight begins leading them on small circuits around the training area.

> "You'd end up with a bird that's flying along, trying desperately to follow you, but always way behind and usually down on the deck. And you realize that that bird has never found the vortices created by the wing. And so you land, you put the rest of the birds away, and you take that bird flying by himself. And you can see the penny drop in his brain—'Oh, look at that! I get it!' And the next time you go flying, he's right up there with the rest of them. It took us a while to discover these things—these little nuances that happen."

On August 30, the birds began flying with two aircraft. The migration would involve three ultralights—two to lead the birds and one to fly as chase plane and to scout ahead.

In the wild, flying in a "V" formation allows each bird to take advantage of the wake left by the next bird ahead. The strongest and most aggressive bird takes the lead, and does all the work, and the most subservient birds are at the back, where they get the most aerodynamic advantage. In the ultralight-led migrations, said Duff,

> "We're not sure whether it's the smartest birds or the most aggressive, but the ones up front are doing the least amount of work. We've reversed the scenario. And sometimes we'll get a weak, subservient bird at the back, where he's doing the most work. It's the worst place for him to be, and he'll drop off."

That is why, on migrations, OM flies two lead aircraft at all times—if a bird drops out of formation on one, the other aircraft can move in and pick up the bird.

---

[33] "Ground effect" is an aerodynamic advantage that occurs when a wing is flying close to the ground. For an airplane, ground effect is a factor when the wing is lower than roughly one quarter of its wingspan above the ground.

ON SEPTEMBER 15, OM FOUNDER AND President Bill Lishman received Canada's Meritorious Service Medal, just one example of the international recognition OM has received for its pioneering recovery work. The medal recognizes a "deed or activity [that] sets an example for others to follow, improves the quality of life of a community, and brings benefit or honour to Canada."[34]

In mid-September, the birds were given thorough health checks, ID leg bands, and radio transmitters. After that indignity, the cranes seemed depressed. It took more than a week for them to regain their trust of the handlers and their enthusiasm for the training.

On October 3, 2000 at 7:30 a.m., Joe Duff led the flock off the runway at Necedah for the last time and headed south toward Florida, with a flock of 13 sandhill cranes. The first leg of the trip was 23 miles (km), flown in 44 minutes. One of the birds dropped out along the way. Over the next couple days, the team tracked the missing crane by radio and eventually found him in the company of wild sandhills. When the humans approached, the OM crane flew off with the wild cranes. That OM crane had been something of a loner all summer. Now his loyalties to the wild flock seemed stronger than his ties to the OM flock. After talking it over with the biologists, the team decided to let the crane go.

Heading south, the OM flock grew stronger each day. Riding the vortices rolling off the ultralight's wings, the birds mostly glided, flapping their wings very little. Two or three birds traded off the point position less than a foot behind the ultralight's wing.

Cold air is thicker than warm air and is easier for the cranes to fly in. Cold, calm fall mornings offer the best flying conditions aloft. But on the ground, those same conditions can bring thick fog that keeps the ultralights grounded. The aim was to launch each morning around 7:30, but fog often delayed takeoff until midmorning, when the winds were beginning to pick up. A typical day's flight lasted 60 to 90 minutes and covered anywhere from 20 to 80 miles, depending mostly on winds and weather.

On a good flying day, the routine went something like this:[35] The pilots pre-flighted their aircraft. That sometimes included de-icing the wings. When lead pilot Joe Duff was ready, a costumed handler

---

[34] Office of the Governor General of Canada.
[35] Operation migration's detailed field notes can be read at www.operationmigration.org

opened the pen and the birds came out onto the runway.

Each ultralight was equipped with an electronic sound system designed Dr. Bernard Wessling, a German chemist and an expert on the vocalizations of Europe's common crane. Encouraged by digitally recorded "follow me" crane calls broadcast from the ultralight, the birds followed Duff into the air. Second lead pilot Bill Lishman took off, and took up station just behind the flock, ready to pick up any birds that broke formation. In the chase ultralight above and behind the leaders, Deke Clark was ready to scout ahead or to follow any birds that dropped out or took off on their own. High above, Don Lounsbury flew top cover in his Cessna 182, keeping an eye on the other pilots, relaying radio messages from the ultralights to the ground crew, and communicating with airports and air traffic controllers.[36] All of the aircraft carried GPS navigation receivers.

Most of the stopping points on the migration were small private airports selected for their isolation from human activity and for the hospitality of their owners. When the flock was about 15 minutes from a stopping place, chase pilot Deke Clark scooted ahead and landed at the airport, to move any people and vehicles out of sight and to check for dogs and other unpleasant surprises. Duff and Lishman landed with the flock, shut down their engines and walked the birds out of sight of the airplanes. The ground crew arrived, set up the temporary pen, and slipped out of sight. Then Duff and Lishman walked the birds back to the pen and tucked them in. Half of the pen wall was open mesh to give the birds a "natural view." The other half had a canvas view block, to hide buildings, vehicles, and human activity.

For the most part, the weather cooperated. Morning fogs and headwinds seemed to be the biggest problems. On October 25, three weeks after leaving Necedah, the flock passed the halfway mark, 625 miles, in northeastern Tennessee.

As the flock moved south, the mornings brought warmer, muggier air that quickly turned rough with thermals. The rough, "trashy" air made it harder for the birds to hold formation, and the warm temperatures tired them more quickly. As they tired, the birds began to pant and splayed their feet to cool themselves. Slowing the lead aircraft helped the slowest birds keep up but the stronger birds might end up in front of the ultralight, and risk getting tangled in its rigging.

---

[36] Don's wife, Paula, has also spent many hours flying top cover for Operation Migration in the Lounsbury's Cessna 182.

At times, the best tactic was a slow descent that gave the birds a chance to glide and rest. Occasionally, the only recourse was to scout a likely spot and land.

At some spots, the ultralights could not taxi close enough to the pen to pick up the birds on the ground, and the pilots used an "aerial pickup." The birds were released and the ultralight flew low and slow over the birds, coaxing them to follow with recorded flight calls. Aerial pickups were always chaotic, with ultralights trying to pick up the birds and birds trying to sort themselves out. During these "aerial rodeos," the pilots needed an acute sense of "situational awareness" to avoid colliding with the birds or with each other.

On November 3, as the ground crew prepared to pack up the pen after the flock's morning departure, they found one of the cranes dead in the pen. It appeared to have injured itself or been injured while in the pen.

The flock crossed into Florida on November 6. Then, just 65 miles from their goal, they were pinned down for five days by strong headwinds from a stationary weather front to the south. On November 11, the day dawned clear and unseasonably cool, with frost and ice on the ultralights' wings. A picture-perfect flight 83 minutes long took them the last 65 miles to their landing site at the St. Martin's Marsh Aquatic Preserve near Chassahowitzka NWR. This would be the sandhills' winter home, but the flight team wasn't quite finished. In 2001, the whoopers would be penned 22 miles away in an area with a slightly different habitat—the kind whoopers prefer. In 2000, the ultralights led the sandhills on one more leg to a temporary pen built out in the coastal salt marsh, near where a permanent pen would later be built for the whoopers. There was no landing strip there, so the ultralights had to deliver the birds with an aerial drop—a technique the team had never tried before. While Joe Duff circled above the pen, crane biologist Dan Sprague, in costume in the pen, began playing recorded brood calls. Duff turned off his recorded calls and climbed hard, away from the birds. The cranes circle the pen twice and landed right on target.

Salt marsh habitat is not suitable for sandhill cranes. Two days after the aerial drop at the salt marsh, the ultralights led the cranes back to their permanent winter pen at a freshwater pond at St. Martins Marsh.

Like the non-migratory whoopers introduced at Kissimmee Prairie, the OM sandhill cranes were allowed to fly out of their pen during the day to forage. At night, food lured them back to the safety of the pen. Gradually, their trips abroad grew longer and farther as the birds became wilder.

In December, the wayward bird that dropped out of the migration on the first day out of Necedah was located by radio signal in Georgia, probably in the company of migrating wild sandhills. Two months later, Dr. Urbanek spotted that bird in the company of 30 or so wild sandhills, in good crane habitat near Osteen, Florida, about 25 miles (40 km) northwest of the Canaveral National Seashore on the Atlantic Coast. He probably migrated south with a flock of wild cranes.

Back at Necedah, Dr. Urbanek and ICF Intern Laura Moore had been working with the third cohort of sandhill chicks, raising them and soft-releasing them into wild sandhill flocks on the refuge. After they were released, most of them followed wild sandhills south for the winter.

THE 11 OM SANDHILL CRANES SPENT THE WINTER loafing at their pen and a nearby cow pasture, where they foraged for an hour or two each morning. Most of each day was spent in or near the pen. At night they roosted in the water inside the pen. Volunteers checked on them each day and the food bin in the pen was filled each day with crane chow laced with antibiotics.

On February 25, 2001, 15 weeks after they arrived at St. Martins Marsh, 10 of the 11 OM sandhill cranes left the preserve and headed north. Urbanek tried to track them without success. Over the next few weeks he drove north to Tennessee and back, then spent hours in a Windway aircraft, trying to pick up a radio signal from the ten birds. For all his efforts, they seemed to have vanished.

The last, reluctant member of the flock of 11 cranes finally left her winter home at St. Martins Marsh on March 17—St. Patrick's Day. Three days later a tracker in a Windway airplane picked up her signal in northern Florida, near Mayo, then spotted her flying alone toward Valdosta, Georgia. The main flock from St. Martins remained missing. Urbanek had planned to track them all the way from Florida to Wisconsin but their sudden, unheralded departure had caught him unawares. Their leg-mounted transmitters had a limited range—only about 15 miles (25 km). That made it impractical to try to locate them in a migration corridor 1,250 miles (2,011 km) long and perhaps 200 miles (330 km) wide. From ground vehicles and Windway aircraft, Urbanek listened for their signals in central Wisconsin. He finally acquired a signal in late April and tracked it north to Necedah.

On Friday April 27, Rori Paloski, a recent graduate in conservation biology from University of Wisconsin/Eau Claire and a Necedah Refuge volunteer, was listening for the sandhill cranes' radio signals as he had every Friday for several weeks. Suddenly, his radio receiver "went crazy," picking up signals from all eleven birds from the 2000 ultralight migration.

The next day, a flock of OM sandhill cranes landed on the grass runway at Necedah from which they had departed the previous November. When Urbanek approached the birds, they took to the air and flew off, just like wild birds. Two more times that day, when humans approached them, they flew away.

It was clear that the experiment was a success. The sandhill cranes had left their wintering grounds on their own initiative and had returned on their own to the place where they fledged. They had completed the migration taught to them by the ultralight, though no one knew what northbound route they had followed or what they had been up to for 62 days. And they were wary of humans; OM's methods to promote wildness appeared to be working.

The "dress rehearsal" was over. And by the time the Class of 2000 sandhills returned to Necedah, everyone was gearing up to repeat the experiment in the fall of 2001—this time, with whooping cranes.

Chapter 18
Come On, Whoopers!

IT ALMOST DIDN'T HAPPEN IN 2001. Messing about with an endangered species requires special dispensation from the powers in Washington D.C. In this case, the Whooping Crane Eastern Partnership (WCEP)[37] needed a new federal rule that would declare the ultralight-led whoopers to be an "experimental, non-essential population" of an endangered species. Permits and authorizations were also required from states along the migration route.

Leading whooping cranes on migration from Wisconsin to Florida also requires a lot of money, between $325,000 and $350,000 for each migration. And nearly all of it has to come from private sources.

WCEP set June 30, 2001 as the "drop-dead deadline" for getting its permits and purse in order. But by the third week of June, both were "hanging fire." If the new rule or the necessary funding missed the deadline, the first whooping crane migration in the eastern U.S. would be put off until 2002.

In Washington D.C., the Bush administration had taken over from the Clinton administration in early 2001. When the new Secretary of the Interior (DOI), Gale Norton, came onboard, all DOI projects and permits in process were halted for review by the new administration. George Archibald hollered to the Kohlers about the problem when it cropped up, Terry recalls. Through some of Mary Kohler's political contacts in Colorado (Norton's home state), the Kohlers found some folks who were political intimates of Norton, and who were able to convince her to expedite the permitting process for the whooping crane project. "Mary and I flew out to Washington, D.C. in the Citation to be interviewed by a DOI staffer there," Terry said, "and suddenly everything fell into place! We later met Gale at a

---

[37] www.bringbackthecranes.org

Windway's Cessna Caravan arrives at Necedah with a load of whooper chicks from Patuxent.

Photo, © www.operationmigration.org

Chicago 'political snake rassle' and thanked her profusely."

The federal rule was published on June 26, 2001. ("We were down to the wire when it passed," said Stehn.) Three days later, OM announced that it was only halfway to raising the $300,000 needed for the migration, but was working hard to close the gap. With most of the pieces in place, WCEP gave the go-ahead for the 2001 ultralight-led migration. At Patuxent, ten whooping chicks were already getting acquainted with the ultralight. At Necedah, workers were lengthening the runways, building a new permanent blind at pen #1, and enlarging the pens at both training sites, to give the young cranes a roomier and more natural environment in the enclosures.

The Windway Caravan brought the ten crane chicks from Patuxent to Necedah on July 10. They were given a health check and released into their pens—the five younger birds in one, the five older birds in the other. After a few days rest, each group was led out to its runway and began running back and forth behind the wingless ultralight. In late July, the wing was added and after some initial misgivings about this strange, new beast, the young whoopers happily followed the winged aircraft up and down the runway.

By early August, both groups of birds were following the ultralight into the air.

A whooper chick, in its crate, is loaded into a van for the trip from the Necedah airport to the training pen. Author's photo

The early flights at the training grounds were simple circuits around the training area and back to the runway. Planners had long assumed that the older chicks would have the advantage and would take to the air sooner than the younger cohort. But, said Tom Stehn, the younger birds have often turned out to be the better students. The younger birds seem to do a better job of following the ultralight during migration, even though they have less "practice" time than the older chicks.

The dreaded "Swamp Monster."
Photo, © *www.operationmigration.org.*

On those early flights, some of the birds had a tendency to drop out of formation early and land near their pen as the ultralight passed over it in the circuit. The trainers wanted the birds to follow the aircraft all the way back to its starting point on the runway. Some way had to be found to discourage the cranes from landing at the pen.

One morning in early August, as the flight passed over the pen, a few birds began dropping toward the ground. Out of the marsh beneath them rose a frightening apparition—the "Swamp Monster!" The wayward birds quickly rejoined the formation and followed the ultralight back to the runway. Mission accomplished, Dan Sprague, draped in a camouflaged-colored tarpaulin, settled back into his hiding place near the pens.

The training followed much the same routine as that used with the sandhills the year before. Whoopers hatch later than sandhill cranes, so the whoopers were younger and less developed than the sandhills at the same stage in the training, but their progress was good. In August, the trainers began allowing the whooper chicks out of the pens during the day, to forage—first in the company of a costumed "parent," and then on their own, watched over from the blind.

In mid-September, the birds were brought out of the pen one at a time for health final health checks. Each bird was hooded to keep it from seeing un-costumed veterinary staff. Each bird received an ID band on one leg and a radio transmitter on the other. The whole process took about 30 minutes per bird. Afterwards, most of the birds were wary of their keepers for a few days but otherwise recovered. But cranes are fragile birds. The day after the health checks, one of the birds appeared to be in trouble. Despite special care, it died around midnight that night from acute capture myopathy, brought on by the shock of being captured and handled.

During the health checks, the biologists found poorly developed flight feathers in two other birds. One of them was removed from the study. The other remained and his progress was watched carefully.

Fog and other bad weather limited the birds' flight training in early September and after 9/ll, all private aircraft were grounded for a week. By mid-October, the birds' longest flight behind the ultralights was just 27 minutes. The first leg of the migration would require 45 minutes.

The scheduled launch date, October 15, came and went. Fog and wind pinned the team down for two days. Finally, on October 17, the three ultralights and eight whoopers took off southbound. Six of the birds made the 44-minute flight in good order, formed up on Joe Duff's wing. Two others lagged behind and were picked up by Deke Clark's aircraft. One of those two dropped out and headed back to the refuge. After some discussion, that bird was put in the trailer for the trip south.

High winds and bad weather persisted. Late on the night of October 25, a storm with strong gusty winds knocked down part of the traveling pen and scattered the birds. With crane suits, radio receivers, crane calls, and night-vision goggles, the team managed to round up all but one by 2:30 am. They paused until first light, and then searched again for more than an hour. They found the bird's body beneath a power line it had collided with during the night.

Between October 17 and November 4, the planes and cranes were grounded or turned back by headwinds on 16 days. On the six days when the bad weather relented, they covered 400 miles. On November 5, in Indiana, their luck finally changed. With five straight days of good flying, the six whoopers (plus one in the trailer) put miles behind them, passing the halfway mark on November 9.

They stood down on November 10 to retrieve a wayward crane that disappeared the day before, and on the 11th due to fog and rain. Then a solid week of good flying days brought them to Terrell

County in the southwest corner of Georgia on November 18.

The weather continued to bedevil the project. Fog kept them grounded on several days. When they could fly, headwinds and "trashy" (turbulent) air kept progress slow, exhausting both the pilots and the birds. A short flight of 21 miles (35 km) on November 26 brought them into Florida and 120 miles from their final destination. But they were moving in "baby steps" when they moved at all, and just 75 miles (125 km) from their goal, the weather pinned them down again. Finally, on Sunday, December 2, on a perfect flying day, they covered 52 miles. The next day, December 3, 2001, the ultralights landed at the Homosassa pen in Citrus County, near Chassahowitzka NWR, with six whooping cranes flying right behind them and a seventh crane riding in the trailer. Two days later, they were moved to their winter pen on an isolated coastal island in the refuge. Their journey had taken 48 days, 23 of them spent grounded. For the first time in more than a century, whooping cranes had migrated in the eastern skies.

Like the Sandhills of 2000, the whoopers quickly settled into a stable winter routine—days foraging around the refuge and nights in the predator-proof pen. They roosted in water when the tides were low, and on land when the water was high. (The oyster bar that allowed good water roosting would come later.) From their costumed keepers, they learned to break up and eat blue crabs. This protein-rich food source is critical to the cranes; recent studies show a direct link between the availability of blue crabs at Aransas and the number of

The whoopers' pen at Chassahowitzka NWR.

Photo, © www.operationmigration.org

whooper chicks hatched the following summer in Canada.

Two weeks after the whoopers arrived at Chassahowitzka, bird #4, the one who had been trailered all the way, was killed by a bobcat just outside the pen. A month later, a second whooper met the same fate farther from the island. Refuge staff trapped and relocated two bobcats in December and January and there were no more losses.

On April 10, the five surviving whoopers left their island and, driven by a timeless urge, flew north. Richard Urbanek and ICF's Anne Lacey tracked them with ground vehicles. By April 16, they were in Indiana. One of the birds, a female, had split from the group but was still heading north on her own.

On the evening of April 19, four whooping cranes landed at Necedah NWR, less than half a mile from their training pen. The fifth bird, the loner female, wandered around southern Wisconsin for another two weeks, tracked by Urbanek and Windway pilots. On May 3, she too returned to the place where she fledged, completing the cycle. In future seasons, she and her "classmates" migrated south and north on their own in the fall and spring.

EACH YEAR SINCE 2001, OPERATION MIGRATION has successfully led a new class of whooping cranes from Necedah to Chassahowitzka. Weather is still the major obstacle, and the ultralight-led migrations have grown longer under weather delays. In 2006, it took a record 76 days to lead 18 whoopers from Wisconsin to Florida. The group arrived at Chassahowitzka without the loss of a single bird along the way.

In 2006, a wild whooping crane hatched and fledged at Necedah—the first wild fledgling of the new migratory population. Its parents were two ultralight-led whoopers from the Class of 2002. They hatched two chicks but one died in September. In December, the female chick and its parents, dubbed "the first family" by ICF biologists, completed the fall migration to Florida.

As of early 2007, Operation Migration has led a total of 92 whooping cranes on the long migration from Necedah to Chassahowitzka, between 2001 and 2006. The 2003 and 2006 migrations were made without the loss of a single chick. In each of the other years, only one chick was lost en route.

Tragically, on the night of February 1, 2007, the worst storms to hit central Florida in years claimed the lives of all but one of the 18 recently arrived chicks at Chassahowitzka. At first it was believed that all 18 birds were dead, apparently either hit by lightning or drowned by a storm surge that hit their pen. But two days later, trackers picked up a radio signal from one of the birds. A local pilot flying the Kohlers' Cessna 206 spotted the bird in the company of sandhills, in a safe area inland from the refuge.

The loss of 17 whooping cranes set the reintroduction back by a year, said Tom Stehn. It's a ten-year effort, he said, and the loss of those birds means the project will have to be extended by a year. He added:

> "Any project that has never been done before requires taking project results and making adjustments in the way operations are conducted. We will adjust our methodology for the soft release of the ultralight whooping cranes in Florida to try to prevent such a loss from ever happening again."

The storm occurred during the annual meeting of the Whooping Crane Recovery Team in Lafayette, Louisiana. And while everyone connected with the project was deeply saddened by the loss of 17 young cranes, no one suggested that this tragedy could invalidate the project's successes or its goals.

The ultralight-led migrations are "surpassing the expectations we had, in survival and in [the cranes'] ability to navigate and establish the correct migration," said Stehn. "Most of the birds are actually going between the Gulf Coast of Florida and Wisconsin, and the nesting pairs we have are returning very close to Necedah."

Some of the eastern migratory cranes have wandered off course, Stehn noted. "But even if they winter in the areas outside where we expected, they're still migrating back to Wisconsin" in the summer.

Once they are on their own, a few of the ultralight-led cranes have gotten way off course, summering in New York. Stehn admitted:

> "We don't really know how concerned we should be about that, because cranes will wander and it doesn't really matter as long as they live, as long as they can find mates. So we talked about, 'What if one of [the cranes that wandered into Michigan] ends up nesting in Michigan?' And we think, well, that might be a positive thing."

With the migratory flock established through ultralight-led migrations, Richard Urbanek and his team began in 2005 soft-releasing isolation-raised whooper chicks at Necedah in Direct Autumn

Releases (DARs). Released among the wild whooping cranes, the DAR birds learn the migration route from older whoopers, just as they would if they were hatched in the wild. In 2006, all four DAR chicks released at Necedah migrated successfully to Florida in the company of older whooping cranes.

"All the indications are that DAR is working," said Tom Stehn. He predicts that the Working Crane Recovery Team will put more and more emphasis on DAR, while still keeping the ultralight program going. "It's going to mean a bigger, wider wintering area," he said, "but we don't think that's a problem."

One of the more complex tasks faced each year by the WCRT is allocating captive-raised whooper chicks to the various breeding and reintroduction efforts. "We really want to get more birds out there for the DAR" said Stehn." I'll be really disappointed if we don't have eight" in 2007.

"We don't know how many we can release in one year," he added. If all eight chicks were released together at Necedah, they would have no inclination to follow another group of birds south, he explained. They need to be released in groups that are small enough that the birds feel insecure staying by themselves. "As we get more whooping cranes out in the wild," Stehn said, "presumably we can have more releases of small groups of birds and get more cranes out into the wild that way." And if it turns out that DAR birds are following sandhills on migration most of the time, that could create a potential for more releases.

Windway pilots continue to transport new groups of chicks from Patuxent each spring and to track migrating whoopers each spring and fall.

At Kissimmee Prairie, release of new chicks into the non-migratory flock remains "on hold," according to Stehn, while the WCRT waits to see how well the existing flock there will reproduce. Crane mortality has been high at Kissimmee, from bobcats and alligators, from disease, from getting tangled in fishing lines, and from power line strikes. Even with a normal reproduction rate, the mortality rate appears too high for successful reintroduction. But, said Stehn, in 2006, the flock fledged four new chicks—the best year yet.

"If some of these older adults keep surviving and keep pumping out chicks," he said, "we may want to reconsider" the prospects for the Kissimmee flock.

Meanwhile, the captive breeding programs have been very successful. They now have the potential to produce more chicks in a year than biologists could release. "We're short on facilities and manpower to really handle a bumper production year in captivity," said Stehn. "It's going to happen some year soon."

At Aransas NWR in late 2006, the whooping crane population hit a record high of 237 birds. The flock has surpassed WCRT's target of 40 nesting pairs. Still, said Stehn, the whooper crane has long way to go:

> "We'd need 1,000 whooping cranes in the wild before we'd even think of downlisting them, and that would only take them to the "threatened" level. That number comes from genetic theory, the idea that until you have 1,000 individuals breeding, you're losing genetic material. And that's a major question down the road: Is the cranes' genetic material adequate to keep the species going? So far, it seems to be."

Chapter 19
Chasing Cranes

APRIL 13, 2005—MOST OF THE MIGRATING whooping cranes returned to Wisconsin from Florida about a week ago. Now they are in their "spring wander," meandering around to various wetlands and agricultural fields before choosing a place to settle down and spend the summer. Lara Fondow, a biologist, graduate student, and ICF intern is in the Kohlers' Cessna 182 "Skylane"—a four-place, single-engine, high-wing airplane—with Windway pilot Mike Voechting,[38] searching for the birds' radio signals. Richard Urbanek, with whom Lara works, called Windway a few days ago to request this tracking mission. Mike took off from Sheboygan in the Skylane about eight o'clock this morning, and picked Lara up at the Mauston airport, near Necedah about an hour later. Today, they'll try to locate several young whoopers that have just made their first migration north from Chassahowitzka, plus a couple of the older birds from earlier classes. "It's always the first-year birds that wander the most," Lara explains, "the females, more so."

From Mauston, Mike points the Skylane east, at an altitude of 5,500 feet (1,675 m).[39] For tracking, he'll stay between 4,500 and 6,500 feet (about 1,400 to 1,900 m). At the higher altitude, Lara can pick up a bird's signal from about 70 miles (115 km) away, if the bird is in the air. If the bird is on the ground, the transmitter's range may be as low as two miles, depending on the terrain. At the lower altitude of 4,500 feet (1,400 m), the Skylane is high enough to avoid spooking the birds but low enough to allow visual contact with birds

---

[38] Voechting flew for Windway for about 8 years, until mid-2005, when he took a job flying for another corporate flight department.

[39] Altitudes given are "MSL"—"above Mean Sea Level." In Wisconsin, ground level averages 1,050 feet (320 m) MSL.

on the ground. At that height, a whooper on the ground shows up as a white dot against the green or brown fields. And though they are pure white, it can take a practiced eye to spot them. "If they're flying," Lara says, "they're harder to spot, because of the relative motion and because the sun reflects off their wings in different ways." She needs to make visual contact to confirm each bird's position and to determine what kind of habitat it's in.

Each of the birds they are tracking today carries a battery-powered transmitter, about the size of a deck of cards, strapped high on its leg, with an antenna stretched down the bird's leg. The transmitters have to be waterproof, shockproof, and able to endure frequent pecking by the bird. Capturing a crane to replace dead batteries or a sick transmitter is a traumatic experience for the bird, so batteries are designed to last for three or four years, transmitters for at least that long. Each transmitter has its own frequency, so individual birds can be identified by their radio signals.

Tracking antennae.   *Photos by the author.*

The Skylane carries an antenna on each side, mounted on the wing struts. In her lap, Lara holds a lunch-box-sized receiver that can scan multiple frequencies or zero in on a single frequency. With the two antennas, her receiver also works as a direction finder. The volume she hears in each ear from her headset tells her what direction the signal is coming from—louder in the direction of the source.

The Skylane's cabin is not a quiet place; pilots and passengers wear headsets that block out engine noise and allow them to talk and listen to each other, to other aircraft, and to ground-based radios. Lara's headset is plugged into the telemetry receiver; she can hear only the signals from the birds' transmitters. Her microphone is plugged into the Skylane's intercom panel; she can talk to the pilot but often uses hand signals instead. She and Mike have spent many hours together tracking birds and their communications are spare and efficient.

Today's search begins near Necedah; later it will move south and east to the Horicon Marsh. Whoopers have been sighted from the ground in both of those areas. "If we have an idea where the birds are," Lara explained earlier, "we'll fly a straight line until we pick up their signals, then we'll circle until we spot them. Otherwise, we'll do a square search pattern" hoping to pick up a signal.

This spring, when the whoopers started their migration from Florida, winds kept them stuck on the east side of the Blue Ridge Mountains for a while. Then the winds shifted, Lara says, "and the birds went from the Carolinas to north of Indianapolis in one day— about 600 miles."

As they near Necedah NWR, Mike points out the area where the birds have recently been sighted. Lara says, "I've driven all through there, but let's check it." They fly over the spot where a family of whoopers was seen last week, but there's no sign of them and no signal. They do spot a flock of egrets in the air below them. "I like flying," Lara says. "It's a different world up here."

East of the refuge, she picks up a radio signal. She gives Mike a hand signal and he begins a 360° turn, in a gentle 20° bank. Banking (tilting) the wings increases the antennas' range and can produce a stronger directional signal. Turning a full circle provides 360° scan. As Lara notes a signal, she tells Mike. After he completes the circle, he'll head in the direction of the nearest signal. During the turn, Lara's concentration is intense as she scans several frequencies, listening for the faint beeps from a whooper's transmitter.

ICF Intern Lara Fondow listens for whoopers' radio signals. Photo by the author.

Wetlands are the best bets for finding the birds, Lara says—better yet if there are cornfields nearby. The older birds will return earlier to their previous nesting sites, she explains. The younger birds will wander until late May or early June. Next to the receiver, she has a book of maps showing wetland areas and the last known locations of several of the cranes. She spots one bird east of Necedah and records it in her log.

Near Fond du Lac, she picks up the signal from one of the cranes that has migrated to western Michigan. The signal is louder than it was last week, she says. That bird is probably still on the east side of Lake Michigan, but she wants to make sure. This spring, eight of the cranes ended up in Michigan. So far, three of them have come back to Wisconsin. Mike points the Skylane east toward the lake and the Sheboygan County Airport. They'll stop there, refuel, stretch their legs, and then take off again.

Over Fond du Lac, Lara asks for another 360° turn, but gets no signals. "The static is really bad here; let's head east."

Near the shore of Lake Michigan, at 5,500 feet (1,700 m), Mike and Lara can see the beaches on the far side of the lake. Lara picks up the signal from the Michigan bird again. "She's farther south than last week," Lara says. That's good; the hope is that she and her mate will work their way around the south end of the lake to Wisconsin. The bird's signal was audible farther west, "so she's definitely flying," Lara says. There's no signal from her mate though.

Later over the Horicon Marsh, Lara picks up a few signals while Mike flies in circles, but the signals are intermittent, too brief to get any directional fix on them. "If the birds are on the ground and one pops up into the air for a few seconds, I'll get a brief signal," she says, "then lose it again." And if a bird is standing in deep water—deep enough to cover the antenna on its leg—"it really burns up the range" of the signal. On the marsh, she sees a few pelicans, but no whooping cranes.

After several hours in the air, they head back to Mauston. Lara will continue searching on the ground around Necedah this afternoon. From the air today, she has spotted only one whooper. Some tracking missions are like that. "I'm frustrated," she says. "But my boss says I'm doing a fine job." The next day is a better day; she and Mike are in the air again and she locates several of the missing whoopers in northern Illinois.

TRACKING THE BIRDS ALONG THEIR MIGRATION ROUTE can be a challenge, too—trying to find and follow them along a 200-mile-wide (330-km) corridor that stretches from Wisconsin to Florida. The trackers usually know where the birds have spent each night. So, each morning, said Mike Voechting,

> "we would track one group of birds for awhile and plot them on the map, and then we'd fly over to another group and that could be 80 to 90 miles

[135-150 km] away. We'd pick up those birds, track them for a while, get a bearing on what they're doing and then go on to another group. And there were times when we were tracking three groups of birds throughout the day."

And it could be a long day, up to 10 or 11 hours of flying.

Windway Chief Pilot Mike Mauer said that tracking missions are all flown in VFR (Visual Flight Rules) weather, because the trackers have to be able to see the birds. He explained:

"Somewhere along the line, someone suggested that we do these [tracking] flights on an instrument flight plan, but when you're working with ATC (Air Traffic Control), they're just not going to allow you to meander around tracking a bird any which way. So it needs to be done VFR, listening to a telemetry signal, in slow flight, doing some S-turns, and seeing the birds visually as you're tracking them. And the ultimate goal is to eyeball the bird, see what kind of habitat it's in, and mark its location very precisely."

There is no ground crew assigned to the aerial trackers. That was tried for one year and was ineffective.

Mike Frakes, who has been flying for Windway for about eight years, holds the unofficial record for the longest whooper tracking flight. On November 19, 2003, Frakes and ICF intern Colleen Satyshur were tracking three whoopers southbound from Bloomington, Indiana. For eight hours, they tracked the birds to near Atlanta, Georgia. Frakes recalls:

"We were pretty tired by then. We followed these birds past Chattanooga, and through Atlanta Airspace. It's one of the biggest, busiest airports in the country and they go through it.

"We were circling and following these birds, and Colleen and I are thinking that this is going to be the end of the day, and we're looking forward to it.

"Who knows what a bird is thinking. The biologists

always say that the birds stop at night. I've since learned that that's not the case. We're near Atlanta and it's busy and crowded and there's nowhere good to roost. And the birds just kept going, and the sun went down, and we had plenty of fuel, and the weather was great.

"We must have stopped for fuel someplace. After that we got back up and we followed the birds for four more hours into the night, to somewhere near Albany, Georgia."

Frakes doesn't know how far they flew that day. The straight-line distance is about 550 miles (875 km), but Frakes probably flew twice that distance or more, through a long day of circling and slow flight to keep the birds in sight. That kind of flying is hard work, and that day Frakes logged 13 hours of it. "As far as I know," he said, "that's a record."

When the pilots are tracking the birds, he added, "Whatever they decide to do, whatever airspace they want to go through, we follow. And who knows where they're going to land?" Tracking migrating cranes is never "routine."

Mike Voechting recalled that he once interrupted a tracking flight to fill in as top cover for Operation Migration for a few days. OM's regular top-cover Cessna 182 had been tracking a wayward bird and had loitered too close and for too long near a nuclear power plant. It was intercepted and escorted to a nearby airfield by F-16 fighter jets.[40]

Frakes once requested clearance to follow a whooper through an artillery range. "The controller asked, 'Can you make it through in five minutes?'" Frakes told the controller he could. He crossed the range and landed just outside it, "and we could hear the shells booming behind us."

Charles Koehler has worked for Windway for 13 years and has logged about 500 hours of telemetry flying. On occasion, he has seen whooping cranes do things that make them seem to him "not very bright," compared to sandhill cranes. He recalled one whooper that landed on an athletic field in Chicago—during a game. And he once followed another whooper along a river, until the bird found a coal-fired power plant in its path. There were open fields to the left,

---

[40] Post-9/11 regulations prohibit light aircraft from "loitering" near nuclear plants or other designated facilities.

Koehler recalled, and open river to the right; either direction should have been safe and unthreatening to the crane. But half a mile from the plant, the whooper began circling. "And it must have used up half a day's energy," Koehler said, climbing high enough to fly right over the tops of the tall smokestacks before continuing on.

Lara Fondow, argues that the question of cranes' relative intelligence is a complicated one:

> "Whooping cranes are actually more socially complex than sandhill cranes. [Social complexity] is one sign of intelligence. And many components of animal behavior can be difficult for humans to understand, given that our perception of the world is entirely different from theirs."

Fondow once saw a sandhill crane lead its chicks to forage in the median strip of an Interstate highway. That, she said, didn't seem very intelligent to her, but to assess the birds' own intelligence on the basis of such behaviors is too subjective. In her four years on the whooping crane project, she has seen the birds do some "truly amazing things," and it seems unfair, she said, to call them 'not very bright.'

TRANSPORTING CRANE CHICKS BY AIRPLANE presents a different set of challenges. Mike Mauer said Windway's Cessna Caravan is the plane most often used. It's not as fast or as comfortable as the Citation jet but it has more cargo space and it can operate on Necedah's short runway. The trip from Patuxent to Necedah or Kissimmee Prairie, takes four to five hours in the Caravan. Mauer usually sends two pilots on each flight. They leave Sheboygan and fly to the Baltimore airport the night before. Early the next morning the cranes are brought to the airport in a van, already in their traveling crates. While they are transferred from van to plane, there is no talking—part of the isolation-rearing protocol. "Once we start the [Caravan's] engine," said Frakes, "it's loud enough back in the cargo area that we can talk on our intercoms and radios, and the cranes won't hear us." However, the pilots can hear the cranes, even over the engine noise. "They sound like crickets back there," Voechting said.

If the winds are in its favor, the Caravan can fly non-stop from Baltimore to Necedah. "When we leave [Baltimore] with those birds on board," said Mauer,

"It's very critical that we complete this flight. "That doesn't mean you can't stop for fuel if you need to, but it's very important not to find yourself going halfway and then having to stop for weather, when you have these very valuable birds with you. So we really watch the weather closely, in the days before the flight."

ASK THE WINDWAY PILOTS TO RECALL AN "ESPECIALLY INTERESTING" tracking flight, and Mauer, Koehler, Frakes, and Voechting all point to the same bird.

During the 2004 whooper migration, this bird was trailered most of the way because of an injury. Finally, near Valdosta, Georgia, the biologists released the bird and it followed the ultralights to Chassahowitzka. In the spring of 2005, that crane started north with its classmates. But when it got to the place where it had been released from its crate six months earlier, it didn't know where to go and it ended up on the wrong side—the east side—of the Appalachian Mountains. Mike Voechting and an ICF biologist tracked the bird into North Carolina and ended up "sitting with that bird for a week, because it just didn't move," he said. Mike Frakes and Lara Fondow took over, following the bird north for several days. Then Charles Koehler relieved Frakes, and Koehler, Fondow, and biologist/ICF intern Sara Zimorski tracked the bird north into Ohio. The two biologists intended to capture the bird for transport back to Wisconsin.

It was challenging flying, involving a lot of work in rough terrain. One night in particular, there was low cloud cover, light rain, and poor visibility as the trackers followed the bird to its evening roost. "Some birds," said Koehler, "will spot something good and land, and it's, 'okay, I'm here. It's an hour before sundown. I'm done, already.'" On this particular night, this bird circled in the foothills and valleys for almost an hour. "It would almost land," Koehler recalled, "and then it would decide, 'this isn't right,' and it would move."

To stay on top of the bird, Koehler slowed the airplane to about 70 or 75 knots. "And you don't want to go much slower" in a Cessna 182. He made "standard rate" turns—360° in two minutes—turning to the right, so the biologist had the good window And as the bird made its way east, he adjusted each turn to move the plane about a quarter mile to the east. He recalled,

"We circled for 48 minutes, making 24 of those standard rate turns. This was at the end of a long day; we hadn't had a good meal; and we were low on fuel, which means that we hadn't been to a bathroom in almost five hours. And it was really strenuous to maintain that constant standard rate turn with all the terrain and the poor visibility. That was a struggle."

After they had tracked it for three days, the whooper came to roost in a restored open pit coal mine in southern Ohio. "We all have this horrific image of an abandoned coal mine," said Koehler. "This restoration was only a few years old, but it was already a veritable wildlife refuge." In the voids that were left when the coal was removed, the restoration created ponds and very good habitat. And in that beautiful green area, teeming with wildlife, the whooper settled for the night. The next morning before sunrise, Fondow, Zimorski, and Koehler donned crane suits and set out to capture the crane. Koehler recalls:

"I found myself in this very surrealistic setting. I'm supposed to be flying airplanes and now I'm trudging into this wildlife refuge with this suit on and a visor I can only partially see through. [In the suit's hood], you're hearing your breathing come back to you—it's like you're watching a bad science fiction movie. And I'm skeptical about this mission; we're three humans in sacks, with a box. How are we supposed to get this bird into a box?"

They hiked in for a while and then spotted the bird about half a mile (1 km) away, he said, "and it immediately turned and looked at us, because we were the only things moving." A few seconds later, it took flight. But instead of flying off, it flew straight to the three costumed humans and landed at their feet. "I guess it was so excited to see something familiar after being all alone for at least a month," Koehler said.

"So here I am with almost no sleep in this silly suit, and I'm staring almost eyeball to eyeball with this whooping crane. And the bird, after sizing us up for about a half a minute, decided to attack us. And the way they attack is . . . they jump in the air, they flare their wings to look scary, and then they rake you with their feet. And they repeat this over and over until you're clawed to death."

One of the biologists motioned to Koehler to hunker down—to look submissive.

"So we lay down on the ground and we've got our little puppet crane heads pointed at the ground, not making eye contact with the real crane. After about a minute of this, the bird decided that he was king, and he fluffed up and started getting all groomed and nice. And one of the biologists unceremoniously jumped on the bird and wrapped her arms around it, and we stuffed it in the box."

Koehler then called Mike Mauer back in Sheboygan. Mauer flew the Windway Citation to Ohio, picked up the bird and flew it home.

"That was a pretty good adventure," says Koehler. "I was a minor hero after that."

Afterword:
Canaries in the Coal Mine?

"In wildness is the preservation of the world."
—Henry David Thoreau

In the days before electronic "sniffers" and high-tech detectors, coal miners took caged canaries into the mines, to warn them of carbon monoxide and methane gas, common and deadly hazards in deep shafts. It was a crude device, but effective. If the air in the mine was good, the canary sang all day. As methane or carbon monoxide levels rose in the shaft, the canary stopped singing. If the canary died, everyone had to get out.

Today, there are many canaries in our coal mine. Species—both animal and plant—are disappearing at an alarming rate. Each one of them holds secrets that we will never know. Each one warns us that, on some level, something in their environments has been damaged or disrupted, maybe by natural change or maybe by human activities. Not every species or habitat that disappears is lost because of humankind's folly or disregard. Countless species came and went before we entered the scene. But whenever a species or habitat is lost, it suggests that our world is becoming a little less hospitable to life.

In the grand scheme of things, does it matter whether or not the Siberians cranes survive? Would it make much difference in our lives if the whooping crane had gone the way of the carrier pigeon 50 years ago? What did we really accomplish by bringing trumpeter swans back to the Midwest Flyway? Asked about the value of whooping cranes, USFWS Whooping Crane Coordinator Tom Stehn had this to say:

> "I always have a two-pronged answer. One is pure economics. Just in the local economy down here in Rockport in the winter, the Chamber of Commerce estimates that about $6 million is brought in by people coming to see the whooping cranes. So, if we're spending $3 million a year trying to save the whooping crane, that's pretty good math to me. . . We get about 8,000 people a year riding the commercial whooping crane tour boats . . . to see whooping cranes, and they're coming from all over the world. So in terms of economic value, the cranes are definitely worth saving.
>
> "If you take a moral stand, which I do, I think mankind has a duty to save fellow living species. And I feel that very strongly, that that's part of being human and having the power that we do. We need to exercise that power wisely and save fellow critters. Whenever we don't, it usually comes back to bite us."

In the Midwest, trumpeter swans are bringing new tourist dollars to communities like Monticello, Minnesota, and serving throughout the region as ambassadors of wildlife conservation and environmental protection.

Not all reasons for saving these birds are quantifiable, nor should they be. Kent Clegg, who completed the first ultralight-led crane migrations, recalled:

> "We released four cranes in Yellowstone and it was almost a religious experience for me to sit on a ridge and watch them spiraling up and riding the thermals to gain altitude and begin their migration. It would be a neat thing to have the whoopers back."

And Clegg could have been speaking about any endangered species when he said:

> "You could say, 'It's just another bird.' But the

278

whooping crane is an important indicator of how well we are managing our ecosystems. And if we don't care about the cranes, what do we care about next, when species start disappearing? If we had English sparrows around the barn and now all the English sparrows are gone, we have to ask, Is there something we should be doing differently?"

The success of the trumpeter swan restorations and of the whooper migrations, and the efforts to save the Siberian crane are icons of faith. They demonstrate to us that we humans are intelligent enough to recognize the mistakes we have made in tending this garden of ours. And they give us hope that maybe—just maybe—we have the capacity and the will to make things right.

Wisconsin DNR Biologist Sumner Matteson pointed out that none of these projects could succeed without diverse coalitions of partners, supporters, and volunteers. If you'd like to get involved, or if you just want to learn more, Tom Stehn suggests that you start by visiting the Web sites of the many organizations working to protect threatened and endangered species.

National Audubon Society *www.audubon.org*
International Crane Foundation *www.savingcranes.org*
Kellogg Bird Sanctuary *www.kbs.msu.edu/birdsanctuary/*
National Wildlife Federation *www.nwf.org*
The Nature Conservancy *www.nature.org*
Operation Migration *www.operationmigration.org*
Patuxent Wildlife Research Ctr. *www.pwrc.usgs.gov/cranes.htm*
Trumpeter Swan Society *www.trumpeterswansociety.org*
U.S. Fish & Wildlife Service www.fws.gov
Whooping Crane Conservation Ass'n *www.whoopingcrane.com*

There are many more.

Learn. Join. Contribute. Volunteer. Only by working together can we hope to keep the trumpeters trumpeting, the Sibes calling, the whoopers whooping, and the canary singing.

ACKNOWLEDGEMENTS

THIS BOOK WOULD HAVE BEEN IMPOSSIBLE without help from a lot of people:

I am deeply grateful to Terry Kohler, whose passion for the cranes and swans inspired this book and whose generous support made it possible for me to write it. Working with him and Mary Kohler on this project has been a rare privilege; getting to know them has been a pleasure, indeed.

My thanks to the staff at the International Crane Foundation (ICF), especially to George Archibald, Jim Harris, Mike Putnam, and Claire Mirande who read parts of the manuscript and corrected my errors. Betsy Didrickson, librarian, and Ann Burke, director of public relations, helped me with countless details.

Tom Stehn, the Whooping Crane Coordinator for the U.S. Fish & Wildlife Service gave generously of his time; he read the draft, tracked down information and sources for me, and contributed much to the veracity of the final work.

Sumner Matteson, of the Wisconsin DNR, offered comments, corrections, and stunning photographs for Part 1.

ICF, Operation Migration, Wisconsin DNR, Kyoko Archibald, Peter Clegg, Greg Erlandson, Harry Burns, Jean Davids, Dennis Poeschel, Emily Spoo, and Marlene Sternberger generously shared their photographs with me.

Dale-Harriet Tate, Kirin Nielsen, and Yuliya Melnyk helped with research.

I'm indebted to my literary editors: to my good friend and fellow writer Kevin Garrison, whose comments and suggestions were very helpful and entertaining; to Evelyn and Gene Kane for their insightful reading of the draft and for their wonderful homemade brandy; and to others who read all or part of the draft—Terry and Mary Kohler, Jerry Baumann, Lara Fondow, Lena Ilyashenko, Shari Voigt, John Schubley, Diane Penzenstadler, and Christal Sakrison.

Bryon Zimmerman and his staff at ZDO worked magic to turn the manuscript into a real book. ZDO's Lee Mauer created the drawings.

Adam Smith, director of the EAA AirVenture Museum in Oshkosh, Wisconsin gave my name to Windway's Jerry Bauman, when Jerry called looking for an aviation writer for a museum project. Jerry introduced me to Terry Kohler and this book is the result. Thank you, Adam. Thank you, Jerry.

To all the people who consented to be interviewed or who provided information for this book, thank you for your help and encouragement.

I've surely forgotten someone. If it's you, forgive me—I didn't mean to.

Christal, my wife of 30 years, has supported this project and its author in so many ways. Our daughters, Ingrid and Robin, cheered me on and were patient with me when the pressure of deadlines made me the family ogre.

First and last, I give thanks to God for the talents He has lent me and for the opportunities and the people He has set in my path. It is His garden that we walk in. Walk with reverence. Soli Deo Gloria.

David Sakrison
Ripon, Wisconsin
February 2007

David Sakrison has been a professional writer and editor for more than 30 years, working for businesses, associations, health care, non-profits, museums, political campaigns, and the press. He is a Private Pilot who often writes about aviation for periodicals and museum exhibits.

He has won awards and professional recognition for his work as a copywriter. On assignment, he has delved into complex social and legislative issues, joined forest fire fighters in British Columbia, ridden with the "Iditarod Air Force" at Alaska's Iditarod Sled Dog Race, tracked cougars in the Florida Everglades, and wrestled a Bengal tiger.

<u>Chasing the Ghost Birds</u> is his second book. He previously co-authored, with Harry Heileman, <u>A Portrait of Ripon: the first 100 years in photographs</u>, published in 2000.

He lives in Ripon, Wisconsin with his wife, Christal, their daughters, Ingrid and Robin, and two cats.

*　　*　　*

The International Crane Foundation (ICF) works worldwide to conserve cranes and the wetland and grassland ecosystems on which they depend. ICF is dedicated to providing experience, knowledge, and inspiration to involve people in resolving threats to these ecosystems.

ICF differs from most nature centers and conservation facilities in that its activities single out a very specific subject—cranes—rather than treating the natural history and general ecology of a region. But the focus on cranes is not limiting; instead it provides ICF an opportunity to address a series of issues not tied to a particular place: endangered species management, wetland ecology, habitat restoration, and the critical need for international cooperation.

To accomplish its mission, ICF relies on a wide range of education and conservation activities directed toward the many countries where cranes occur.

International Crane Foundation
E-11376 Shady Lane Rd. P.O. Box 447
Baraboo, Wisconsin 53913 USA
Phone: 608.356.9462 / Fax: 608.356.9465
www.savingcranes.org